KING'S NORTON

NORTON

A History

The north range adjoining the old Saracen's Head inn and St Nicolas church, 2009

Photograph taken in 1868 by Sir Benjamin Stone (1838-1914) of the north end of the village with the Saracen's Head *inn on the left, St Nicolas church, and the old Malthouse on the edge of the churchyard.*

KING'S NORTON

A History

George Demidowicz
& Stephen Price

Phillimore

2009

Published by
PHILLIMORE & CO. LTD
Chichester, West Sussex, England
www.phillimore.co.uk
www.thehistorypress.co.uk

Printed and bound in Great Britain

Contents

List of Illustrations

Acknowledgements

*O*ur first debt is to the librarians and archivists in whose care the primary documentary source material is entrusted. Staff at the following institutions have been especially helpful: Birmingham Archives & Heritage Service (Patrick Baird and Sian Roberts and their respective teams, in particular Fiona Tait and Richard Albutt), King's Norton Library, Mike Byrne of Birmingham Libraries, Worcestershire Record Office and the Worcestershire Library & History Centre (especially Robin Whittaker and his team), Worcester Cathedral Library (David Morrison), the National Archives, the British Library, the Society of Antiquaries of London, Staffordshire Record Office, Warwickshire County Record Office, the Local Collections of the Shakespeare Centre Library and Archive and the Gloucestershire Record Office.

Special thanks are due to the following individuals for sharing information with us: members of the King's Norton History Society, especially Frances Hopkins, Jim Melling, Wendy Pearson and Claire Simpson; the Committee of the Birmingham & Warwickshire Archaeological Society for supporting our fieldwork in the Rea Valley and at Hawkesley; Roy Pearson of Wythall; Canon Rob Morris, the Rev. Heather Flack and the team at St Nicolas Place for giving us the opportunity to monitor the restoration of the Old Grammar School and *Saracen's Head*; Jo-Ann Curtis of the City Museum & Art Gallery, Birmingham; Bryony Halsted for allowing us to use her illustrations of the Roman site at Longdales Road; Marvin Lee and Chris Higgins of CTTM Ltd for giving access to Primrose Hill Farm and saving the house and barn from destruction; Alan Bridge, works manager at Sturges, for archival material, co-operation and funding for the excavation at Lifford Mill II; Pridie Langard and their staff at Lifford Hall for providing access and funding for excavations at Lifford Mill I over many years; Julian Pritchard, chairman and CEO of the Patrick Motors Group and the staff at King's Norton Business Centre for providing information; Don Gilbert of Kidderminster; the late Stan Budd for his invaluable work indexing the building plans for King's Norton; the late Helen Goodger and Phyllis Nicklin for instilling in one of the authors a lifelong interest in King's Norton; Dr Chris Upton; Professor Christopher Dyer for helpful advice over the years; Malcolm Hislop of Birmingham Archaeology; Nicholas A.D. Molyneux of English Heritage for discussing with us the interpretation of some of the historic buildings, for commenting on drafts, helping with photography and compiling the index. Simon Thraves, Kate Wilks and Heather Robbins at Phillimore have been very patient in waiting for this book which has been produced under difficult circumstances.

As we were putting the finishing touches to the book we heard of the death of Margaret Gelling, one of the country's leading experts on place-names. We were lucky that she lived and worked locally and we owe a great debt to her for sharing her knowledge over the years and teaching us about landscape and the precision of place-names.

Thanks are due to the many other people who have written to us over the years and shared information. However, the usual author's caveat applies: we alone take responsibility for any errors in the text.

Finally, we dedicate this book to Toni Demidowicz, who has had to live with King's Norton's past for very many years and in the process has helped us develop and clarify some of the ideas set out in the following chapters.

Picture Credits

Illustrations 32, 40, 47, 52, 56-7, 60, 62, 64-5, 67, 69, 72, 76-9, 81-3, 86, 92-4, 97, 99-100, 102, 105-7, 109, 111, 113, 116-18, 125-6, 129, the front endpaper and Appendix maps pp. 210-13 are reproduced by permission of Birmingham Central Libraries; front cover and illustrations 36, 53-4, 59, 74, 85, 88-9, 108, 114,-15 and 123 are reproduced by permission of Birmingham Museums & Art Gallery; illustrations 17, 98, back cover and Appendix map p. 209 are reproduced by permission of Worcestershire Record Office; illustrations 96 and 128 are reproduced by permission of the *Birmingham Post & Mail*; illustration 24 is reproduced by permission of Stanley Jones; illustration 5 is reproduced by permission of Cambridge University Collection of Air Photographs; illustrations 33 and 68 are reproduced by permission of King's Norton History Society; illustration 49 is reproduced by permission of Humphrey Bartleet; illustration 7 is reproduced by permission of Bryony Halsted; illustration 8 is reproduced by permission of Birmingham Archaeology/Peter Leather; illustrations 104 and 106 are reproduced by permission of the National Monuments Record at English Heritage; illustrations 80, 119 and 120 are reproduced by permission of St Nicolas Place, King's Norton; illustrations 26 and 58 are reproduced by permission of Wendy Pearson; Nicholas Molyneux took photographs for us of King's Norton today and these are reproduced with his permission: frontispiece, 23, 27-9, 37-8, 42, 44-6, 50, 61, 66-7, 71, 75, 87, 91, 110, 122, 124. He also supplied his own drawing of illustration 42; illustrations 34 and 48 from the Prattinton Collection are reproduced by permission of the Society of Antiquaries of London; the following illustrations belong to the authors: George Demidowicz's maps – 1-4, 6, 9-15, 18-20, 25, 35, 51, 63, 101 and back endpaper – and images – 95 and 127; Stephen Price drew map 21 and supplied the following images – 16, 22, 30, 31, 39, 41, 43, 55, 70, 73, 84, 87, 90, 105, 121. The authors and publishers are grateful for permission to reproduce the materials in which they hold copyright. Every effort has been made to trace the copyright holders; apologies are offered for any omission, and the publishers will be pleased to add any necessary acknowledgement in subsequent editions.

Introduction

Standing in front of the former *Saracen's Head* inn, with the tower and spire of St Nicolas church ahead, the visitor to King's Norton is presented with a classic image of the English village – a fine medieval church and a spectacular timber-framed house fronting a village green. It is a scene that has inspired generations of writers, artists and antiquarians. Today visitors express surprise that such a remarkable survival of the rural past exists in a south Birmingham suburb. This book attempts to explain how King's Norton developed from earliest times to become a small trading centre in the medieval period with a high level of freedom, and was eventually dominated and swallowed up by its northern neighbour, Birmingham.

Until 1911 King's Norton was part of Worcestershire and throughout the 19th century was recognised as one of the most picturesque villages in the county. When John Noake, one-time journalist, mayor of Worcester and writer on Worcestershire history, visited in 1854 he was enchanted by its ancient 'cross-timbered' houses around The Green, 'where pigs and geese, and donkeys, and boys with their hoops, and little girls with babies nearly as heavy as themselves have rejoiced in rustic felicity from time immemorial'.[1] Yet even as Noake was describing this bucolic scene the signs of change and the growing influence of Birmingham were apparent; the population of the parish was increasing rapidly and factories with their attendant chimneys were being established in the Rea valley. But while industry followed the arrival of the canals and railway, the environs of the village remained remarkably rural until the 1930s, when housing began to spread along the major roads. It would be followed by vast housing developments in the 1960s and 1970s.

There is, however, still much evidence of a rural past. Even today it is a well-wooded landscape with many old trees from ancient hedgerows remaining, medieval and later farmhouses have been preserved among the new estates, and less than a mile south of The Green the countryside begins. The industrial archaeology of the canals and factories, as well as the late Victorian and 20th-century housing, all provide evidence to show the later changes that have taken place. Wherever possible we have combined the physical evidence with the documentary sources to help us understand how the landscape evolved and how people reacted to change.

But first we must define King's Norton as a place. The village centre, known as The Green, lies 5½ miles south of Birmingham city centre and seven miles north of Bromsgrove from which the Norton or *north town* element of the place-name derives. The manor of King's Norton was combined with that of Bromsgrove until separation in the 16th century. Both were royal manors – hence the King's element of the place-name, seen also in King's Heath and King's Wood. King's Norton remained a royal manor until 1804 when the Crown sold it to John Taylor, whose father had made a fortune in the Birmingham button industry.

The boundaries of the ancient parish and the manor were co-terminous. They covered approximately 11,500 acres and stretched seven miles from Balsall Heath in the north to Inkford at Wythall in the south and another seven miles from Rednal on the slopes of the Lickey Hills to Solihull Lodge on the east. It was the largest parish in the county

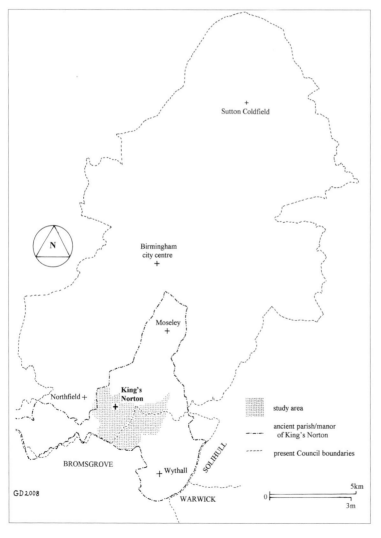

1 *Location of the ancient parish of King's Norton and the study area within Birmingham.*

and its boundaries were 40 miles long. Not surprisingly, the ceremony of beating the bounds in the early 19th century took four days to perform and was relieved by frequent stops for refreshment at local hostelries.[2]

Within the main manor a series of sub-manors developed. Of these the manor belonging to Worcester Priory was the most important, having been given to the monks with the rectory of Bromsgrove by Henry III in the early 13th century in memory of his father, King John.

Until the 19th century the population of the parish was scattered, with a nucleated settlement around the parish church and Green, and smaller settlements of hamlet size at Moseley and Wythall. The vast majority of people, however, lived in isolated farms. King's Norton village in fact developed into a small trading centre by the end of the medieval period, but never quite reached the status of a town, though the grand scale of its church would suggest otherwise. At the same time Moseley and Wythall obtained their own more modest chapels of ease. During the 19th century the population grew enormously. In 1801 the parish contained 2,807 people, but a century later this had rocketed to 74,617. Development began first in Balsall Heath, then submerged Moseley in the third quarter of the 19th century and only really spread out to the village area within the last seventy years.

From at least the 15th century the manor or parish was divided into five yields or taxable divisions for administrative purposes – Moseley (from Balsall Heath to the edge of King's Heath), Lea (King's Heath to Lifford and the village itself), Moundsley (Lifford to Gay Hill and Warstock), Headley (Primrose Hill to Inkford) and Rednal (Longbridge to Rednal). Some time in the early 19th century Lea was abolished and Moseley and Moundsley yields were expanded accordingly. A plan of the original five yields is published for the first time alongside the four used in the tithe survey (1838-40) for comparison.

Given the huge size of the ancient parish of King's Norton we have decided to focus on the modern ecclesiastical parish of St Nicolas. It equates with the western end of Moundsley Yield, the south side of Lea Yield and the northern part of Headley Yield, and stretches from Northfield Road, Cotteridge in the north to Headley Heath and Forhill in the south, and from the edge of West Heath on the west to the Maypole on the east. The Green and parish church are roughly north-central to this area. Despite the expansion of Birmingham during the 20th century, approximately one third of the area remains rural.

Physically and historically our study area lies in border country. Nowadays it straddles the suburban limits of south Birmingham with rural north Worcestershire. But geographically King's Norton lies close to the watershed separating the drainage basins of the major rivers of central England. King's Norton's principal water course, the Rea, and the upper reaches of the Cole on the margins of our area eventually join the Tame and Trent. Below Wast Hill, in Alvechurch parish, the River Arrow flows south to join the Avon and Severn. The steep divide between the two follows the line of the Clent-Lickey ridge, which extends via Cofton as far as Weatheroak

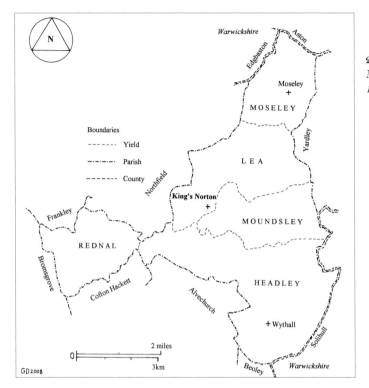

2 *The five yields of King's Norton before the early 19th century.*

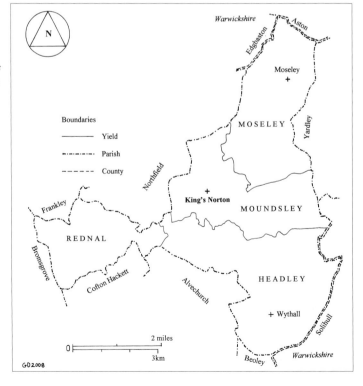

3 *The four yields of King's Norton from the 1830s.*

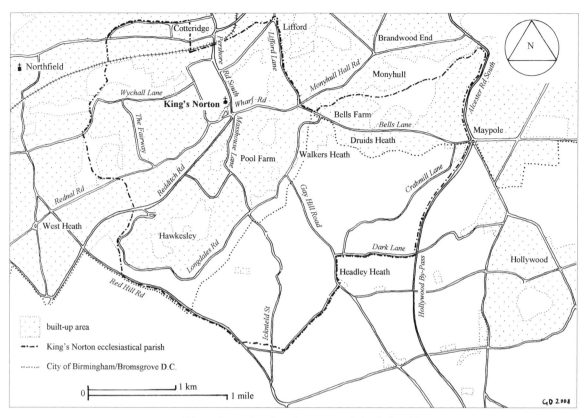

4   *The study area based on the present ecclesiastical parish.*

Hill. This physical division is thought to have been a tribal boundary in Saxon times. North of this ridge, King's Norton is a land of gently rolling topography cut by minor headwater streams, the Rea having only been graced with the name 'river' in modern times. The highest ground rises via Gay Hill to Headley Heath from where a plateau, dissected by streams, descends very gradually south-eastwards to Wythall and east to the Cole valley. It is here that the historic landscape which characterised the much larger manor of King's Norton can still be appreciated. The underlying geology is Triassic Keuper marl, now known as Mercia mudstone, which produces a thick heavy clay, which is relatively impervious and would have supported fairly dense woodland. Where glacial deposits of sands and gravels occur, as at Walker's Heath and West Heath, the soil sustained more open woodland with gorse and other heathland species.

In the following chapters, which are arranged chronologically, we present the story of King's Norton through a number of themes – evolution of the landscape, landownership and tenure, population, houses and homes, the village, church and religion, agriculture and trade and industry. Our intention is for those who wish to pursue these themes consistently to be able to choose the appropriate sections of each chapter. Inevitably this arrangement has meant that the chronology within each chapter is not rigid, so that rather than a sequential account of events we present recurrent themes. We have paid particular attention to the *Saracen's Head* and the Old Grammar School, two of King's Norton's finest timber-framed buildings, which have recently been the subject of a Lottery-funded repairs programme having won the BBC Two *Restoration* series 2 in 2004.

The growing influence of Birmingham emerges as a main theme from the end of the 17th century. In the late medieval period King's Norton's connections had been with towns like Bromsgrove, Worcester, Coventry and even Bristol, rather than northwards to Birmingham, the city that would eventually envelop it. But by the early 1700s King's Norton's rich pastures were supporting a thriving dairy trade and its mills and watercourses were increasingly being used for semi-industrial purposes, especially blade-grinding in the production of edge tools. In the 18th century King's Norton became a convenient rural retreat for the successful Birmingham merchant and his family looking for a healthier abode than the town centre or its immediate environs. Victorian industrialists like the Lanes of Moundsley Hall followed that pattern, taking on small country estates and became the new squirearchy. By the end of 19th century manufacturers and tradesmen were moving into the new villa residences at Middleton Hall Road, and houses for skilled artisans were edging further south to Cotteridge. The old rural community was increasingly under threat but agriculture persisted, albeit in a modified form, well into the 20th century.

We are very conscious of not being the first to write about King's Norton's history. The antiquary William Hamper wrote an article on its antiquities in *The Gentleman's Magazine* in 1807.[3] Late Victorian writers included William Salt Brassington, who published accounts of the church and manor in the *Transactions of the Worcestershire Archaeological Society*, while J.R. Holliday lambasted the then vicar and the diocesan architect for their over-enthusiastic restoration of St Nicolas church and the loss of original fabric in the early 1870s in the equivalent journal for Birmingham.[4] Hilda Light contributed the King's Norton entry to the authoritative Victoria County History in 1913 and in 1924 E.A.B. Barnard, the Cambridge scholar with Worcestershire origins, joined forces with H.M. Grant, the King's Norton builder, to publish a selection of local material from the National Archives.[5] Slightly later came Arthur Lock's *History of King's Norton and Northfield Wards*, published by the Birmingham Branch of the Historical Association.[6] After the war two librarians made substantial contributions: firstly, Charles Parish wrote a series of useful articles on the history of the parish for the *Redditch Indicator* in 1951. These were followed by John Edmund Vaughan's guide to the church, which went through many editions, and his account of researches on the Old Grammar School.[7] In 1963 the Worcestershire Historical Society published a volume on the court rolls of the combined manor of Bromsgrove and King's Norton for the decade 1494-1504 with a scholarly introduction and commentary by A.F.C. Baber.[8] From the 1970s the present authors highlighted the physical remains of King's Norton's history, while the formation of the King's Norton History Society in 1980 spawned a host of small publications on various aspects of local history.[9] At the same time Helen Goodger compiled her history of the parish, drawing on much of the research undertaken by a University of Birmingham Extra-Mural class started by Phyllis Nicklin in the 1960s and continued into the 1970s by one of the authors.[10] More recently two compilations of old photographs of the area have appeared in print.[11]

Fuller references appear in the endnotes to each chapter, but a note on the principal sources may be helpful here for those wanting to undertake their own research. Because of the sheer size of the parish the sources for the study of King's Norton's history are vast, a fact that has deterred writers from attempting a comprehensive history. There are, for instance, over 800 wills and inventories from the 16th to the 18th centuries in the Worcestershire Record Office and the National Archives. The archives relating to the royal manor and its eventual sale are partly in the National Archives, but important collections are held by the Shakespeare Birthplace Trust because an 18th-century architect, Thomas Archer, leased the manor from the Crown and inherited much earlier material. The archives relating to the Rectory Manor owned by the Priors of Worcester are in Worcester Cathedral where they were produced. Historians have overlooked them, but they contain a very detailed survey of the Priory estate enabling us to reconstruct the layout of The Green in the late medieval period. Meanwhile Birmingham Central Library (Birmingham Archives and Heritage Service) holds important collections of title deeds, copies of the Tithe Apportionment and Map (1838-40), maps and building plans. It needs to be stressed that plans of King's Norton, or parts of it, are relatively rare before the Tithe Map, inhibiting research on the physical appearance and layout of the manor. The control by the distant royal landlord was relatively light, the manor too large and most of it freehold to justify the expense of a traditional estate map.

The parish church's own archive has been deposited in Birmingham Central Library and contains detail about the later history of the *Saracen's Head* and the Old Grammar School. There are many archives with local relevance which now have homes far removed from their origins, but these are currently more easily traceable through the powerful Access to Archives (A2A) website, part of the UK Archives Network administered by the National Archives. By painstaking searches over the years, aided recently by A2A, nearly 30 surveys and rentals of King's Norton, although scattered in many repositories, have been located. Together they provide a framework from which to plot the ownership and occupation of the majority of 'sub-manors', estates, farms and pieces of land in the parish between *c*.1500 and 1820. Several owners of private deed collections have also generously made them available to us.

Visual evidence provides essential information in a parish which has witnessed so much change. The principal collection of photographs is held by Birmingham Central Library, but important private collections are held by members of King's Norton History Society. Paintings and drawings, which are especially useful before the age of photography, are held by the City Museum & Art Gallery, Birmingham.

The Prattinton collection in the Society of Antiquaries of London contains Dr Peter Prattinton's account of his field visit to King's Norton in 1826, his transcripts of numerous medieval deeds as well as the drawings he instructed his assistant, John Instan, to produce of St Nicolas church and the Old Grammar School.

The study of King's Norton history can be enhanced by combining the documentary with the physical evidence. In 1974 field work was conducted by the Birmingham and Warwickshire Archaeological Society before the development of Hawkesley, and in the early 1980s a survey of the Rea valley, from its source down to Hazelwell, was organised through a successor field group of the same society.[12] Archaeological excavations were a rare event locally until pioneering work by one of the authors, who grasped the opportunities evolving in the late 1980s for combining archaeology and planning. Three excavations took place at Lifford Mills, which were all developer-funded. Our agitation for such work to be placed on a more formal footing eventually succeeded in the creation of the post of planning archaeologist for Birmingham. As a consequence great strides have been made in recent years in the understanding of the early history of the area through further developer-funded archaeology. An important Roman farmstead site at Walker's Heath has led to a reassessment of early settlement history and the role of the Roman road, Icknield Street. Similarly, excavations at various points around The Green have thrown much light on the form of 13th- and 14th-century houses in the centre of King's Norton, as well as providing evidence for widescale trade. Birmingham City Museum holds archaeological finds and excavation archives from the area as well as post-medieval items such as the carved frieze from the panelling once in Bell's Farm.

The full potential of museum collections to local history has yet to be realised, but one instance will suffice. Three-dimensional evidence for the local dairy trade is represented by the 18th-century cheese press from Wychall Farm and for the 20th century by the milk cans and ephemera used by Jack and Fanny Bullock on their horse-drawn milk rounds in the inter-war years. Mrs Bullock's memories of King's Norton and her work in the milk trade were recorded by one of the writers in the 1980s and are part of the City Sound Archive in the City Museum & Art Gallery in Birmingham. The Sound Archive contains several other recordings made in the 1970s and 1980s with King's Norton people, especially those involved in local agriculture and allied trades earlier in the 20th century.

The physical remains of farmhouses, cottages, Georgian canals, Victorian factories and villas can all be studied to reveal their structural development and can be linked to documentary sources. In the past it has been difficult to date timber-framed buildings precisely enough to correlate them with the names of owners or occupiers. However, over the last few years dendrochronology has been successfully applied to some of King's Norton's historic buildings, giving us exact dates for their constructional phases and enabling the links with their builders to be made with some confidence.

I

Prehistoric, Roman and Anglo-Saxon

For the majority of the time man has occupied the King's Norton area little can be said of its earliest inhabitants or landscape. We know nothing of the hunter-gatherers of the Old Stone Age (Palaeolithic *c.*450,000-10,000 B.C.) and the Middle Stone Age (Mesolithic 10,000-*c.*4,500 B.C.). The landscape changed dramatically several times during the Old Stone Age, veering from the extremes of the glacial periods (when the land was covered with thick ice) to dense deciduous woodland. Any clearings in woodland were caused by nature or natural catastrophe and the impact of humans on the landscape was minimal. Settled life associated with agriculture began around the fifth millennium (the New Stone Age or Neolithic) and this phase, defined by a continuing reliance on stone tools, lasted just over two thousand years. All that has been found from this period is a single stone hand axe at Druid's Lane.[1]

The use of bronze began around 2,300 B.C., but few bronze artefacts have been found in the Birmingham area and none around King's Norton. By contrast numerous Bronze-Age sites known as 'burnt mounds' have been identified along the streams of south Birmingham. Two of these mounds of heat-shattered and fissured pebbles in charcoal were spotted in the banks of Chinn Brook to the south and north of Monyhull Hall. There is another by the Rea in Wychall Lane.[2] Burnt mounds could have been created by pouring hot water onto stones, creating billows of water vapour. It has been suggested that shelters were erected on the mounds to be used as sweat houses, often described as the equivalent of Bronze-Age saunas.[3] This is not as strange as it may seem, as sweat houses or lodges were popular with North American native peoples into modern times. Apart from the practical side of cleansing, the practice has been recognised as having ritual or symbolic meaning. Alternatively burnt mounds could have been the sites for cooking food, the water quickly heated by the immersion of heated stones, or the sites of some industrial processes. Unfortunately no Bronze-Age settlements associated with these mounds have been identified anywhere in Birmingham, but their density suggests the area was not as thinly populated as thought only a few decades ago.

Prehistoric settlements or farmsteads are difficult to find in built-up areas such as city suburbs. Most are detected by examining aerial photographs of open land in rural areas, a few by earthworks in the field. Many are likely to have been destroyed in the

Birmingham area including King's Norton. Even if some traces still lie below the ground, they are obscured by modern buildings, roads and car parks and will only be discovered by chance. Iron-Age (700 B.C.-A.D. 43) settlements were numerous elsewhere, surviving as groups of circular ditches representing round huts. In King's Norton only a few suspected Iron-Age pottery sherds have turned up. It is worth mentioning, however, the Iron-Age fortification, known as Berry Mound, situated about three miles east of King's Norton village in open country at Wythall between Major's Green, Hollywood and Solihull Lodge. It consists of an oval-shaped ditched and banked enclosure about 11 acres in area. The ramparts, much eroded by ploughing, encircle a low gravel hill standing about 50 feet above the River Cole that flows to the west. This modest Iron-Age hill-fort measures 450 feet from north to south and 200 feet in width. Excavations in the 1950s found no dating evidence.[*] Iron-Age fortifications were generally not situated in wilderness, but represented a place of refuge, assembly and even a status symbol for a local tribe, the majority of whom lived in farmsteads in the hinterland of the fort. Despite the lack of evidence in the immediate area of King's Norton, this monument and fieldwork in neighbouring rural areas of Worcestershire and Warwickshire have demonstrated a well-established pattern of settlement in the Iron Age. The Birmingham region may have been significantly more wooded than further south in Worcestershire and Warwickshire, but it was not empty of people, settlements and fields.

5 *The Iron-Age hill-fort of Berry Mound, looking north-east towards Solihull Lodge. The ramparts follow the oval-shaped enclosure.*

Only a few decades ago it was widely believed the Romans cut their new straight roads through vast tracts of primeval forest. The Birmingham plateau was regarded as basically empty, with the Roman roads constructed here heading elsewhere, to Droitwich, Wall and Alcester for example. The isolated Metchley Roman fort, situated on the site of the present Queen Elizabeth Hospital in Edgbaston, existed only because of the strategic junction of roads in the West Midland forest. Again recent fieldwork and aerial reconnaissance have radically altered our view of the Roman landscape, indicating that it was perhaps as open and exploited as that of the medieval period.

The most obvious Roman feature in the study area is the road, laid out in the mid-first century A.D. and known from the medieval period as Icknield Street, and sometimes Ryknild Street. It ran more or less north to south from Metchley fort to Alcester. Today it can be traced with minor deviations as a lane, still called Icknield Street, heading from Forhill in rural Worcestershire towards built-up King's Norton. It passes east of the village as a longer diversion (Walker's Heath Road/Broad Meadow Lane). The actual line of the road was west of this diversion, crossing Parson's Hill roughly halfway down to the canal bridge. Lifford Lane and Pershore Road return to the original line of the Roman road. The name Stirchley is a corruption of Street-ley (*streat-leah*), meaning 'clearing on the Roman road'.

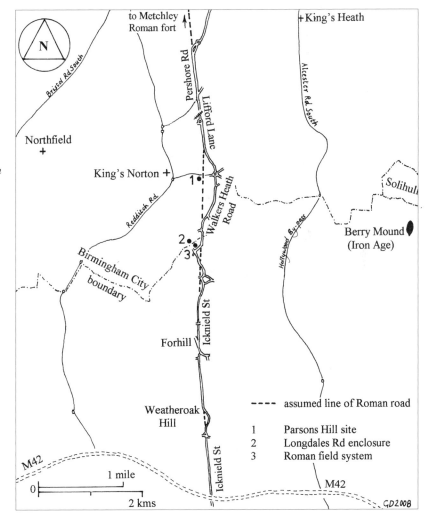

6 *The Roman road, Icknield Street, through King's Norton with associated sites.*

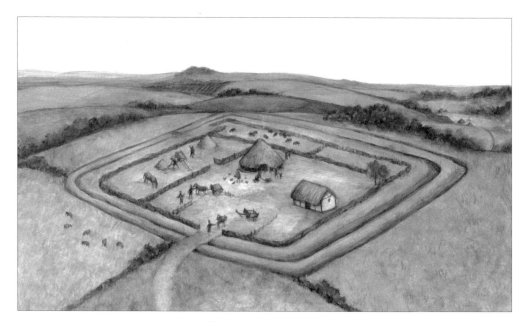

7 *Artist's reconstruction of the Roman enclosure at Longdales Road from the air.*

Roman coins and pottery have been found by chance within a mile or two of King's Norton village, and these are no longer considered to have been dropped by travellers, but by people living and working in the area.[5] In 1949 Michael Nixon noticed Roman pottery in a bank created by bulldozers less than a mile south of Parson's Hill on the presumed line of the Roman road. The significance of this find was that subsequent excavations in the 1950s revealed features of an occupation site alongside Icknield Street that lasted for a considerable period of time, with pottery dating from the first to the third centuries A.D.

More recently a major Roman site has been discovered farther to the south along the Roman road at Longdales Road, again demonstrating that the road attracted settlement and considerable activity. Excavations here in 2002 and 2003 before the construction of the new municipal cemetery revealed a large triple-ditched enclosure measuring about 230 x 197 feet, containing pebble surfaces and a circular and rectangular building. It lay immediately to the north-west of Lilycroft Farm. Due to the number of ditches and their size it has been interpreted as a livestock compound, although there may also have been a homestead within. The pottery found in the ditches dates from the second to fourth centuries A.D. The enclosure appears to have been connected by a trackway 26 feet wide running south-east to Icknield Street. There were other buildings located to the north and south of the enclosure. More excavations in 2006 discovered ditches running at right angles to Icknield Street, which correspond to the modern field boundaries. It appears therefore that these field boundaries date back to the Roman period and give us a glimpse of a wider landscape that may have been laid out to respect the line of the Roman road. Other boundaries away from the road, however, were curved.

What does all this mean for Roman King's Norton? Strictly speaking it should be described as Romano-British, with the emphasis on the latter. Most of the population were Celtic and the degree of local Romanisation is unknown. It is unlikely that settlement and fields were confined to a narrow strip alongside Icknield Street, but the proportion of field to woodland is impossible to determine. The Longdales Road site has been interpreted as a collecting and storage depot for animals and crops, and also as a rural roadside market with booths providing food and drink for visitors.[6] The site lies in an elevated position on the ridge between the Lint Brook and the Chinn Brook. To the north on the hill that rises from the Lint Brook lies the present village of King's Norton. The topographical correspondence is fascinating – could this have been proto-King's Norton, the main settlement within our district in the Roman period? Roman pottery was found at the *Saracen's Head* in 2007, but has not so far been associated with any structural evidence. It is possible, however, that in the Roman period there was at least one farmstead near the site of the present village.[7]

After the departure of the Romans and the collapse of the Roman Empire the arrival of Anglo-Saxon invaders and settlers brought about a significant alteration in the ethnic composition of the King's Norton area. Place-name evidence for the first three centuries of the Anglo-Saxon period can cast a little light and even take us further back into the Romano-British period. Substantial evidence is not available until the beginning of the eighth century when it appears that the Roman site at Icknield Street had been long abandoned and woodland re-established over the area.

8 *Aerial photograph of the Roman enclosure with possible Roman field boundaries running towards Icknield Street. Longdales Road is to the left.*

The name, Norton, was created in the Anglo-Saxon period, in the language called Old English introduced by invaders from north Germany and Frisia from the fifth century onwards. Celtic names were almost entirely wiped out in the area, leaving only some stream and river names, e.g., the *Leontan* (Lint Brook) and the Cole (the earlier name for the Rea). The name of the present-day River Cole further to the east and south has the same origins. *Leontan* is possibly derived from the Welsh, *lliant*, 'a torrent, flood or stream'.[8] Until the 17th century at least the Rea was known as the 'Col(l)e' for much of its length, including the area around King's Norton. The name has its origin in the old Celtic word for hazel (Welsh, *colle*). The two river Coles in the district are intriguing, and it has been suggested that their survival as stream names may reflect the existence of a Romano-British territory based on the Tame/Cole/Rea/

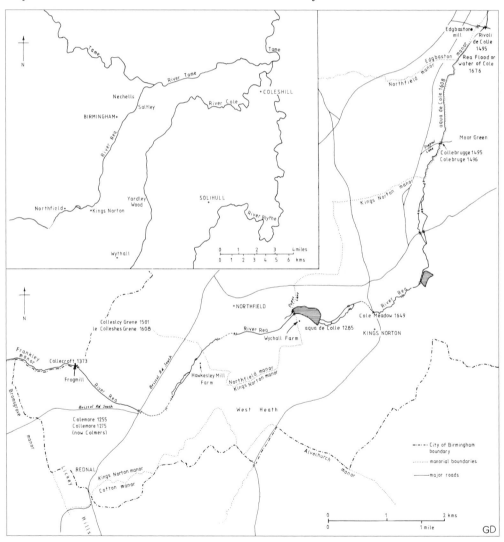

9 *Location map of references to 'Cole' or 'Colle' indicating the earlier name of the river Rea.*

Blythe basin with its base at Coleshill.[9] If there is any truth in this proposition, then in Romano-British times King's Norton was part of a territory or administrative area that lay to the north and east.

The name Norton, however, means a settlement or homestead to the north of another settlement (north-*tun*). This other place was usually the more important and, in the case of King's Norton, it has been speculated that this was Bromsgrove. If so, the coining of the name possibly reflects an administrative re-orientation to the south, a link that was to last until the end of the medieval period. It is not known, however, when Norton was created or named. It may even have been the site of an earlier Romano-British farmstead. The formation of names with *tun* was common throughout much of the Anglo-Saxon period and all that can be said is that *tun* was used in more open country.[10] The *leah* ('clearing') names which are found in the many places around King's Norton ending with '-ley' are considered to reflect a wooded environment (Headley, Moundsley, Stirchley).

King's Norton is fortunate in having two Anglo-Saxon boundary charters, *Hellerelege* (A.D. 699-709) and Cofton (A.D. 849). Both boundaries have proved difficult to plot on maps. The three hides of the *Hellerelege* charter lie entirely within the modern parish of King's Norton. It was a grant by Offa, King of Mercia, of wooded country to the church of Worcester. The estates of the Cofton charter, on the other hand, lie entirely outside the parish to the south and west, but with boundaries coincident with *Hellerelege* along Redhill Road. Bishop Ealhun of Worcester has leased the 20-hide estate to King Berhtwulf.

The earliest charter, the *Hellerelege* wood, was first mapped by Della Hooke in 1990.[11] Her interpretation of the charter boundaries included the village of King's Norton and stretched from the Chinn Brook in the south to the stream that runs through Bournville in the north, which she interpreted as the *Leontan* stream of the charter. Although the names Chinn Brook and Lindsworth can be confidently recognised within the charter, this was not the case for a stream called the *Leontan*, previously identified as the river Rea.[12] The discovery of the Lint Brook name brought about a re-interpretation of the boundary clause, the *Leontan* being recognised as its earlier version. The Lint Brook flows from the watershed at Redhill Road north-eastwards through the present Hawkesley and Pool Farm estates to join the Rea. Here on King's Norton playing fields the Lint Brook can be most easily seen. Wharf Road and Parson's Hill descend into the valley of this stream, now followed in part by the Worcester and Birmingham Canal. The Lint Brook solution to the boundary clause was offered in 2003.[13]

According to this interpretation, *Hellerelege* consisted of three hides of woodland occupying the ridge between the Chinn Brook and the Lint Brook. With the southern boundary the present Redhill Road, and Lindsworth (Farm) centred on the northern limits, the village of King's Norton is thereby excluded. This conclusion carries some conviction, as Norton was likely to have been more important than Lindsworth and in existence at least at the same time. It would therefore have been mentioned.

The 10 places listed in the charter give us our first view in any detail of the topography of the King's Norton area based on documentary evidence. They are listed below and mapped on Fig. 10 following the boundary clockwise from the north-west corner.

1. 'First from (the) *liontan/leontan* so that it comes to (the) black mere'
2. 'from (the) black mere so that it comes to the spreading lime-tree'
3. 'from the spreading lime-tree so that it comes to Lindsworth'
4. 'from Lindsworth so that it comes to (the) *ciondan*'
5. 'from (the) *ceondan* so that it comes to (the) reed marsh'
6. 'from (the) reed marsh so that it comes to the great oak'
7. 'from the great oak so that it comes to the red slough'
8. 'from the red slough so that it comes to (the) cress-pit'
9. 'from (the) cress-pit so that it comes to *usan* mere'
10. 'from *usan* mere so that it comes again to (the) *leontan*'

Water figures prominently with the two streams and two pools called black mere and *usan* mere and a cress-pit. It is not surprising that the land is undrained and swampy (the reed marsh and red slough). In the great tract of woodland the two trees mentioned must have been very prominent, the spreading lime tree and the great oak. Only one habitation is mentioned on the northern edge of the wood, Lindsworth, later to become a berewick (see Chapter 2) along with Norton. Two thirds of the way up the *Hellerelege* ridge lay the site of the former Roman enclosure close to Icknield Street. Part of the Roman road, however, must still have been visible as the original course north and south of the Walker's Heath Road diversion has survived to the present day. The woodland should not be regarded as a single tract of dense forest. The trees had naturally regenerated after the abandonment of the settlement following the Anglo-Saxon invasions, and clearings and grassland may have given *Hellerelege* the appearance of a wood-pasture landscape.

The *Hellerelege* charter may not give quite the right impression of the typical landscape of King's Norton at the turn of the eighth century, for not all of the area should be seen as regenerated woodland or wood pasture. A substantial open area, including arable, may have existed around Norton itself, and other fair-sized 'clearings' are likely to have been centred on Lindsworth, Moundsley and Headley. The Cofton charter bound (Fig. 11), however, mentions little cultivated land (*earthlande*), perambulating an extensive area which now embraces Rednal (later a yield of King's Norton) Cofton Hackett, Hopwood and Wast Hills, and the southern extremity of the later King's Norton manor near Wythall.

The watershed between the Lint Brook/Cole and the River Arrow forms a distinct line of hills from West Heath via Wast Hill to Weatheroak Hill. This can be clearly seen from the M42 motorway north of junction 2 – the road to Hopwood. A former Romano-British territory north of this watershed, fossilised in the name 'Col(l)e,' was hinted at earlier. The watershed would have acted as a convenient boundary with tribal areas to the south centred on Worcester (the Anglo-Saxon Hwicce territory). Near West Heath the Cofton charter refers to the boundary of the *Tomsaetan* and *Pencersaetan*, two

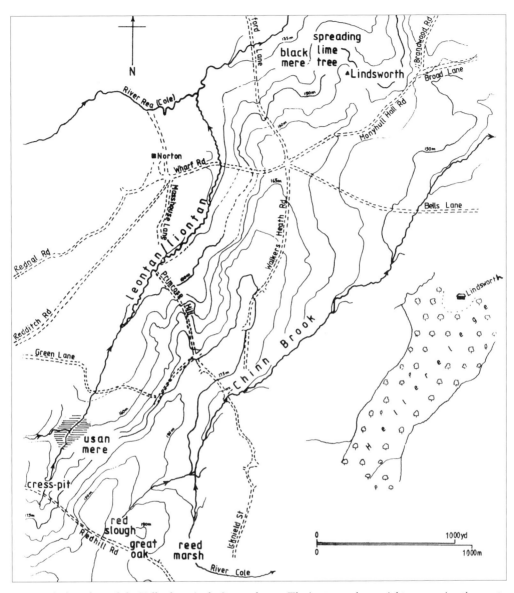

10   *The boundary of the Hellerelege Anglo-Saxon charter. The inset map, lower right, summarises the grant of the woodland, whose boundary points are shown on the larger map.*

Staffordshire folk-groups. The transfer of Norton from these Staffordshire tribal areas to Bromsgrove took place at an unknown time in the Anglo-Saxon period. The boundary point mentioned was probably once the southernmost extent of the folk-groups based on the rivers Tame and Penk, but this was not necessarily the case when the charter was compiled (A.D. 849). As a result of this switch from north to south, the later diocese of Worcester, mostly coincident with the territory of *Hwicce*, stretched well north of the watershed to include not only Norton but also Northfield and Yardley.[14]

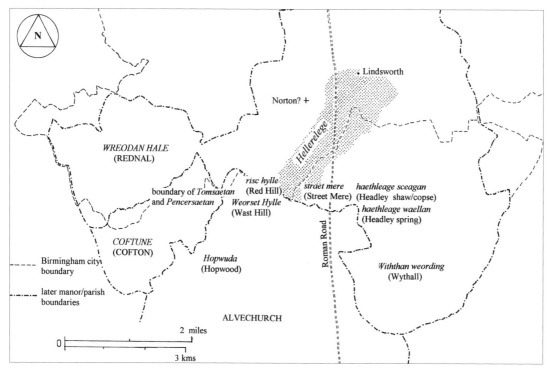

11 *The boundary of Cofton and Wythall Anglo-Saxon charter in the King's Norton area, including the area of the* Hellerelege *charter.*

The watershed was also the local boundary between Hopwood and *Hellerelege*, and the Roman Icknield Street, on its way south from the wooded *Hellerelege*, was noted and recorded in the charter (see *straet mere* Fig. 11). The charter also records for the first time Headley (*haethleage* – heath clearing) and Wythall (*withthan weorthing* – the enclosure of the willows). These areas were later to become part of the extensive medieval manor of King's Norton as well as Rednal (*wreodan hale* – nook of the thicket). The remainder of the charter area evolved as independent Cofton Hackett and the north part of Alvechurch manor.

For well over two hundred years after the Cofton charter of A.D. 849 there is no information available on the people and landscape of Norton. The manor of Bromsgrove and King's Norton, first recorded in Domesday Book, must have been created in this period, gathering together extensive lands to form one of the largest manors in Worcestershire. The manor had also become royal, but it is not known when it came into the king's hands. As part of this process the church at Worcester (later the cathedral) must have given up its *Hellerelege* woodland to the king. It is possible moreover that Norton and a considerable area around it were already Crown territory at the time of the charters, but no charters have survived to confirm this. The immediate consequences of the Norman Conquest in these parts were not chronicled, and it is not until 1086, through the compilation of Domesday Book, that a new light is brought to bear upon Norton and our study area.

II

Medieval King's Norton

The Middle Ages were a formative period for King's Norton. Over four centuries from Domesday to the end of the 15th century the landscape was created. It endured for another four hundred years until the city of Birmingham, which seemed so far away, spread to the village and beyond during the 20th century. It is remarkable that the relics of the medieval period, in the shape of a village green with timber-framed buildings, can still be seen in suburban King's Norton. The tower and spire of St Nicolas church are a landmark in this area of south Birmingham, much as they were when they dominated the rural landscape of medieval King's Norton.

DOMESDAY BOOK

King's Norton is recorded for the first time in Domesday Book in 1086. Norton (Nortune) is listed as one of 18 berewicks of the manor of Bromsgrove (Bremesgrave) held by King William. The area of the later manor of King's Norton contained nine berewicks including Norton. Presumably the most important berewicks were dependent or subsidiary areas of a large estate. Bromsgrove was one of the largest estates in Worcestershire at this time (23,000 acres or 36 square miles), stretching from what is now the Avoncroft Museum of Buildings on the south side of Bromsgrove to Belgrave Middleway in Balsall Heath, Birmingham.

The naming of a berewick at Norton in Domesday Book suggests there was already an identifiable settlement at this time, probably where the present village is located today. It may have been only a small cluster of farms, with one of these perhaps acting as a local administrative base for the royal estate. Norton can be understood to have been both a settlement and an administrative territory, but there were no definite boundaries for this period. A list of neighbouring berewicks gives an impression of its reach, although not all berewick locations are certain.[1] Just less than a mile to the east-north-east was Lindsworth (*Lindeorde*, present Lindsworth Road). Moseley (*Museleie*) lay just over three miles to the north east and *Lea* much closer, about 1.25 miles to the north. There is still some doubt over the location of *Lea*, possibly centred on the former Leys Farm off Bournville Lane, but a later administrative district known as a Lea Yield was most likely named after it. Tessall (*Thessale*, near the present Tessal Lane) was situated about 2.5 miles to the south west. *Witeurde*

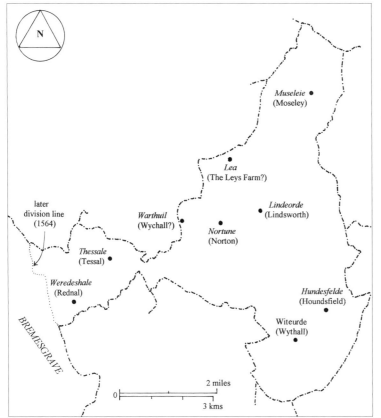

12 *The Domesday Survey berewicks of Bromsgrove within the later manor of King's Norton.*

berewick has been identified as Wythwood, which would place it just north of Wythall church, nearly three miles to the south east of Norton. Dividing these distances by two would create a territory for Norton with a maximum reach of roughly 1.5 miles from the present village.

The Lindsworth berewick, lying so close to Norton, is in the study area of this book. Lindsworth, as discussed in the previous chapter, was already in existence in the early eighth century, being mentioned in an Anglo-Saxon boundary charter.[2] In contrast to King's Norton, it appears not to have grown as a settlement, and by the 19th century was only a single farm. It was demolished between the wars to make way for Bradstock Road and the eponymous Lindsworth Road.

Four hawks' nests are listed in Bromsgrove in Domesday Book. Confined to woodland, and reflecting both the Anglo-Saxon and Norman love of hunting and the nature of the local landscape, there is a possibility that two of these nests or eyries are reflected in surviving place-names: the present Hawkesley estate, named after the demolished Hawkesley Hall, and Hawkesley Drive, Longbridge, where the moat of Hawkesley Farm can still be seen.[3]

Although it is difficult to interpret the composite Domesday statistics for Bromsgrove (the plough team totals are unfortunately not divided among the berewicks), it has been estimated that about one third of the area of the estate was under plough, leaving two-thirds as commons, waste and woodland.[4] The Domesday Survey confirms the wooded environment of the royal estate, itemising a wood seven leagues long by four leagues wide. Some indication of the inroads made upon the forest is given by references to the 300 cartloads of wood which annually supplied the salt works at Droitwich. Most interestingly a road called *Wychewey* in the 15th century and now Silver Street, Wythall, led only as far as Houndsfield, indicating its purpose as such a supply route to Droitwich.

TENURE AND LANDOWNERSHIP

LANDLORDS

1. THE CROWN ESTATE

The Emergence of the Manor of King's Norton

Norton means 'north farm' and, as an outlying dependent part of a large estate, this orientation reflects an origin in the Anglo-Saxon period between Norton to the north and Bromsgrove to the south.[5] By the 13th century Norton, as part of a royal manor, had become known as King's Norton (Norton Regis in some Latin documents) and the process by which the great royal manor of Bromsgrove eventually divided into two halves had already begun. Although remaining part of Bromsgrove throughout the medieval period, King's Norton had emerged as a separate entity so that the estate from the mid-13th century was known as the 'manor of Bromsgrove and King's Norton'.[6] The expansion of the territory of King's Norton had been aided by the establishment of a chapel at the settlement sometime in the 12th century (see below).[7] The relatively small territory that had probably been associated with the berewick had extended to cover an extensive area stretching from the Lickey Hills in the west to Balsall Heath in the north west, an area of 11,726 acres.[8]

The Manorial Succession

The manors of King's Norton and Bromsgrove did not remain the direct property of the Crown. The succession of owners and leaseholders is long and complicated and there is no room to repeat it here.[9] Suffice to say that over the centuries the manors passed backwards and forwards between the Crown and members of the royal family, household and officials for the usual favours rendered and expected. Sometimes it went to men of little distinction and on one occasion in 1261 it was even leased to 'the goodmen of Bromsgrove and Kings Norton'.[10] From the mid-13th century to the end of the 14th century the Mortimer family, Earls of March, held a major interest in the two manors, though it was granted intermittently to royal ladies, often in dower with a large number of other manors. By 1460 Bromsgrove and King's Norton had once again become part of the Crown estates. In the following century the practice of granting the manors to female members of the royal family was resumed, culminating with the many wives of Henry VIII, Anne Boleyn excepted.

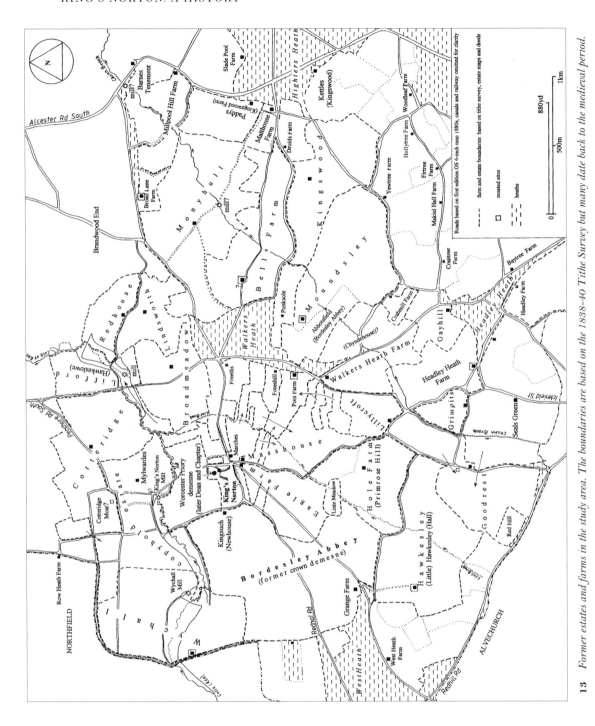

13 *Former estates and farms in the study area. The boundaries are based on the 1838-40 Tithe Survey but many date back to the medieval period.*

Bromsgrove manor was finally separated from King's Norton in 1564, when it was sold by Queen Elizabeth to Ambrose, Earl of Warwick.[11] King's Norton, however, remained royal until the beginning of the 19th century. King's Norton parish, by contrast, did not become independent of Bromsgrove until 1846.[12]

2. BORDESLEY ABBEY'S GRANGES

When Bordesley Abbey, a Cistercian house, was founded in 1138 near what is now the northern edge of Redditch, Empress Maud gave a substantial block of royal land at King's Norton to the monks as part of its endowment. The land had formed part of the Domesday berewicks of Norton and Houndsfield in Wythall. The gift comprised 'the whole demesne of Norton with the land of the forester and beadle' as well as the land of Godric de Hundesfelde. We can trace these early monastic holdings with some precision because land acquired by the Cistercians before 1215 enjoyed exemption from the payment of tithe. This privilege was closely guarded throughout the Middle Ages, retained at the Dissolution and recorded in the Tithe Apportionment of 1838. From this it is clear that the 'whole demesne of Norton' comprised what had become Newhouse and Grange Farms by the mid-19th century. In 1838 the combined acreage of these two farmsteads amounted to 245 acres, a figure which corresponds very closely to the estimated 256 acres occupied by Bordesley's monastic farms, known as Norton Grange and Kingsuch Grange in the 14th century. Together they formed a solid block of farmland stretching from Wychall Lane in the north to Green Lane, off Redditch Road, in the south. Further small grants of land from local people followed, but they did not alter the overall picture of three main granges – Norton, Kingsuch and Houndsfield.[13]

Their stricter interpretation of the Rule of St Benedict of Citeaux meant the Cistercians of the early 12th century attempted to throw off all superfluous and feudal accretions to the monastic life and return to a life of material and spiritual simplicity with a new emphasis on manual labour. One of the means of achieving this was by a total separation from the world, reflected in their policy of isolationism from existing settlement. Wherever possible the Cistercians sought remote situations for their abbeys and farms. In the first century and a half of operation, from the 1130s to the end of the 13th century, it can be argued they were largely successful in achieving this monastic ideal. In their search for solitude they are credited with reclaiming vast stretches of waste and wood beyond the existing margins of cultivation. At some sites they even moved existing settlements to ensure the isolation they sought. However, at King's Norton the evidence suggests they were given demesne land that was almost certainly already in cultivation. Far from achieving the solitude they sought, they were prepared to compromise by working the granges in what was fast becoming a relatively densely settled rural landscape. For the lay brothers at Norton and Kingsuch granges there were an increasing number of neighbours: to the east a nucleated settlement was developing around the chapel and a triangular green, while on the south and north early enclosed moated farmsteads at Hawkesley and Wychall were established in the 13th century. Only on part of its south-western boundary towards Northfield did the Bordesley land adjoin waste, West Heath, and conform to Cistercian ideals of seclusion.

In the 12th and 13th centuries the Cistercians worked their granges directly with lay brothers and hired workmen. In theory, no grange should have been further than a day's journey from the monastery, but in reality a permanent base was needed for the efficient running of outlying farms. The grange therefore comprised domestic accommodation for the labour force, a chapel or oratory for worship, and farm buildings for the storage of crops.[14] In the 13th and early 14th centuries Bordesley Abbey enjoyed a high reputation nationally for the quality of its wool. It is likely, but cannot be proved, that its lands at King's Norton were in part used for the production of these high quality fleeces. Monastic sheep farming may well have encouraged the growth of King's Norton's wool trade.

By the early 14th century, however, Bordesley's direct involvement with its King's Norton estate changed. In 1329 the monastery withdrew its workforce in the granges of Norton and Kingsuch, preferring to let them to the neighbouring landowner, Richard de Hawkesley, who was then able to treble the acreage of his farmland. At the same time he acquired an estate with a mill at Lifford as well as land at Inkberrow and Dormston. The source of his wealth that funded this expansion has yet to be explained but involvement in the wool trade is very likely. De Hawkesley took on high office: he was a Sheriff and MP for Worcestershire several times between 1328 and 1344 and steward of the Mortimer estate in King's Norton. He had a town house near the cathedral in Worcester and through endowments became 'a dear friend to the Priory of Worcester'.[15]

3. The Worcester Priory Estate in King's Norton

The origins of this important estate lie in a royal grant. In 1232 Henry III gave the church of Bromsgrove to the Prior and monks of Worcester.[16] Henry's father, King John, had been buried in Worcester Cathedral and Henry wished to have the anniversary of his father's death commemorated by the monks so encouraged them by the generous gift of one of the richest rectories in the county.[17] By 1237 all the revenues from the rectorial estate income had been appropriated by the Priory, including the considerable tithe.[18] Included with Bromsgrove church were the chapels at King's Norton and Grafton.

Unfortunately there is no description of any land that was granted to the Priory at this time, except that the vicar had a house both in Bromsgrove and in King's Norton.[19] As was often the case, the rector in Bromsgrove had already delegated day-to-day pastoral care and duties to a vicar, while retaining the principal tithe revenues and rents. It is not until 1514 that we obtain reliable information on the holdings of the Priory estate in King's Norton.[20] This consisted firstly of a compact area of glebe between the church and the river Rea to the north, now mostly contiguous with King's Norton park and the playing fields on either side of Pershore Road South. This is not unexpected, as this large parcel equates with the rectorial glebe that belonged to the Dean and Chapter of Worcester recorded in the 1838 Tithe Survey. After the Dissolution of the Priory in

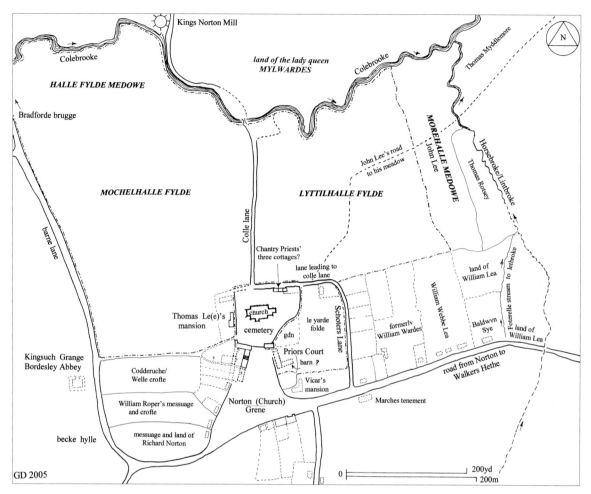

14   *King's Norton in 1514 – a reconstruction of the Worcester Priory estate survey.*

1540, Bromsgrove rectory, which included King's Norton church, was granted in 1542 to the newly created Dean and Chapter at Worcester Cathedral.[21]

It was not suspected until the recent discovery of the 1514 survey at the Worcester Cathedral archives that the Priory estate also included much of the village and its backland on the east and west side of The Green and on the north side of the present Wharf Road down to the canal bridge. In the same way that the Priory became 'firmly established as a landlord at the centre of Bromsgrove', so did the Priory come to dominate King's Norton village.[22] The 1514 survey has been plotted on Fig. 14. The principal house of the estate, and one of the most important buildings in the village, was called Prior's Court. It was situated in a prominent position on the east side of The Green opposite the *Saracen's Head*. This was the home farm for the demesne or glebeland that lay on the north side of the church, which in the mid-14th century was directly cultivated by the Priory, their local bailiff probably living in the house.[23] It is not known when this glebeland was created.

It is possible that it existed before the grant to the Priory and may have been part of original royal demesne given to the chapel at King's Norton when it was first founded in the 12th century. In the middle of the 15th century the demesne was leased (a common practice at this time) to local inhabitants and divided into two, with a new house built on the west side of the churchyard by one of the leaseholders, the Lee family.[24] In 1514 John Middlemore of Hazelewell Hall leased Prior's Court and the field east of Colle lane while Thomas Lee leased the land west of the lane and the 'mansion' house that his ancestors had built by the churchyard. This latter house was demolished in the late 19th century, Prior's Court having disappeared some time earlier, in the 17th century.

The Priory estate also consisted of about ten houses with gardens and crofts situated in and around the village. These were held freely, as was most land on the King's Norton royal estate, and owed only a small chief rent. Among the most important were a couple of houses called 'Bosshemore' and 'Ronkes', which formed the rear buildings of the *Saracen's Head*, constructed by the Rotsey family on their 'forecourt' on the opposite side of The Green to Priors Court. The survey also tells us that several of the neighbouring houses were owned by the various chantries in the church.

The Priory estate also had outlying land to the north near King's Heath, a larger block in the area of Newland Road and Lewis Road based on the later Bullies Farm (the eponymous Priory Road is not quite accurately located), and a separate field off the west side of Grove Lane.

4. WESTBURY COLLEGE ESTATE (MONYHULL)

Although Monyhull is located on the edge of the study area, it is worth mentioning this other estate with ecclesiastical connections, established in King's Norton in the late medieval period. Monyhull is first recorded in the 13th century as a family name;[25] in 1286 Richard de Monhull is mentioned along with his King's Norton lands and watermill on the Chinn Brook.[26] By 1424 Monyhull had been acquired by the Wybbe family along with a scatter of holdings to the north spreading towards King's Heath.[27] This was only a small part of an extensive Worcestershire estate with a house in Hanbury that still bears their name (Webhowe or Webbhowse).[28] Thomas Wybbe had leased or 'farmed' the 'manor of Monhull' to John Belne and Richard Kettel for a considerable annual rent of £7 8s. 4d. It appears that a daughter of Thomas or a John Webbe married Thomas Haukeslow, whose daughter married Nicholas Middlemore, beginning the Middlemore of Hawkesley line.[29]

Thomas Wybbe or a relative of the same name appears to have fallen on hard times and sold his lands in the mid-1460s to Bishop John Carpenter of Worcester.[30] John Carpenter had been born at Westbury-on-Trym near Bristol where there had been a monastery since before the Conquest. It had been founded by Saint Oswald, Bishop of Worcester around 961.[31] By 1194 it had been reformed into a collegiate church with a dean and canons (secular priests rather than monks). Bishop Carpenter became Westbury's most important patron, rebuilding much of the present church and constructing new separate college buildings of which the gatehouse still stands.

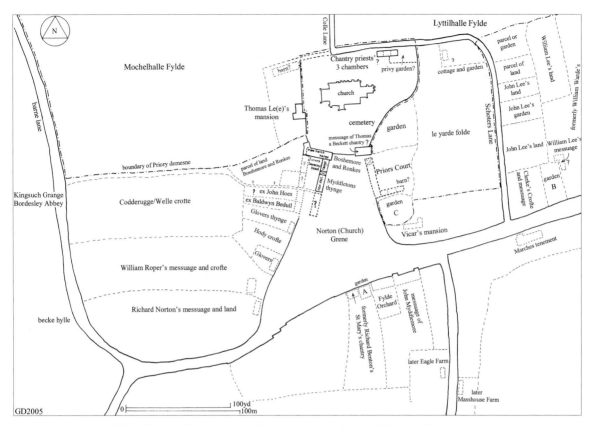

15 *King's Norton village in 1514 with tenants' names from the Worcester Priory estate survey*

He reorganised the college and styled himself Bishop of Worcester and Westbury and acquired lands in Worcestershire and Gloucestershire to endow his beloved establishment. Gannow near Frankley was purchased as well as the Monyhull estate.[32]

Monyhull remained in the ownership of Westbury College until the college was dissolved by Henry VIII in 1544. The valuation carried out just nine years before shows that the main holding or 'manor' was leased for an annual sum of £15 17s. 6d., over twice the amount in 1424, and that the rents received from the free tenants amounted to only 17s. 6d., only a shilling more than in 1424.[33] It was clear that the leasing of property at commercial rates was more profitable than collecting ancient fixed rents (rents of assize) from tenants. There was also land at Grovelly and near Icknield Street in Alvechurch attached to Monyhull. William Sparry was Westbury's local bailiff and it is possible that he was the leaseholder of Monyhull at this time.

TENANTS

The fact that King's Norton was part of a royal manor of Bromsgrove at the time of Domesday Book meant by definition it was part of 'ancient demesne', conferring particular rights and privileges on the tenants. The origins of ancient demesne are obscure but by the late 13th and 14th century the concept was fully developed.[34] Tenants of the king did not attend the county court and were exempt from the jurisdiction of the sheriff. They did not pay any toll in local markets and were not taxed with the country at large; they held their own court independent of the common law assizes. In return for this franchise, tenants were levied directly by the Crown, but despite this link the tenants of King's Norton and other ancient demesnes enjoyed a freedom that even the new boroughs of the realm would envy.

In King's Norton the vast majority of tenancies were free; there were a few customary tenancies, that is those held by custom of the manorial court. Traditionally, most servile (unfree or villein) tenants held by custom and could only transfer their land by the authority of the manorial court. In King's Norton the customary tenancies do not appear to have originated in servile tenure, which was also frequently associated with arable cultivation in scattered strips in common or open fields. By the time records appear in the 16th century, the few customary tenants appear to have their origin in escheated land,[35] property confiscated by the Crown for lack of heirs, or serious misdemeanours such as treason. The location of customary tenures in King's Norton cannot be seen as indicators of early medieval common arable fields, as they are elsewhere; the difficult question of the extent of the open fields in King's Norton will be discussed later.

POPULATION

According to the figures estimated from Domesday Book, north Worcestershire and Warwickshire had one of the lowest populations in the country (the north of England excepted), with an average of 2.5 to 5 people per square mile.[36] In addition, the very large size of the Bromsgrove and King's Norton manor is accepted as a marker of low population density. Looking at the Bromsgrove data, however, a different picture emerges. There are 128 people listed, and applying the normal multiplier of five to a household would give a total of 640. Bromsgrove's area of 36 square miles provides a figure of 17.7 per square mile, well above the level calculated in the Domesday Geography series and in close agreement with Anne Baker's recent work on King's Norton.[37] The discrepancy could be explained by the very low populations in the neighbouring Worcestershire and Warwickshire manors.

Giving the Domesday berewick of Norton an average radius of one mile results in an area of 3.1 square miles and a population of 54 people or nearly 11 households. In the whole of the later manor of King's Norton, roughly the same area as the reduced Bromsgrove, there would have been a population of 320 people or 64 households. If these latter figures are divided equally between the eight berewicks of King's Norton, an average population per berewick of 40 people or eight households is obtained. Norton is slightly above average based on an estimate of area, but too much reliance should not be placed upon the analysis of the Domesday population statistics beyond the very basic level.

More direct information on population is not available until the 13th century. In a rental of chief King's Norton rents compiled in the reign of Henry III (1216-72) 103 names are listed. If this is a true representation of the number of households it implies a population of about 515. This is an increase of 60 per cent over the unreliable Domesday levels and much less than the doubling or more of the population that might be expected by the 13th century.[38] It is possible the Domesday statistics are too high; it is also likely that the rental undercounts the number of households. In later centuries, when rentals can be compared to other taxation lists, it is clear that many households did not pay a chief rent.

The 1275 Lay Subsidy Roll lists 147 taxpayers for King's Norton, giving 735 as the total population.[39] Unfortunately the Lay Subsidy Roll omits a considerable number of people, such as anyone with less than 15s. worth of goods – in other words the poorest. The total must be increased by an amount not easy to calculate. Nationally the population had at least doubled since Domesday. Locally the maximum would be eight hundred. It is more likely to have been higher, taking into consideration the under-enumeration of the Lay Subsidy roll, and perhaps over a thousand. The 1327 Lay Subsidy Roll, however, lists only 53 taxpayers for King's Norton, a decrease of 64 per cent.[40] Such a steep decline could have been expected after the Black Death of 1348-50, but it appears that this taxation was not efficiently collected, with the resulting serious under-enumeration of the taxable population. Some decline might have been expected following the severe famine of 1315-17.

Nationally the population did not start to recover from the Black Death until the 1520s. The epidemic was responsible for reducing the population of England from about 5 million to 2.5 million. There is no evidence chronicling this catastrophe locally but there are some indicators of its impact on church and house building.

The next listing of King's Norton inhabitants is dated roughly 1460. It is a chief rental of the royal tenants and therefore understates the total number of households due to composite entries, sub-tenancies, unlevied small holdings and tenants belonging to other estates such as the Worcester Priory. A total of 141 tenants are recorded in five yields, for which the rental is the first known record.

Rednal	14
Headley	43
Moundsley	27
Lea	25
Moseley	32
Total	141

This figure is close to the 1275 Lay Subsidy total but the lists are not comparable. All that can be said is that about 700 people may be represented by this rental; a large, but unknown, percentage of households did not pay the king's chief rent.

We are fortunate in having a detailed military survey or muster for the manor of King's Norton dated 1522.[41] Excluding six priests, there were approximately 210 households recorded, giving a population of approximately a thousand.[42] This is the same number calculated using the 1275 Lay Subsidy Roll, quite contrary to the trend that could be expected nationally. In the country as a whole the population in the 1520s was still about half the total of the late 13th century.[43] If we can rely on these statistics then something significantly different happened in late medieval King's Norton, bucking the national trend. Perhaps the Black Death was not so virulent and recovery was much faster. Maybe the dispersed farms and the less intensive pasture economy inoculated the population from the pestilence that decimated populations in the over-exploited arable areas further south in the county. The 1524 and 1525 Lay Subsidy Rolls record 152 and 148 names respectively, down by over a quarter on the military survey of a few years before. A fall in population of this order is unlikely in these few years, confirming the unreliability of Lay Subsidy rolls in general. If the population of King's Norton manor was around a thousand in the 1520s then it took another 400 years to reach four thousand.

In none of the medieval lists is there any way of identifying those who lived in the village of King's Norton, and in fact this problem persists with records well into the 19th century. The post-medieval rentals and hearth tax returns do not identify the village, and our first view – fortunately detailed – is contained in the 1514 Worcester Priory survey.

THE EVOLUTION OF THE RURAL LANDSCAPE

1. FIELD AND FOREST

The rural landscape of King's Norton evolved in a distinctive way, due in no small part to the considerable freedoms enjoyed by the tenants of the Crown. This freedom of action, however, may merely have intensified a long process, only completed in the medieval period, whereby a 'woodland' or enclosed type of landscape was created over large areas of north Worcestershire and Warwickshire (known as the Arden in the latter county). This landscape stood in contrast to the southern parts of the two counties: in Worcestershire along the Severn Valley and in Warwickshire in the area known as Feldon. Feldon literally means field in the arable sense, and the term 'champion' is often used interchangeably. In the Feldon large common or open fields with few hedgerows dominated, subdivided into furlongs and in turn into strips, or 'selions'. The strip was a unit of landholding and could contain one or more ridges, commonly known as 'ridge and furrow', created by ploughing. Woodland and waste were relatively scarce.

Settlement patterns were also distinct. In the woodland landscape hamlets and individual farmsteads predominated, connected by a dense network of winding lanes set within irregularly shaped and relatively small hedged fields. Many of the farms were surrounded by moats. In champion countryside, large nucleated villages were the norm and unhedged roads ran more directly across the fields.

In King's Norton open field agriculture appears not to have developed to any great extent, and what little area was given over to common fields may have shrunk

significantly during the medieval period. Open fields may be expected to have existed around the settlement of King's Norton itself, but there is little evidence of them. The survival of 'ridge and furrow' within the present King's Norton Playing Fields is due to 19th-century ploughing techniques and the ridges distort to fit the shape of the field. They are, in fact, later in date than the boundary hedgerows, while in champion countryside, much affected by Parliamentary enclosure in the late 18th century, the characteristically thin hawthorn hedgerows post-date the ridges.[44]

There is a hint of a field (Size Field/Sisefield) formerly divided into strips on Dougharty's 1731-3 map of Masshouse Farm.[45] The field lay south east of the village between Wharf Road and Masshouse Lane. To the west, between the latter road and Rednal Road, two narrow rectangular fields survived into the 19th century, part of the larger Eagle Field.[46] The remainder of the land around the village appears never to have been tenants' arable and formed an extensive area of demesne land, which the Crown granted to Bordesley Abbey as early as the 13th century and to the Worcester Priory in the 14th century.

Elsewhere there is evidence for selions, but it is confined to small scattered areas. Much farther to the east, near Crabmill Lane, a certain croft in 1467 called 'Newelond' (Newland) had within it four selions.[47] The name 'croft' in this area usually means a field enclosed by hedges. Newland is usually interpreted as newly cleared land and it appears it was initially ploughed into ridges. Further to the east and south at Houndsfield (the present area of Hollywood) is the best evidence in King's Norton manor for intermixed holdings in strips. At the end of the 13th century John Baudrey gave 22 selions with headlands to his son in 'his field called Middlefield'.[48] Next to these strips was a furlong called ' Hale Furlong'. Another son, Robert, held more selions, two in 'Hale Furlong' and nine in 'Well Crofte'. But none of this points to a fully-fledged open field system, with crop rotation in two or three large fields, one lying fallow, and the complete intermixing of strip holdings. 'Welle Crofte' was hedged and ditched, and Middlefield was regarded as the private property of

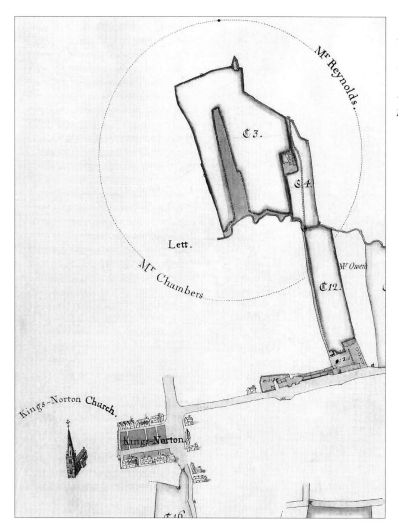

17 *An extract from John Dougharty's plan of 1731-2. This is the first known plan of the village, but shows The Green inaccurately as a rectangle; the strip fields may suggest the position of former open fields.*

John Baudrey rather than communally held. It is possible that an earlier open field system associated with the Domesday berewick of Houndsfield had begun to collapse with amalgamation of strips and enclosure by hedges. The same process may have taken place at the berewick of King's Norton itself, in the fields to the south, and at Moseley where two selions were recorded in 1491 near Lady Pool Lane.[49]

During the period from the Norman Conquest to the mid-14th century the landscape of King's Norton manor changed significantly to accommodate the growing population. Large areas of woodland were cleared, including *Hellerelege*. This clearance, or 'assarting' as it was called, did not add greatly to the open fields that perhaps lay immediately around many of the berewicks, but was conducted on an individual basis and encouraged by the freedoms enjoyed by the tenants of the royal manor. A network of isolated farms was created, many moated, located within their own enclosed fields. The process of 'assarting' can be detected through the names of the fields created, e.g.

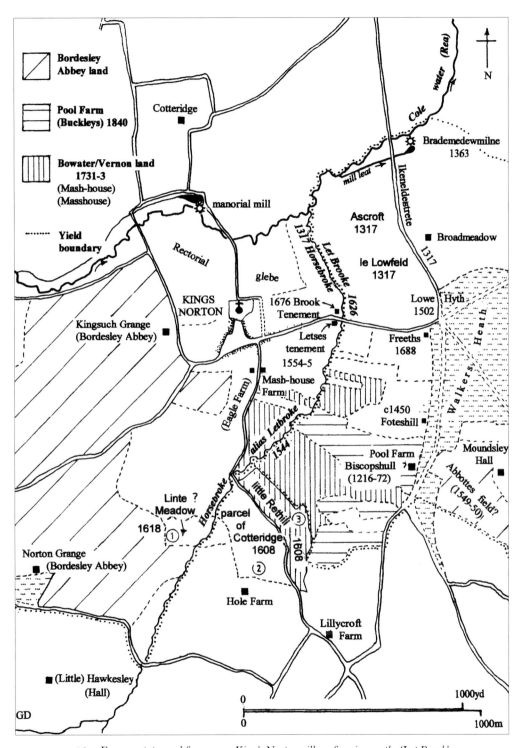

Bordesley Abbey land

Pool Farm (Buckleys) 1840

Bowater/Vernon land 1731-3 (Mash-house) (Masshouse)

Yield boundary

Cotteridge

Cole water (Rea)

Brademedewmilne 1363

mill leat

Ikeneldestrete

manorial mill

Ascroft 1317

Broadmeadow

Rectorial

Let Brooke

1317 *Horsebroke*

glebe

le Lowfeld 1317

1317

KINGS NORTON

1676 Brook Tenement

Lowe 1502

Hyth

Kingsuch Grange (Bordesley Abbey)

Letses tenement 1554-5

Freeths 1688

Walkers Heath

Mash-house Farm

(Eagle Farm)

alias Letbroke

1544

c1450 Foteshill

Pool Farm Biscopshull (1216-72)

Moundsley Hall

Abbottes field? (1549-50)

Linte ? Meadow

1618

Horsebroke

parcel of Cotteridge 1608

little Rethill

1608

Norton Grange (Bordesley Abbey)

Hole Farm

Lillycroft Farm

(Little) Hawkesley (Hall)

GD

N

0   1000yd

0   1000m

18   *Former estates and farms near King's Norton village focusing on the 'Let Brook'.*

25

Newland (see above), Ridding, Stocking, Breech.[50] Nevertheless, a generous cover of woodland remained in the manor and much of the extensive heath (about 2,000 acres, 1772 Enclosure Award) that survived into the late 18th century should be seen as representing a significant remnant of the medieval woodland. Not all should be seen as thick forest; a more open landscape of wood pasture was perhaps more normal. Here denser woodland was intermixed with open areas of grass, where animals could graze.

The evidence of place-names shows how the woodland was eventually converted into heath, with a 'wood called Kyngesheth' still in existence in 1519, 'Kingesnorton Wode' (1330-1), transforming into the east part of Highter's Heath, and Kingswood becoming the west part of Highter's Heath and Bateman's Green.[51] In the study area were part of West Heath, Walker's Heath, Headley Heath and the fringes of Highter's Heath and West Heath.

The clearance of woodland and wood pasture in King's Norton caused competition over the shrinking resource. Tenants resisted further enclosures by their superior lord or were in conflict with the tenants of neighbouring manors where the woodland straddled boundaries.

In the 1320s a lessee of the royal manor, Roger Mortimer, Earl of March and one of the most powerful magnates in the country, built a huge bank and ditch across common land between Warstock and Hollywood. The inhabitants of King's Norton, Solihull and Yardley, who claimed that they had 'time out of mind inter-commoned for all animals and cattle at all times of the year in the pasture of Kyngesnorton Wode', filled up the ditch. They were pursued in court by the Earl's steward in King's Norton, Richard de Hawkesley, and an enormous fine of £300 was imposed upon them. Roger Mortimer had led the opposition with Queen Isabella to Edward II and was seized as a criminal and imprisoned in Nottingham Castle and directly executed at Tyburn. The tenants of the three manors then petitioned Edward III and eventually won a substantial reduction. Until the late 18th century Mortimer's Bank was still an impressive linear earthwork and one that the antiquary William Hutton noted. Between 1772 and 1774 parliamentary enclosure of the common east of the Alcester Road at Hollywood changed the landscape to such an extent that Hutton struggled to find the earthwork after enclosure, but its line can still be traced running north-south between Trueman's Heath and Warstock.

Where the precise boundary on the common land lay between King's Norton and Alvechurch may not have been important in the early medieval period, but it had taken on some significance in 1273 when a dispute broke out between the shared grazing on West Heath and *Dodenhaleshay*. The tenants of the Bishop of Worcester's manor of Alvechurch were known to be vigorously assarting the land in the north of the manor and causing the 'men of King's Norton to destroy the new banks and fences'. The conflict rumbled on until September 1287 when an agreement was reached between the warring parties. The King's Norton community was paid 10 marks (£6 13s. 4d.) and gave up rights to *Dodenhaleshay* in exchange for retaining common rights on what remained of West Heath.[52]

2. THE EXPANSION FROM NORTON BEREWICK

The clearance of large areas of woodland and woodland pasture in the manor of King's Norton from at least the 13th century to the mid-14th century was mostly achieved by individual families creating relatively compact holdings. These consisted of small irregularly shaped fields, hedged and ditched, with the farmstead placed within them.

The settlement of Norton itself, one of two berewicks in the study area, appears to have had two open fields to the south (the later Size Field/Sisefeild and Eagle Field), although the evidence is not conclusive. Each of these fields was later associated with an individual farm, Eagle Farm and Masshouse Farm respectively, both situated on the fringes of the present village on Masshouse Lane. Masshouse Farm in fact shared the Size Field with another village farm, Marches Tenement, once situated on the present Wharf Road, and with farms located on the western edge of Walker's Heath (Pool Farm, Freeths, Footshill). It is possible that the disintegration of the open field system at Norton was accompanied by the creation of farms along the edge of Walker's Heath, a convenient way of gaining a foothold within the fields themselves. It is not certain, however, whether this process was completed before or after the Black Death.

The demesne that was situated to the west and south west of Norton village, as discussed above, was granted to Bordesley Abbey in 1138. The Cistercian monks may have taken over an existing royal demesne farm, called Kingsitch/Kingsuch (later Newhouse Farm), located on the west side and on the summit of the present Westhill Road. Sitch means a small stream (OE *sic*), and this was probably the stream to the west of Kingsuch that flows north to the river Rea and on which there is a pond situated today near Beaks Hill Road. It is unlikely that the name would have arisen during the four centuries of Cistercian ownership and therefore reflects its earlier royal origins. On the other hand, Grange Farm to the south on Redditch Road might have been a Cistercian foundation. The land immediately to the north of the village, which was granted to Worcester Priory in the 13th century, was farmed from Prior's Court, situated on the east side of The Green. It may also have originally been royal demesne.

The demesne and suspected open field area formed the core of the settlement of Norton by the end of the 12th century. There is no evidence of any open fields around the berewick of Lindsworth and its immediate landscape appears no different to the large areas cleared beyond Norton in the 13th and 14th centuries. Lindsworth may only have ever been a single isolated farm with demesne land and no tenants. Another farm was created to the west, between Lindsworth and the Lint Brook – Broad Meadow (near the eponymous Broad Meadow Lane today). To the north a small estate was developed around a watermill, later known as Lifford (see below).

Moving west along the river Rea, or the Cole as it was called in this period, we encounter a block of land on the north side that was held by custom of the manor. There were three subdivisions. The first, Millwards, was Crown land and was associated with the *Saracen's Head* from the early 16th century.[53] In the early 18th century a dwelling, High House, was constructed upon the summit of the land, but it may have been the location of 'millerstenement' in the medieval period.[54] The manorial estate with the

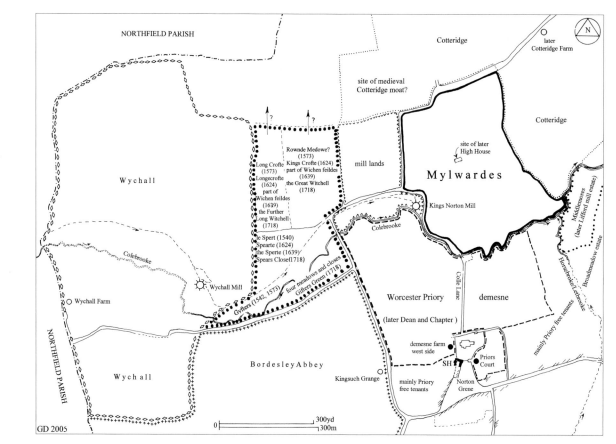

NORTHFIELD PARISH

Cotteridge

later
Cotteridge Farm

site of medieval
Cotteridge moat?

Cotteridge

Rownde Medowe?
(1573)
Long Crofte   Kings Crofte (1624)
(1573)   part of Wichen feildes
Longecrofte   (1639)
(1624)   the Great Witchell
part of   (1718)
Wichen feildes
(1639)
the Further
Long Witchell
(1718)

mill lands

M y l w a r d e s

site of later
High House

Wychall

Kings Norton Mill

le Spert (1540)
Spearte (1624)
the Sperte (1639)
Spears Close(1718)

Colebrooke

Colebrooke

Wychall Mill

four meadows and closes
Gyfters Green (1718)
Gyfters (1542, 1573)

Wychall Farm

NORTHFIELD PARISH

Wych a l l

B o r d e s l e y A b b e y

Kingsuch Grange

Worcester Priory

(later Dean and Chapter)

demesne farm
west side

mainly Priory
free tenants

SH

Priors
Court

Norton
Grene

Colle Lane

demesne

mainly Priory free tenants

Middlemores
(later Lifford mill estate)

Horsebroke/Lythroke

Broadmeadow estate

GD 2005

0   300yd
300m

19 *Former estates and farms to the north of King's Norton village: 'Mylwardes', King's Norton Mill,*
Wychall and Worcester Priory ('SH' represents the Saracen's Head).

working mill itself formed the next small unit. West of this, a larger block stretched
from Row Heath to the river but did not appear to have contained a farmstead; with
Millwards and the mill it was held by the owners of the *Saracen's Head* at the very end
of the medieval period. North of the customary land was an important estate known as
Cotteridge, which gave its name to the present suburb.[55] This contained a moated site
in the medieval period (field names 'Far Motts' and 'Near Motts') which was situated
to the north of Middleton Hall Road.[56] An estate of comparable size to Cotteridge,
Wychall, straddled the river as it entered King's Norton from Northfield manor. It
represents one of many compact estates in this area that changed little in size from the
original grant given by the Crown.

Leaping south over the former royal demesne given to Bordesley Abbey we
reach Hawkesley (Hawkesley Hall, Little Hawkesley), much confused with the
other Hawkesley further west on the other side of West Heath (Great Hawkesley,
Hawkesley Farm).[57] Both might have had their origins in two of the four recorded
Domesday hawks' eyres and been, by implication, isolated places buried within

woodland. The eastern half of Hawkesley lies in fact within the former area of the *Hellerelege* woodland of the Anglo-Saxon charter, confirming the original sylvan environment. Immediately to the north of Hawkesley Hall was a compact estate called Hole Farm (the house surviving as Primrose Hill Farm), entirely surrounded by roads and probably one of the most stable units of landholding in this area. It also represents the clearance of part of the *Hellerelege* woodland. Other farms created out of this great wood include Goodrest Farm, Lilycroft Farm, Walker's Heath Farm and Moundsley Hall. North of Hole Farm, one of the farms in the Size Field area, Pool Farm, may have once been known as Bishopshill. This medieval name possibly originated in the eighth century when the Bishop of Worcester owned *Hellerelege*. Walker's Heath itself was probably the last tract of *Hellerelege* left after the colonisation of the woodland had spent itself before the mid-14th century.

A large number of small farms were established between Hawkesley Hall and Moundsley Hall, with less compact and stable boundaries: Grimpits Farm, Gay Hill Farm, Headley Heath Farm, Crabtree Farm, Makiel Hall Farm, Hollytree Farm, Woodleaf Farm. Returning north towards Lindsworth, we pass four large farms, compact but elongated in an east-south-east direction: Moundsley Hall, Kingswood Farm, Bell's Farm and Monyhull Hall give the impression that they spread in this direction from the west, clearing a large area of early medieval Kings Wood in the process.

In a relatively short period of no more than a century and a half, the landscape in an area up to a mile and a half from the Norton settlement had been transformed. There is not enough information surviving to tell us whether the new fields that had been created were predominantly arable or pasture, nor how the landscape might have changed in the remainder of the medieval period. Animal husbandry certainly became characteristic of a large area of north Worcestershire, as towns and local trading centres were established, allowing the exchange of surpluses of grain and animal products and reducing the need to devote the land to cereal crops for subsistence. Specialisation of the economy was beginning to develop.

3. Moated Houses and Farmsteads

A distinctive feature of the medieval landscape of King's Norton is the moated site. Moats existed around the houses of the more prosperous tenants at Hawkesley Hall, Monyhull Hall, Headley Heath Farm, Wychall Farm and Cotteridge ('The Moats'). Across the whole parish there is evidence for no fewer than 19 moats. Most have long been infilled, ploughed out or built over. William Hutton, Birmingham's 18th-century historian, left the earliest description of one site at Cotteridge which was known simply as The Moats, but had been destroyed by ploughing.[58] 'The numerous buildings which almost formed a village are totally erased, and barley grows where the beer was drank'. The moated sites in the northern part of King's Norton parish disappeared as housing and industrial development spread from Birmingham in the later 19th century, but many of them are traceable from field-name evidence (Moat Close or Leasow) on the Tithe Apportionment of 1838 and from a study of the accompanying

Tithe Map of 1840. The latter shows all water-filled ponds and ditches, which are sometimes indicators of once completely moated enclosures.

In 1971 a field survey recorded the remains of eight moats in the entire parish. Those in the study area were largely fragmentary but at Wythall, in the extreme south, four moated sites survived virtually complete. Since then considerable damage has been done to earthwork sites; many have been infilled and the ground levelled. The most complete example now is at Blackgreves (Blackgrave) Farm, Wythall, where a roughly square moat encloses an island between 40 and 50 metres wide on which now stands a 19th-century farmhouse. The width of the moat varies between 12 and 17 metres and today is crossed by a stone bridge. The clay dug to form the moat was partly used to raise the level of the platform but it was also dumped on the outer perimeter to build up the old ground surface.[59] As such, Blackgreves reflects the typical plan of moated sites in King's Norton – square or sub-rectangular enclosing an island of just over half an acre, providing ample space for several buildings and yards. Within the old parish, excavation has taken place inside the moated platform at only one site – Hawkesley Farm, Longbridge. Although the sub-rectangular moat may have been begun in the early 13th century, the first buildings found were not earlier than *c.*1300 and comprised two barn-like structures.[60]

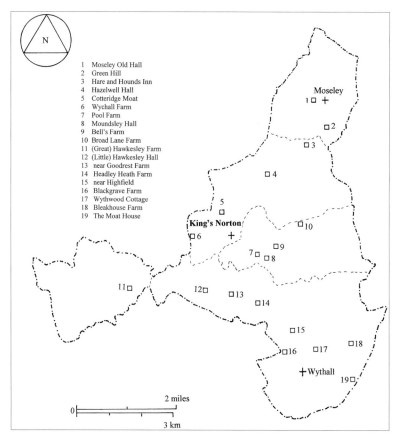

1 Moseley Old Hall
2 Green Hill
3 Hare and Hounds Inn
4 Hazelwell Hall
5 Cotteridge Moat
6 Wychall Farm
7 Pool Farm
8 Moundsley Hall
9 Bell's Farm
10 Broad Lane Farm
11 (Great) Hawkesley Farm
12 (Little) Hawkesley Hall
13 near Goodrest Farm
14 Headley Heath Farm
15 near Highfield
16 Blackgrave Farm
17 Wythwood Cottage
18 Bleakhouse Farm
19 The Moat House

20 *Location of moated sites within the ancient manor of King's Norton.*

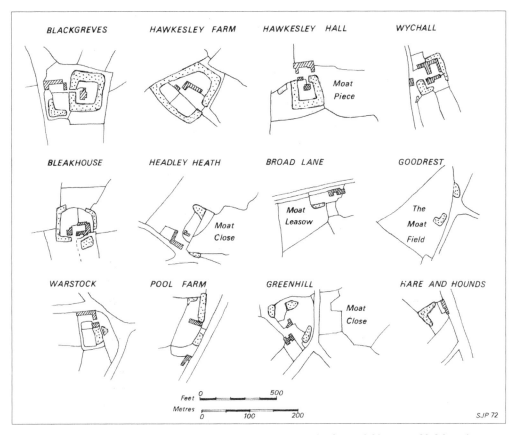

21 *Moated sites in King's Norton from the Tithe Map of 1840 with relevant field names added from the 1838 Tithe Award.*

The moats of King's Norton should be seen in the wider context of their distribution in the West Midlands. Both Warwickshire and Worcestershire, and the Birmingham area in particular, have a high concentration of moated sites. There have been many explanations offered for their popularity; some have argued that digging a moat provided a dry platform for building a house, and while this is true at Blackgreves, at Hawkesley Farm the material excavated from the moat was dumped outside the moated enclosure, not on the island. The evidence from King's Norton, where tenants enjoyed a high degree of freedom, supports the theory that adding a moat to a holding conferred social status by imitating the grander moats associated with fortified manor houses.

Despite the large number of recorded moats it is clear that they were not associated with every medieval farmstead. At Primrose Hill and Gay Hill Farms there is no evidence of a moat around the substantial surviving 15th-century houses. Both farms were probably created in the late 13th century, pottery evidence from Primrose Hill Farm providing the earliest indications of settlement. In the 15th century the earlier houses at Gay Hill and Primrose Hill were replaced by timber-framed hall-houses. The medieval house at Gay Hill now lies behind a late Georgian front block, while

31

22   *Blackgreves Farm, Wythall, photographed c.1925 when the edge of the moat was more clearly visible than it is today. The farmhouse on the island dates from 1827.*

23   *Primrose Hill Farm after its recent restoration. The open hall on the left was built in 1440 and the cross-wing to the right in 1475. The barn (extreme right) was erected in 1457.*

a brick re-fronting of the hall range at Primrose Hill conceals one of the finest examples of an open hall farmhouse in the West Midlands. Attached to the hall range is a timber-framed cross-wing which provided service rooms off the cross-passage and chambers above. Excavation has shown that another wing once existed on the eastern end of the hall range, thus making an H-plan. Primrose Hill Farm was originally known as Hole Farm, and from recent tree-ring dating we now know that the main part of the house was built in 1440 by the Field family. Baldwin Field was owner in about 1450 and was one of the leading freeholders in the parish. The barn followed in 1457 and the cross-wing has two phases, 1475 and 1521.[61]

24 *Reconstruction drawing by Stanley Jones of the open hall at Primrose Hill Farm as it might have appeared in the mid-15th century.*

THE VILLAGE

1. EVOLUTION

The earliest plan of the village is dated 1731-3 but is unfortunately distorted – The Green is rectangular rather than tapering northwards towards the church. John Dougharty was making a map of the Masshouse Farm lands to the south of the village and such inaccuracies often happen at the edge of a surveyor's area of work. Unfortunately, the buildings are not shown in plan but merely as flattened elevations and there are no back gardens or closes drawn. We must rely, therefore, on the much later Tithe Map (1840), and the large-scale drafts of this map have luckily survived (Fig. 67).[62]

Is the map recent enough to conclude anything reliable about the form of the village in the medieval period? The shape of The Green is distinctive, an irregular triangle. Two of its apexes lead into ancient highways – Rednal Road, west to West Heath, and Wharf Road, east to Walker's Heath. The north apex has its point blunted to form a boundary with the churchyard and the present Back Road exits awkwardly north-eastwards to connect with the later turnpike road, Pershore Road South. Before the latter was constructed, in 1825, the road from Birmingham took another course southwards from King's Norton mill, the site today of a petrol station on the corner of Camp Lane and Pershore Road South. The earliest we can track it with confidence is in 1449 (Fig. 25); instead of swinging to the east of the church, as it does now, the ancient road headed directly up the hill to the spire of the church.[63] This would take it through the present King's Norton park and the 19th-century graveyard extension lying immediately above. It was called Colle Lane after the local river name, 'water of Colle'.[64] On reaching the north side of the cemetery, the road appears to have turned sharp left (east) to run below the present Old Grammar School and then turned sharp right (south), into 'Schoters Lane', to connect with Wharf Road in front of the present *Navigation* inn. The lost lane ran at the back of what is now King's Norton Primary School. The awkwardness of this route from Birmingham might suggest an earlier diversion.

On The Green itself the simple lines of the triangle appear to be distorted by the buildings of the *Bull's Head* and *Saracen's Head*. They have the classic look of an encroachment. If the building line is set back to the south of these buildings, then the triangle becomes more regular, but with a lost north apex. If the building lines of both sides of The Green are projected northwards, they appear to converge upon the south end of Colle Lane. Is this only coincidence, or have we the original shape of Norton Green?

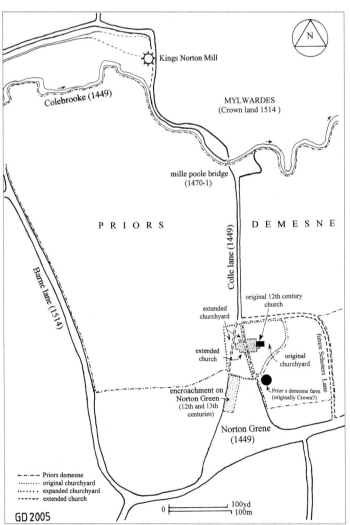

25 *A hypothetical reconstruction of King's Norton Green and St Nicolas churchyard in the early medieval period.*

In support of this idea is the fact that the original 12th-century church, the present chancel, would sit comfortably on the east side of The Green in the centre of a graveyard. It is possible that it was the expansion of the church in the following centuries, culminating with the construction of the tower and spire in the 15th century, that caused the loss of The Green here and its incorporation into the graveyard. Colle Lane would still have needed to connect to The Green, but it was forced in a roundabout way via 'Schoters Lane'. This lane appears to have been abandoned when Prior's Court was demolished sometime in the mid- to late 17th century. The cleared site of these buildings provided the opportunity of creating a new, more direct, link between Colle Lane and The Green – the present Back Road. It is no surprise that the existence of Prior's Court on The Green was not suspected until recently, as it disappeared from the village at least 300 years ago.

2. Medieval Secular Buildings in King's Norton Village

Until the late 19th century King's Norton was famed for its picturesque timber-framed and brick cottages surrounding The Green and extending eastwards along Wharf Road. Many of these were medieval and their early form was concealed behind later brick fronts, but successive rebuilding and redevelopment have reduced their number to just two examples – the *Saracen's Head* and no. 10 The Green (Spar Shop alias Hiron's Bakery). A Victorian photograph of no. 3 The Green (Fig. 26) reminds us what has been lost. It shows a substantial H-plan late medieval hall-house with jettied cross-wings either end of the hall. One wing and the hall were demolished in the 1890s despite protests from the Society for the Protection of Ancient Buildings. The western cross-wing was demolished in the 1930s leaving fragments of just one wall with a jetty post until its final clearance in 1982. Further along the south side of The Green a complete medieval cross-wing lies behind a late 18th- or early 19th-century façade at no.10, the upper parts of a close-studded gable being visible above the brick wall (Fig. 27). The accompanying open hall has long disappeared but enough remains of the cross-wing to show that at first floor level it originally consisted of a most impressive chamber with an arch-braced open roof. In the 18th century the house was known as St Mary's Hall and it is possible that its early history is associated with one of the chantries established in the late medieval period.

The Lost History of the Saracen's Head

More impressive still are the buildings at the north-western end of The Green, generally known since the 18th century as the *Saracen's Head* after the central part had become an inn. Facing the churchyard is a complete medieval house built of timbers felled in 1492, arguing for a construction date in that year or very shortly afterwards. A continuous jetty, indicating that it has always had a first floor, distinguishes the north elevation towards the church. The jetty continues round the east side fronting The Green and its corner is decidedly ostentatious. It is supported by a carved post and diagonally set dragon beam into which the richly moulded floor joists are tenoned for both elevations. In plan-form this range comprised richly painted grand rooms at the front on both floors, a centrally placed floored hall with a chamber over it, a cross passage entered by a two-storey porch from the churchyard, and service or storage rooms behind. The east range is structurally later than the north range but tree-ring dating proved the trees were also cut down in 1492, so the east range must have followed very soon after. It once extended as far as the *Bull's Head* inn and, like the north range, the frontage was jettied. In the centre was a projecting gabled entrance with high doors to allow loaded wagons and carts into the yard. It is likely that when it was built in the late 15th century the yard was surrounded on the other sides by outbuildings. Altogether the *Saracen's Head* complex represents an extremely good example of what is recognised nationally as a high-status late medieval house built on the courtyard plan.

26 *Nos 2-3 The Green. The timber-framed gables represent medieval jettied cross-wings to the central section with its sweeping low roof which demarcates an open hall. They were photographed c.1895 just before the demolition of the left-hand wing. The right-hand wing was demolished shortly after 1936.*

The builder must have been a person of great importance in the parish, but until recently his identity was a complete mystery. When the *Saracen's Head* won the BBC Two *Restoration* series 2 in 2004, little was known about the building's history before the Tithe Survey of 1838-40. The major new changes proposed for the building prompted the authors to seek its lost history. Curiosity apart, any new information could be useful in guiding the restoration.

The recorded story of the site begins in 1341 when an Adam Bisshemore is listed as a tenant of the Priory of Worcester.[65] Before 1379 John Bisshemore had acquired some land (a toft) from a priest, Robert in the Holys, and apparently built a house (messuage). John had also dug a ditch between his property and the Prior's demesne, an action which hints at its position at the northern end of The Green.[66] By 1423 the holding had passed to John Colmore and Richard Mydelton and consisted of three houses.[67] The Colmore family held a large rural estate

27 *No. 10 The Green. Externally, the close-studded gable is the only indicator that a medieval house exists behind a much later brick front. Internally, at first-floor and attic levels the timber frame is remarkably complete. An open hall lay to the left-hand side.*

in Rednal, later known as Colmers Farm, and an important link between the village property and the estate was thereby created. In 1431-2 Colmers Farm, and presumably the village houses, were sold to Robert Rotsey.[68] In 1508 Humphrey Rotsey, probably son of Robert, held a house, formerly John Bisshemore's, and another cottage called 'Ronkesse Thynge'.[69] These houses can be identified with the *Saracen's Head* because a few years later, in the 1514 Worcester Priory survey, Richard Rotsey, son of Humphrey, was now holding two houses called 'Bosshemore and Ronkes'.[70] The survey noted the boundaries of the property: on the north they ran with the 'cemetery of the church' and on the east with 'Norton Grene'. This location is unique to the *Saracen's Head*.

The dendrochronological dates obtained from the *Saracen's Head*'s north and east ranges of 1492 would mean that Humphrey Rotsey was the builder; he died about 1510. The north range and east range do not correspond with 'Bosshemore and Ronkes' of the Priory survey. Part was probably demolished by the new Rotsey ranges, part perhaps left standing at the rear. In fact the former 'Bosshmore and Ronkes' alignment may have been preserved in the later wing which projects from the north range into the churchyard. The awkward angle between the two ranges suggests this was dictated by a pre-existing property boundary.

28 *The east elevation of the* Saracen's Head. *Apart from the gable of the north range (right) most of the frame is concealed by later brick.*

It comes as no surprise that the Rotseys built the *Saracen's Head*; Richard Rotsey was the richest man in the village in 1522-3.[71] It is a piece of ostentatious timber framing located in a prime position next to the church and directly opposite the other great house on Norton Green, Prior's Court. It was probably one of the 'faire howsys of staplears', seen by Leland, 'that use to by wolle'.[72] The Rotseys, as well as trading in wool grown on their extensive Colmers estate, also ran a legal and accounting business with wealthy local clients such as the bishop of Worcester.[73] The *Saracen's Head* had to serve many functions: a grand house befitting the owner's status, a counting house, a place to receive clients and customers and a warehouse to store wool and other goods.

29 *By any standards the churchyard elevation of the* Saracen's Head's *north range is impressive, with close studding, jettying and carved pilasters. The doorways two-thirds along mark the position of the storeyed porch.*

30 *Reconstruction of the original east range of the* Saracen's Head. *The centrally placed gateway led to the courtyard at the back.*

31 *Bird's eye view of the* Saracen's Head *complex, showing the courtyard plan and the separate entrances for business via the cartway and to the owner's premises from the churchyard.*

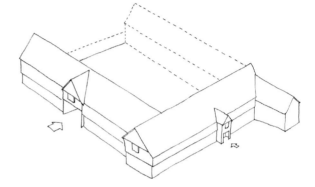

Archaeological Evidence

All the secular medieval buildings described so far belong to the late 15th century and were timber-framed on sandstone plinths. Evidence for earlier structure is derived from excavations in 2005-7.[74] At the *Saracen's Head* the existing buildings overlie 13th- and 14th-century structures. The earliest, using post-holes, was discovered towards the rear of the site and may represent the old building line to The Green. Today this can be seen in the row of shops south of the *Bull's Head* and in the *Saracen's Head* wing that projects into the graveyard. The fragmentary remains of the other buildings were found under the north range, which appears to have respected their alignment. Below these in turn one of the earliest features discovered was a ditch that followed the same east-west alignment. It is likely to have functioned as a northern boundary to the earliest buildings discovered on the site and it is possible, though the evidence is slight, that it turned southwards to form a boundary with The Green. All this suggests that the 'Bushmore and Ronkes' encroachment onto The Green had taken place by the 12th or 13th centuries, supporting the assumption that this was the early settlement focus for the Norton berewick recorded in Domesday Book.

In 1992 demolition of 15 The Green, a 19th-century structure, provided the opportunity to open a large area fronting the south side of The Green. Trenches for sill-beams laid directly on the ground surface indicated the outline of an L-shaped timber-framed structure built *c.*1250-75, which has been interpreted as a single-storey peasant's house with a thatched roof and an enclosed yard facing The Green. Successive rebuilding was followed in the late 14th century by a period of abandonment. It is tempting to link this sequence to the economic and social changes associated with the Black Death of 1349-50.[75]

THE CHURCH

St Nicolas Church

The earliest architectural evidence for a church in King's Norton is the survival of two re-set 12th-century round-headed windows in the chancel. From these writers have speculated that the Norman chapel comprised a single-cell building occupying little more than the area of the present chancel. This modest building was radically extended in the late 13th century when the present nave and its north aisle were built. A second aisle was added in the early 14th century when the chancel was rebuilt and its distinctive arch decorated with ballflower ornament. So far the architectural evidence reflects what was happening at the time to King's Norton's growing population and its economic prosperity up until the middle of the 14th century. There is no direct evidence for the Black Death of 1349-51 in King's Norton, but the breaks in building activity at both St Nicolas church and the excavated site on the south side of The Green are highly suggestive of economic recession. But when church building did resume at King's Norton in the 15th century it was done on a large scale. The addition of the impressive south porch with its vaulted roof and the magnificent tower and spire are the glories of the church. It dominated a wide area of the parish and is prominent from many locations today, such as at the new cemetery at Longdales Road. The tower, with its crocketed niches, arcaded upper

S.E. View of KING'S NORTON CHAPEL, Worcestershire.

32 *This engraving of St Nicolas church and the Old Grammar School was published to illustrate William Hamper's article on King's Norton's antiquities in* The Gentleman's Magazine *in 1807.*

33 *The late 15th-century tower and spire of St Nicolas church photographed by the Rev. J.M.L. Aston in 1870 from his vicarage. In the foreground is Birdcage Farm.*

stage, battlements and pinnacles, surmounted by an octagonal spire, would be worthy of many a small town, rather than what was still a chapel to the mother church at Bromsgrove. It is at Bromsgrove that the closest parallel to King's Norton's tower and spire is to be found. Very similar towers were built at Coleshill, Yardley, Sheldon and Kidderminster, and scholars have speculated that they were all the work of one master mason. At Sheldon the name of Henry Ulm and the date 1461 are recorded within the tower. Henry has been identified as a mason operating extensively in the West Midlands in the second half of the 15th century.[76]

While the development of King's Norton's medieval church can still be traced by a study of the standing structure and its architectural detail, understanding what its interior looked like in the Middle Ages is more difficult due to the extensive restorations undertaken between 1863-72. The Victorian architect W.J. Hopkins replaced the nave and aisle roofs and stripped the internal walls of plaster, thus losing all medieval wall and ceiling paintings. Insight into the rich appearance of the medieval church before the stripping of altars, rood screens and imagery can, however, be gleaned from pre-Reformation wills. When Humphrey Field of Inkford died in the early 1540s he made a bequest 'to the four altars' of the church at King's Norton, and from other contemporary wills we learn that they were known as the High Altar, Our Lady's Altar, the Jesus Altar and St Michael's Altar. The lower section of what may have been the rood screen has been re-set between the chancel and the nave and is richly carved with flowing foliage. Fragments of its upper section remain in the Old Grammar School where they were inverted to provide supports to the master's desk. A gilded tabernacle surmounted by a painted timber tester was a very prominent feature of the interior. It held an image of Our Lady of Pity and recalled the 13th station of the Cross. Church music was provided by an organ, for which bequests for the repair and replacement of bellows, soundboard and pipes were occasionally made.

Chapels of Ease

Because King's Norton chapelry covered such an extensive area, church attendance for those living far from The Green was difficult. During the 15th century medieval chapels were founded at Moseley and Wythall and served these outlying areas. In the petition for the establishment of a chapel at Moseley in 1405 the inhabitants had set out the difficulties: 'the said church [at King's Norton] is so distant that especially for old men and pregnant women and other weak persons access at certain times of the year on account of the said distance and floods is impossible without danger.'[77] Foundations of a single-cell chapel at Moseley were discovered within St Mary's in 1909. It was extended in 1513 by the erection of a stone tower with a bell frame. At Wythall the medieval chapel was probably a timber-framed structure. It was much more modest than Moseley's, and Thomas Habington, the Worcestershire antiquary, described it in the early 17th century as 'a poore thinge affourdinge neyther Armes nor monuments'. A number of late medieval wills make bequests to the chapel at a place called Gorshaw, a name that survives locally in Gorsey Lane. It is likely to have been on the site of the post-medieval and present Victorian church at Wythall, but the possibility that it moved from the Shawbrook area should not be ruled out.

The King's Norton Chantries

From their obscure origins in the 14th century the medieval chantries penetrated deeply into the religious, economic and cultural fabric of King's Norton society. The church acquired three chantry altars, perhaps needing some rebuilding to accommodate them.

It was common for the inhabitants of the parish to embellish the altars during their lives and, after death, through their wills. King's Norton acquired three priests to sing mass at each of the altars. The priests were supported by gifts of land assigned to each altar, and by the 1540s the estate, which had been built up perhaps over 200 years, formed one of the largest in the manor. One of the chantry priests eventually took on the duties of a teacher and the first school in King's Norton came into being.

In 1344 William Paas, a chaplain, was permitted to assign some land in King's Norton to a certain other chaplain to celebrate divine service at the Altar of the Blessed Virgin Mary in the church of King's Norton.[78] Seven men contributed 32 acres altogether to create possibly the first chantry in King's Norton. A monument to one of the later priests of the Blessed Virgin Mary chantry survives in the south aisle. It commemorates Humphrey Toye who died in 1514 and, although much worn, depicts him in his robes with a book and chalice. In 1522 the three chantry priests are known by name: Sir Harry Locock, priest of 'our Lady Service' (Blessed Virgin Mary), Sir Thomas Gardfeld, priest of 'St Thomas service' (Thomas à Becket), and Sir Nicholas Coterrell, the [Holy] Trinity priest. It is clear from the wills in this period that the

34 *Pencil sketch made in 1826 by the antiquary Dr Peter Prattinton of the monument in St Nicolas church to the chantry priest Humphrey Toye.*

dedication of the altars could change a number of times, hence the names mentioned previously in the wills.

In 1481 Sir Thomas Lyttleton in his will gifted a book of grammar to King's Norton church, the first indirect reference to the school. Following the dissolution of the chantries in 1547 the Commission that visited King's Norton reported that when there were three priests then one 'dyd alwayes kepe a free Schole', but when there were only one or two, the revenues from the chantry estate were used instead to maintain bridges and highways and relieve the poor.[79] We are fortunate to know the name of the priest who was 'scole master on the Dissolution', Henry Saunders, Master of Arts, aged forty. For the previous two years he had been assisted by John Peart, a usher 'well learned' but not ordained.

It might appear obvious that the teaching took place in the Old Grammar School, but not in the building as we know it, which only took its present form in the middle of the 17th century (see Chapter 3). It has been suggested that the church served this purpose and its generous proportions could have accommodated the pupils, the aisles doubling up as schoolrooms as well as chantry chapels. The Commissioners' report of 1548 claimed that 120 scholars were being taught and instructed. If this statement were true considerable space would have been required, but the numbers are probably an exaggeration.

The three priests lived in three cottages just before the dissolution of the chantries: 'le Soole Prest Chambar', the 'lady Preste Chamber' and 'le Trinitie P[r]este Chambr'.[80] It is possible that these three chambers were conjoined and situated on or near the site of the present Old Grammar School, a position on the edge of a churchyard being not unusual for the houses of chantry priests. The medieval upper part of the Old Grammar School may be a survivor of their original accommodation, albeit rebuilt in the 17th century.

The extensive estate that was acquired in the late medieval period consisted of 48 rents granted by owners from their own properties and 64 properties in the actual ownership of the chantries, leased out to tenants. These included several houses in the village, which are also mentioned in the 1514 survey of the Worcester Priory estate. This represented a considerable material investment by parishioners in their spiritual life and in the education of their children, all of which was confiscated by Edward VI in 1547.

TRADE AND INDUSTRY

The question remains whether King's Norton in the Middle Ages should be regarded as a town or a village. Legally the definition of urban status is associated with the acquisition of a market charter, and since this was not granted until 1616 it has always been assumed that the place was a rural settlement around its large triangular green. However, a number of other indicators show that King's Norton certainly met many of the criteria for urban status and was a significant trading and manufacturing centre.[81]

The late 13th-century Lay Subsidy Roll gives the names of taxpayers, which are indicative of their respective trades. We find Adam Smith, Thomas Miller and Alan of the Mill, as well as Richard and Nicholas Baker, all occupations that we might expect to find in a rural community. These millers ground corn at two sites – the manorial mill situated north of the village, and at Lifford downstream, then known, among other names, as Hawkeslowe Mill, due to its being a detached outlier of Great Hawkesley Farm, Longbridge. More specialised were names associated with the leather trade – Amicia, wife of John the Tanner – and, for the woollen cloth industry, William and Richard Fuller, John Walker, John the Dyer, William Weaver.

Understanding the processes of medieval cloth production will show how these men specialised in the various stages. After carding to straighten the fibres, wool was spun by spinners or spinsters and then woven on a loom (William Weaver). To get rid of oils, dirt and other impurities the cloth was then fulled in a tub of water by trampling or 'walking' it underfoot (John Walker's family no doubt gave its name to Walker's Heath). Mechanisation of the process in the 13th century led to the introduction of fulling mills, where water-driven tilt-hammers replaced the traditional foot-walking process. By the 15th century Wychall mill had become a fulling mill and appears to have been the only one in King's Norton during the Middle Ages. The cloth was then stretched on tenterhooks and the nap raised and sheared. John the Dyer specialised in using madder, woad, and perhaps more expensive imported dyes to produce a wide range of coloured cloth. The supply of wool for export and processing elsewhere was another essential part of the sheep farming industry.

Of the clay industries pottery and tile-making were ideally suited to local resources, the parish having a plentiful supply of clay and sand, water and wood fuel. Richard the Potter of the 1327 Roll no doubt supplied the parish with everyday wares, but it is clear from excavations at 15 The Green that in the 12th and 13th centuries peasant households in King's Norton also had pottery from much further afield: from Birmingham, the Dudley/Bridgnorth area, Chilvers Coton in north Warwickshire and Boarstall/Brill in Buckinghamshire. It has been argued that these wares would have been traded at a local market and the likelihood is that it was held on The Green.[82]

The making of clay roof tiles was also an important local industry, and one that became increasingly significant as demand for clay tiles in towns instead of thatch increased. The late medieval court rolls repeatedly record tenants being fined for digging clay and sand to make tiles. The regularity of the offence suggests that rather than fining misconduct the court was extracting a licence fee for established practice. In the early 15th century King's Norton tiles were being sent to Stratford-upon-Avon, some 25 miles away, for building the school and almshouses there.

One of the privileges of ancient demesne was the right of tenants to sell their produce within any market within the king's dominions. It is therefore not surprising to find in King's Norton a number of men involved in trade well beyond the parish. At first sight Walter le Mercer (merchant), who appears in the 1275 Subsidy Roll, would perhaps be expected in an established market town, like Birmingham or Coventry, rather than rural King's Norton. In the late 15th century a number of King's Norton men and women were members of the Guild of Knowle, a fraternity that brought them into contact with merchants from Coventry and Birmingham. It is also clear that by the early 16th century a number of merchants from Bristol, one of the most important towns in the country, had established bases in King's Norton and were using them as distribution points for trade with the Midlands. Goods were sent on trows (Severn barges) from Bristol up the Severn to Worcester or Bewdley, and then overland via Bromsgrove to King's Norton. One of the great roads of medieval England, linking Hereford and Worcester with Coventry and Leicester, passed through the southern part of the parish at Wythall and would no doubt have facilitated such trade. These transport links encouraged a Bristol family, the Nortons, to acquire a local base at The Moats, Cotteridge, and a house in the village. The trade with Bristol continued into the early 16th century when King's Norton men like Edward Rowley, Richard and John Chambers, William Reynolds, Richard Grevys and John Lyndon were buying Spanish iron from John Smythe, one of the richest Bristol merchants. It has yet to be established whether these local men were then selling it on to the smiths of Birmingham, but it is apparent that the traditional story of Birmingham's early iron industries relying solely on iron from the Black Country needs revision and that the part played by King's Norton entrepreneurs needs recognition.[83] Links with Coventry can be seen in Richard Benton's purchase of more than 100 gallons of wine from that city.

All this suggests that medieval King's Norton can no longer be regarded as a typical rural community. It was a centre of trade and formed part of regional networks that stretched as far as Bristol and Coventry. King's Norton occupied a quite specific position, transitional between village and town.

III

Tudor and Stuart

The dissolution of the monasteries in the late 1530s, and of the guilds and chantries a decade later, brought about major changes in landownership and institutions in King's Norton and acts as a convenient division between the medieval and what is often called the early modern periods.

TENURE AND LANDOWNERSHIP

Apart from a brief period during the Commonwealth, King's Norton manor remained a royal possession; Bromsgrove was separated from the Crown estate by a sale in 1564 to Ambrose, Earl of Warwick, and the manorial histories were different from thereon. King's Norton continued to be treated as a dower for each new queen, most notably for Henrietta Maria, wife of Charles I, in whose name an attempt was made to enclose part of the commons. There is insufficient space to deal with the detailed landownership of the study area in the 16th and 17th centuries, even though the sources are now sufficiently reliable to do so.

The vast majority of land continued to be held freely, an annual chief rent being paid to the Crown. As Thomas Habington, the 17th-century antiquarian, noted, 'Now this lordship of Kingsnorton streachethe out wider then almost any in our shyre, so hathe it conteyned as many freehoulders, beeinge Knightes, Gentellmen, and others, as any paryshe of ours.'[1] Of the upper echelons of King's Norton society, Habington commented that 'manie weare the tytells of gentlemen and esquires and have and maie aspire to the dignitie of knighthood …'[2]

Most of the freeholders came from local families living in King's Norton, but there were also absentee freeholders who lived in the surrounding parishes such as Northfield, Yardley and Alvechurch and beyond. In these cases the land would be leased to local farmers, who also took the opportunity of renting land from the more prosperous King's Norton families. The latter had accumulated land by purchase and inheritance and usually dwelt on their principal holding, and for this reason it is not always possible to distinguish in the chief rent rolls the freeholder from the tenant. The lands owned in King's Norton by the dissolved monasteries retained a peculiar jurisdiction after they were sold by the Crown, exempt from paying chief rent and the duty to attend the local manorial court. They were for all practical purposes equivalent to the freeholds, but were nominally attached to the royal manor of East Greenwich, east of London.

King's Norton must have been an attractive place to buy land due to the privileges enjoyed by free tenure. By the time property deeds become numerous in the 16th century, it is clear there is an independent and vigorous land market in operation. A great deal of land exchanged hands as a result of the dissolution of the monasteries and chantries. This land was initially transferred to royal ownership, administered in London through the Office of Augmentations, and in most instances quickly sold by the Crown to obtain sorely needed finance. This gave the opportunity for outsiders with little connection with the area, or even with the Midlands, to acquire land in King's Norton.

Bordesley Abbey and Westbury College were dissolved in the 1530s. A few years later they were sold to men connected with the royal court, members of the urban merchant class rather than landed aristocrats. A 'lucky dip' may have operated in some instances during the unseemly land grab that characterised this period, but it is certain the commercial, political and social networks inhabited by those close to court must have played some part. Inter-county connections were also responsible for outsiders acquiring land in King's Norton after the initial burst of post-Dissolution sales.

The Bordesley Abbey granges were granted in 1544 to Thomas Broke, a merchant tailor of London,[3] and a large area of land immediately to the west and south west of the village was permanently transferred to private ownership. Thomas Broke typically held the land for a short time only, in this case one year, before selling to Richard Rotsey, the owner of the *Saracen's Head*. In 1584 Kingsuch Grange came into the hands of Anne (*née* Field) of King's Norton and her husband William Whorwood of Sandwell Hall, West Bromwich. An important connection with this Staffordshire manor was thereby established. John Turton of West Bromwich and his son William bought Kingsuch from the Whorwoods in 1622. John had already purchased Lifford Mill in 1604, an acquisition which may have been influenced by the Whorwood foothold in King's Norton.

The Bordesley grange called Norton stayed with Thomas Broke until his death and passed to his sister and heir, Jane Arrowsmith. Her son, John Arrowsmith, sold the grange to Alexander Avenon in 1580. The Avenons had resided in King's Norton from at least the 15th century and Alexander developed a successful business career in London, reaching the rank of alderman and holding the office of Master of the Ironmongers Company of London a number of times. He was one of a small group of local Tudor men who saw greater opportunity beyond the confines of the manor, perhaps encouraged by the development of King's Norton as a trading centre.

Monyhull had belonged to Westbury College, Bristol, before the Dissolution and was sold to Sir Ralph Sadler in 1544.[4] He was a soldier and diplomat and held several major offices of state, using his position at court to amass a fortune. Gifts of former monastic lands came from a monarch who was grateful for services rendered. The house he built in Hackney in 1535, Sutton House, still stands, and is in the ownership of the National Trust.[5] Sadler was another London-based absentee landlord with little interest in King's Norton, except making a quick profit. He held onto Monyhull for only three years and in 1547 sold the estate to William Sparry, formerly the local bailiff for Westbury College and probably the sitting tenant at the time.[6]

Men at court also took leases of the small amount of King's Norton land that lay beyond the jurisdiction of the Crown. After the Dissolution, the Worcester Priory estate, including their King's Norton lands, was transferred in 1542 to the newly formed Dean and Chapter.[7] In 1547 William Paget obtained a lease of King's Norton and Bromsgrove Rectory.[8] He had been a major figure at Henry VIII's court, holding the offices of Secretary of State and Privy Councillor. In 1559 (when he became Comptroller of the Royal Household, Chancellor of the Duchy of Lancaster and Knight of the Garter) Paget relinquished his lease and it was reassigned to Thomas Cox, a servant to the bishop of Worcester. This family virtually monopolised the leases of the Dean and Chapter estate in King's Norton for the next two hundred years, but as they lived elsewhere they sub-let to local families.

Cotteridge had been in the ownership of the Norton family from at least the mid-15th century, and a hundred years later they had become important merchants in Bristol, emphasising the long-distance trading links between King's Norton and the rest of the country that had probably been established through the wool trade.[9]

Wychall is a good example of a King's Norton estate purchased for investment in the 17th century by local 'outsiders'. In 1621 Richard Rotton, from a family with King's Norton, Bordesley and Birmingham roots, sold a half share of Wychall to Thomas Smalbroke of Handsworth and the other half to John Marston of Yardley. The Smalbroke interest passed to youngest son Josiah, of Handsworth, who bequeathed it in 1667 to his half-brother Richard Smalbroke, a mercer in Birmingham.[10] The Marstons were still in control of their half of Wychall in the early 17th century.

Despite the outside investment in King's Norton during this period, a number of local families remained prominent on the landownership map, including the Middlemores of Great Hawkesley and Hazelwell (just outside the study area) and the Grevis and Field families. The complexity of inter-related local ownership affected Cotteridge, Bell's Farm and the Hole Farm (Primrose Hill).

In the 15th century a small number of dispersed holdings in the manor were leased or 'farmed' by the Crown, which regarded the land as royal private property, unlike the mass of freeholds.[11] From the 1530s they were described as escheat land,[12] the term referring to property that has been confiscated by the Crown; the usual causes being treason, bankruptcy, and the minority of an heir or death of a tenant without an heir. The latter appears to be the main reason for the creation of the escheat holdings. Some time in the 14th century a Thomas Henley, illegitimate, died without heirs and his land was confiscated by the lords of the manor, the Earls of March.[13] The first known escheat rent roll dates from the mid-16th century and lists both free and customary tenures of escheated land.[14] This implies that any land in the manor could be forfeited to the Crown. Although there were fewer than 20 holdings altogether, they contributed about a third of the manor's rental income, the rents fixed at contemporary commercial levels.

From the early 17th century the freehold escheats are not listed and the term is used exclusively as a synonym for customary tenancies. The latter, also known as copyholds, could now be passed to heirs by registration at the manorial court ('by copy of the court roll'). In a manor so dominated by free tenure, customary holdings are not easy to explain and their legal status was the subject of much dispute between royal officials and local tenants.[15] In other places customary holdings can represent previously unfree or villein tenures, often based on scattered strips in large open fields. There is little evidence of such arrangements in King's Norton where the customary holdings were scattered throughout the manor, except in a single block to the north of the village around King's Norton mill. It is very likely that most originated in the random process of land forfeiture or escheating to the lord of the manor.

King's Norton Mill was a customary holding, which was not unusual for a manorial mill. Since it was valuable property, landlords often elected to keep closer control through this type of tenure. It is possible the mill land formed the last remaining fragment of the original demesne around the village, most of which had been granted to Bordesley Abbey and Worcester Priory in the early medieval period. In 1514 another escheat holding, Millwards, was described as being the 'lady queen's land [Catherine of Aragon]'. It lay immediately adjacent and to the east, on the opposite side of the road from King's Norton to Birmingham, and was associated with the *Saracen's Head* in the late 16th and 17th centuries. The escheat land as a whole was leased out by the Crown several times in the late 16th and early 17th centuries.[16]

POPULATION

Calculating the population of King's Norton after the Dissolution relies on careful and cautious use of a variety of sources, none of which was intended to supply statistical data. In 1522 the population is thought to have been about 1,000, based on a total of about 210 households. The Chantry Surveys of 1548 estimate the population to have comprised 900 'housling people'.[17] 'Housling' people are equivalent to adult communicants and usually leave out those not yet confirmed, basically children below the age of 12 to 15. Estimates of this percentage of the population have varied between 25 and 40 per cent, giving a result for King's Norton at the mid-point of the 16th century of between 1,200 and 1,500.

In 1671 the Hearth Tax counted 264 households. Using a multiplier of 4.5 and adding another five per cent for the exempted poor, this gives a total population of about 1,250.[18] The Compton Census of 1676 produces a higher figure of 1,623 for the same decade.[19] We would cautiously suggest a figure around the 1,500 mark for the late 17th-century population – a figure which seems remarkably close to the mid-16th-century level.

But any notion of a static population during this period can be dismissed immediately when we examine the parish registers, which begin in 1546 and provide a fair guide to trends.[20] By plotting the yearly number of births and deaths we can identify periods of high mortality and, conversely, growth. In 1557 and 1558 the number of deaths were 52 and 50 respectively, in contrast to the previous five years when the maximum number recorded was fifteen. This reflected a nationwide famine following disastrous harvests. Stability had resumed by the 1560s, and from then until the 1630s the moving nine-year average number of births exceeded the number of deaths by 50 per cent.

Burials reached peaks in the years for which plague is known to have affected neighbouring communities, and its impact on King's Norton can be inferred. In 1625, when plague struck the town of Redditch, the parishioners of King's Norton contributed nine shillings towards relief, but they also suffered a doubling of burials that year compared to the average of the previous five years. The conclusion must be that plague also visited King's Norton. Similarly in 1636, when King's Norton's burials reached a peak of 52, it is known there was plague in both Northfield and Birmingham. Between 1640 and 1700 the population continued to grow, but a serious crisis with 65 burials in 1684 may indicate another plague.

THE RURAL LANDSCAPE

For the first time we can speak with some confidence about the appearance of the rural landscape. John Leland gives us the first description of the King's Norton area in about 1540:

> Good plenty of wood and pasture and meatly good corne betwixt Alchirch
> [Alvechurch] and Northon. And lykewyse betwixt Northon and Bremisham
> [Birmingham] that be distaunt from [each] othar 5.miles.[21]

We can also estimate the extent of land that was either open, as arable and pasture fields, or waste. The latter was most likely the location with most of the tree cover. In 1638 it was claimed there were 4,000 acres of arable in King's Norton.[22] The arable was cultivated by 102 plough teams of draught oxen or horses, each on average ploughing nearly 40 acres. King's Norton had a total area of 11,726 acres.[23] Adding at least 3,000 acres of common (see below) to this arable total would leave nearly 5,000 acres of enclosed land under pasture mixed with a small quantity of woodland. Leland's impression of the landscape seems therefore to be supported by the statistics a century later. In 1638 the pasture maintained 8,000 sheep, 1,500 cattle and 500 horses, although some of these animals would have been grazed on the commons. A thousand young cattle were bred each year, but in the spring most had to be sold or sent out of the parish to be fattened for 'want of sufficient pasture in the ... wastes'. It is unlikely that in these circumstances there were large quantities of woodland in private hands in the 17th century. This impression is confirmed by the contemporary property deeds that rarely mention any woods. Leland's 'plenty of wood' was probably seen for the most part on the wastes and commons of the manor.

The names of the commons and wastes were listed in the mid-17th century and have been mapped in Fig 35.[24] They belonged to the Crown and could vary significantly in tree cover from open heath to woodland. They had been major areas of woodland in the medieval period and in 1594 there were nearly three thousand oaks on the waste, sufficient to support a Keeper of the Woods.[25] Seventeenth-century estimates of the size of the waste vary wildly from 1,200 acres to 3,000 acres.[26] A figure in the upper estimate seems more likely because there were 2,044 acres available for enclosure in the 1770s. The commons were gradually being nibbled away by small encroachments.[27] This process was, however, strictly controlled by the manorial court and many were removed on pain of a fine.

The tree cover must have thinned out as a result of over-grazing animals, for which offenders were also fined in the manorial court. In 1519 King's Heath was still being called a wood.[28] In 1608 a 'wood … called Kingswood' was still worth leasing to Edward Field for £3 per annum (1608 Rental). By 1661, however, the commons were described as 'generally very bad, cold and barren'.[29]

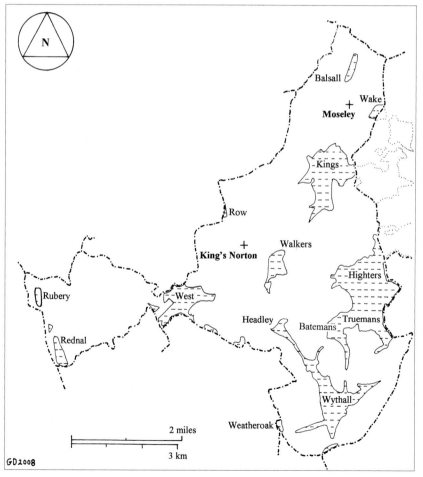

35 *Commons and heaths in the ancient manor of King's Norton.*

King's Norton's heaths all survived into the late 18th century when they were finally enclosed. We cannot be sure how much they shrank in the 17th century but they were heavily exploited for growing flax and hemp in 'plecks' (small enclosures); in addition, traditional grazing rights left few trees. Additional pressure was caused by squatters' cottages and the pragmatic decision was finally taken to accept many of these. The manorial court at first took fines for the cottages, but in the 18th century it was decided to formalise the situation and compile a new rent roll of cottages and plecks.

Enclosure of Kingswood

Although most of the commons were in poor condition, an attempt to enclose 669 acres of them by Henrietta Maria in 1638-9 met with fierce resistance by the tenants of King's Norton. It appears the enclosures that were created were destroyed and the plan in the end was never implemented. The idea had been to enclose 'one greate parcell of the … wast grounds called Kingswood' that had been 'within the memory of man yet living soe full of woods and trees' that the tenants were not able to graze their cattle upon it. The remainder was to be partitioned among the tenants of King's Norton to enclose themselves. The 669 acres were considered to be about a third of the waste but there was much less than 2,007 acres in fact in existence at the time. The local tenants, acting in a 'forcible and tumultuous manner', threw down the fences and banks that Queen Henrietta's officials had erected. They proposed to the Queen that she enclose only one quarter of the waste and that this be distributed throughout the various commons scattered around the manor rather than be concentrated at Kingswood.

The Queen Henrietta enclosure of Kingswood has been commonly accepted to have taken place despite the resistance of local people. An area of fields south-west of the Maypole was marked as Kingswood on early Ordnance Survey maps and was considered to have been part of this enclosure. This area is, however, no more than one fifth of the required 669 acres, which is equivalent to the extensive heath that lay immediately to the east, containing Highter's Heath, Trueman's Heath, the area around the Maypole and Hollywood and Bateman's Green. There is no other heath big enough in King's Norton to account for Queen Henrietta's acres and it is reasonable to assume that it was originally intended to enclose this, the largest area of waste in the manor, using the Kingswood's name as shorthand. The farms and fields immediately to the west cannot be seen as new enclosures, as Monyhull, Bell's Farm and Moundsley had been created in the medieval period out of the waste. Fields in the area of Crabmill Lane and Slough Lane (in the heart of the area marked as Kingswood on the Ordnance Survey maps) are known to have existed in the 15th century.[30]

A survey of 1661 confirms that the enclosures did not take place, but that an attempt was made to respond to the wishes of the King's Norton tenants. The document refers back to the events 21 to 22 years earlier and lists a series of separate enclosures in the various wastes around the manor intended to be enclosed, this time totalling 636 acres. The job was 'never particularly and fully fenced nor inclosed' and the banks and hedges were 'afterwards privately thrown down'.[31]

Agriculture

During the 16th and 17th centuries King's Norton's farmers practised mixed husbandry with an emphasis on pastoral farming. We can see in probate inventories how new crops, such as peas, beans and clover, were introduced and how draught oxen used for ploughing were replaced in the 17th century by horses. Dairy farming led to the development of significant specialisation in the production of cheese, a business that continued into the 18th and 19th centuries. The proximity of the growing town of Birmingham created an increasing demand for these consumables. Dairies and cheese rooms became essential elements of the farmhouse, and even today we can find remains of the trade in the large cheese press stones sometimes abandoned in farmyards as well as the complete cheese press from Wychall Farm now in Birmingham Museum's collection.

36　*This cheese press was used at Wychall Farm. By turning the screw the heavy stone between the guide posts of the frame applied pressure to the cheese vats, forcing out the whey and solidifying the cheese.*

Before the widespread use of lime in the early 19th century marl was used extensively to improve the fertility of topsoil. The digging of marl subsoil has a long history in King's Norton, with references to the practice in the late medieval court rolls. By the 16th and 17th centuries almost every court recorded the names of tenants fined for digging marl, indicating that it was by now a well-established practice which earned income for the manor court. The Tithe Map of 1840 shows that pits were still common features of the whole parish and were usually sited at the junction of two or more fields. Until the 1970s there were innumerable marl pits from Walker's Heath to Kingswood, but many have since been filled in with rubbish. To one side a ramp provided access for carts, but fencing was essential to prevent accidents, especially when pits flooded and became a drowning hazard.

During the 17th century there was considerable encouragement nationally to grow hemp and flax as a means of providing useful employment for the poor and contributing to the diversification of agriculture. A major boost was given in the mid-century with the publication of a number of influential treatises on the value of the crop. Of these, Henry Robinson's pamphlet of 1652 was the most far-reaching, advocating the growing of flax and hemp at home rather than importing them from Holland.[32] It promoted a more productive use of wastes and their enclosure for flax growing. The growth of the trade locally is exemplified in the court rolls: in the first half of the century a handful of flax plecks were approved by the court, but from the 1660s the number rises dramatically to around one hundred reported at each court, which was in fact licensing the enclosers rather than trying to prevent the nibbling away of the waste by the creation of flax plecks.

HOUSES AND HOMES

In the 16th and 17th centuries many of the timber-framed houses of King's Norton underwent major refurbishment or rebuilding. Contemporary English chroniclers commented on the improvements in housing which took place between 1570 and 1640 that economic and social historians have dubbed the Great Rebuilding. However, this should be seen as part of the cycle of successive waves of building activity. In King's Norton, as elsewhere, it took two forms: the conversion of open halls by the insertion of first floors and fireplaces, or the complete rebuilding of an old house in the new style of a storeyed timber-framed house with integral stacks. Among the first group, floors were inserted into medieval halls at Wychall and Gay Hill Farms. At Primrose Hill Farm recent tree-ring dating has shown that the new chamber over the hall was created in 1555.[33] Good examples of the new type of post-medieval farmhouses are to be seen at Malthouse Farm, Alcester Lanes End and Hollytree Farm, Hollywood, where the medieval wing was retained.

The Hearth Tax returns of the late 17th century provide a valuable insight into the comparable wealth of the population as reflected in the number of hearths in their homes.[34] The 1671 returns are most useful in breaking up the parish into its yields. In Moundsley Yield 66 people were taxed on 133 hearths and it is tempting to average this to two hearths per household, but the returns demonstrate the wide variations. Of the population of Moundsley Yield, 75 per cent had only one or two hearths, while another 16 per cent had between three and four hearths. Three people had six hearths, and at the apex were Edward Field at Bell's Farm with seven hearths and Francis Palmer at Moundsley Hall with eight. In the whole parish they were exceeded only

37 *Hollytree Farm, Hollywood: the timber-framed wing on the right is medieval, the long range to the left, although refronted in brick, is a 17th-century rebuilding of the open hall.*

38 *Malthouse Farm is hidden behind 1930s housing fronting Alcester Road South. Although much of the external timber frame has been refaced in brick it is a good example of the lobby entry type of farmhouse built c.1600.*

by Edward Edmonds, gent., at Colmers Farm, Rednal, with 12 hearths and Richard Grevis Esquire at Moseley Hall with thirteen.

These wide variations in wealth are reflected in both the physical evidence of standing buildings and probate inventories, which list rooms in individual houses. From the 1560s the inventories start to describe the contents of the deceased's house room by room, although this pattern was not universally adopted by all local appraisers. Some preferred simply to value the goods as a continuous list rather than giving any indication where they were in the house. A full statistical study of the 800 inventories surviving for King's Norton between 1550-1750 has still to be done, but it is clear that they reflect wide social divisions expressed in the parish's buildings.[35]

When Edward Field, gentleman, died at Bell's Farm in 1686 his house contained no fewer than 29 rooms. Trying to equate the house described in the inventory with the surviving building is difficult. Clearly not all the house in the 1686 document exists today. A close study of the building itself proves it was once larger; another bay on the southern end of the main range and an extra wing at the back, matching that on the north east, formed a U-plan house. Its date is early to mid-17th century, with the addition of the parlour chimney stack in 1661. Until the devastating fire in 1980 there was a highly decorative plaster ceiling in the parlour chamber which was clearly one of the best rooms in the house. The principal rooms on the ground floor – the two parlours and the hall – were panelled. Stone gate piers with ball finials and a brick garden wall were added at the time of the 1661 alterations and completed the setting of this wealthy gentleman's residence.

Nearby Moundsley Hall was home of the Palmer family in the 17th century. In 1630 Henry Palmer, gentlemen, died there and his inventory lists the contents of 23 rooms. Old Moundsley Hall was demolished in 1945 and we have only a few photographs and a brief wartime record of the timber-framed house that was discovered as the Victorian mansion was being demolished.[36] Embedded within the later brick house was clearly just one wing of what must have been a much larger and most impressive timber-framed building.

39 *Bell's Farm, an early 17th-century timber-framed house and home of Edward Field, gentleman, who died in 1686. The house originally extended another bay to the right.*

40 *The early 17th-century frame of Moundsley Hall was exposed during demolition of the Victorian hall in 1939 (for which see Fig. 72). It was just one wing of the once much larger house of Henry Palmer, gentleman, who died there in 1630.*

The house of Thomas Featherstone, gentleman, was not far behind those of Edward Field and Francis Palmer in terms of comfort, and in some areas it exceeded them. Featherstone lived at Headley Heath Farm, a timber-framed house erected *c.*1600 but demolished in the 1960s. There were 16 rooms in the house and the whole of his goods were valued at just over £500. Of this, almost one tenth was made up by the luxurious furniture and furnishings of the Best Chamber, comprising:

> One bedstead, one Feather bed, one pair of Blankets, Curtains and Counterpain, one Bolster and two Pillowes, Four Window Curtains, Six Searge Chairs, two stands, a Glass case, a Liverie Cupboard and a French Table £30
>
> A Silver Kan, three Silver Spoons, a Watch, a Clock, two Gold Rings, a Silver Tobacco Box and Stopper £18 13s. 4d.

The inventories enable us to chart in the upper echelons of society the introduction of luxury items such as Thomas Featherstone's looking glass, his silver tobacco box and watch. They also inform us about his tastes in music, reading and recreation. There was a harpsichord ('a harpsigall and frame') in the parlour, and card tables and a pair of bowls in his study, which also contained £5 worth of books. By the early 17th century painted cloths, which had hung in the main rooms of late medieval and Tudor homes, were replaced by wainscot or panelling. Gradually the move to sleeping upstairs in bedchambers was completed, although the tradition of still using the parlour to house a bed continued well into the 18th century. By 1725 the first dining room has appeared (in part of the *Saracen's Head*) and the long tables, forms and stools of inventories of the 16th and 17th centuries have been replaced by oval dining tables, leather covered chairs and dressers or sideboards.

In sharp contrast to the comfortable surroundings enjoyed by the gentlemen of King's Norton were the modest homes of people like John Anderton, who died in 1699 and occupied just three rooms – hallhouse, chamber over the hall and another room. The total value of his goods was £33 2s. 6d. In 1674 the nailer William Greves had four rooms – hallhouse and parlour, each with a first floor room or chamber over.

The inventories demonstrate that craftsmen such as nailers, blacksmiths, wheel-wrights and weavers invariably combined their trade with agriculture and lived on what were in effect smallholdings. A good example of this type of small house is Maypole Cottage at Hollywood. The timber-framed house measures just 30 feet by 17 feet and comprises two rooms on each floor. A rare feature is a smoke bay or narrow-framed space between the main room (the hall or kitchen) and end gable created to house the hearth. This is the predecessor of the brick chimney stack and is a development from the open hall of earlier times.

One-bay cottages and hovels made of timber and mud are known from the documentary record. Some may have started as squatters' cottages which began as encroachments on narrow roadside plots or plecks. By tradition such cottages were permissible if the builder could erect the cottage and get smoke issuing from its chimney within 24 hours. It is possible that examples of these poorly built homes may still exist in the Hollywood and Kingswood area but they will be embedded within much later brick walls. In the documentary record labourers are the most elusive of the social groups. Their lives are recorded in the barest detail and the wills and inventories of only three labourers have come to light. Some may have lived within their employer's house but others with a family of their own lived in property that was sub-let to them. Roger Cottrell, a day labourer who died in 1600, lived in a two-roomed house consisting of a hall and chamber. The home of another day labourer, Richard Benton, who died in 1622, was larger, with a hall, kitchen and two chambers. Both men supplemented their work as day labourers by keeping small quantities of farm stock on their smallholdings. The value of these three labourers' goods and chattels averaged just over £10 each.

In between the gentlemen at the top of the social hierarchy and the craftsmen, lesser husbandmen and labourers towards the bottom, were the yeomen. With family members they still worked their own land directly but would often employ resident farm labourers or servants to help. There was considerable variation in the wealth of a

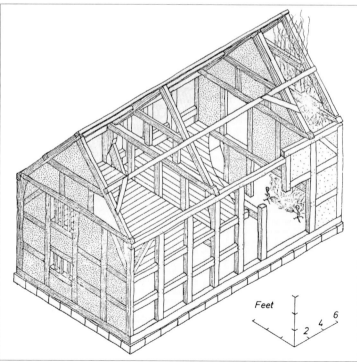

41 *Tucked away between 1930s houses in Crabmill Lane and the Hollywood By-pass is Maypole Cottage. It is a modest late 16th- or 17th-century timber-framed cottage with later brick chimneys at either end. It was photographed in 1966.*

Feet

6
4
2

42 *Maypole Cottage: reconstruction of its original form by Nicholas Molyneux, showing the smoke bay on the right-hand side.*

yeoman. The most successful, in multi-roomed houses, were almost indistinguishable from the lower levels of minor gentry. Thomas Baggaley lived at Lindsworth Farm in the mid-17th century in a 13-roomed house, and when he died in 1673 the contents of his house and farm buildings amounted to £323 10s. His farm was well equipped with two dairies and a cheese chamber containing free-standing cheese shelves and 84 cheeses. The ambitious yeoman often aspired to the status of a gentleman; one testator signed his will as 'gent', but his neighbours who took the probate valuation had no doubt of his real position and described him as yeoman.

THE VILLAGE

Legally, King's Norton was still not a town, although its status as a commercial centre with a significant number of merchants involved in local and regional trade is well documented. Tudor merchants, like the Nortons, Lyndons and Rowleys, had by the eve of the Dissolution developed trading links between King's Norton and Bristol, Coventry, Worcester, Birmingham and London. But King's Norton traders were keenly aware of the need to protect their interests. When, in 1554, Parliament passed an Act to remedy the decay of corporate towns, three King's Norton men – John Field, George Field and Thomas Fulfarde – petitioned the sovereign, Queen Mary, setting out how the new Act would affect their livelihoods. They submitted that having lived in King's Norton 'of longe tyme', and supported their wives and families 'by the selling of grocery ware marcery ware haberdashe wares lynen and woollen clothe', the Act would prevent them from trading. In the course of their plea they acknowledged that King's Norton 'is neither Cytie towne corporate nor market towne'.[37]

Formal market town status was finally secured in 1616 when James I granted King's Norton the right to hold a weekly Saturday market and two annual three-day fairs, one in April and the other in August.[38] Within a generation the weekly market was struggling and by 1661 it was described as having not been kept for many years. It is from this formal market charter of 1616 that King's Norton's modern farmers' market and the ever-popular Mop Fair can trace their origins.

The study of the transition between a village and a town in this period has many difficulties, not least being the lack of any survey. There is no map that tells us who lived in which house before the Tithe Map of 1840. This deficiency is mostly explained by the unwillingness of the Crown, as overlord, or any other owner to survey a village in which they had very little financial interest from rent income. Most villagers owed no chief rent to the king or queen, unless they possessed fields and farms outside the village. A good few of the villagers were either free tenants of the Dean and Chapter of Worcester, or owner/occupiers of former chantry properties. The latter had been confiscated by the Crown after the dissolution of the chantries in 1547, sold to Richard Field and Ralph Woodward in 1549 and then re-sold to individuals, some without doubt sitting tenants. The map reconstructing the village in 1514 has therefore no equivalent until the 1840s (Fig. 14).

It is possible that the first part of the Hearth Tax return of 1671 lists the houses in the village. After listing 32 names in the return, the rural properties in Moundsley Yield can be identified, such as Bell's Farm and Moundsley Hall, and the remainder of the yield appears also to be farms. If this conclusion is correct then we have at least the names of villagers and a rough guide to the size of their properties.

Some of the names can be linked to wills and inventories and a picture of the village in the late 17th century built up. It was predominantly a centre for specialist craftsmen, especially shoemakers and other leatherworkers, tailors, weavers and a dyer, whose premises were probably in Wharf Road. In addition there were at least two inns, one in Swine Street (the earlier name for Masshouse Lane), and the *Cross*, run by several generations of the Potter family. The *Saracen's Head* was not an inn at this time. The village was the site of a number of manorial adjuncts – the Court House, pound and stocks – all of which appear regularly in the court records as requiring regular repair.[39]

Prior's Court and the Saracen's Head

The top of The Green by the church was dominated by two great houses, the *Saracen's Head* and Prior's Court. The first had been built in 1492 by Humphrey Rotsey and the second, perhaps a considerable time earlier, by the Prior of Worcester. Little is known about the latter house after it was taken over by the Dean and Chapter of Worcester. It seems likely that it had disappeared by the mid-17th century, perhaps due to the neglect of its absentee leaseholders, the Cox family. The back road that now runs north east out of The Green to Pershore Road South may in this period have been taken through the empty curtilage of Prior's Court.

At the *Saracen's Head* the rich and powerful Rotsey family eventually ran into financial difficulties. It had descended via Richard Rotsey to Thomas, Humphrey's grandson, who was outlawed for debt although subsequently pardoned in 1556.[40] At the same time Thomas had to sell his King's Norton and Cofton property and the *Saracen's Head* ended up by unknown means in the hands of the Field family.[41] In 1584 Henry Field, brother of John, bequeathed to William Whorwood and his wife Anne Field, daughter of John, two houses in the village (including the *Saracen's Head*), land called 'Millwarde[s]' and King's Norton Mill (Hurst).[42] As early as 1523-4 Millwardes had been leased from the Crown by Thomas Walshe, brother-in-law of Richard Rotsey, probably creating the link between this land and the *Saracen's Head* for the first time.[43] By 1535 Richard Rotsey was leaseholder. Millwards, together with a 'grate messuage' (large house), was granted in 1551 to Lord Clinton as part of a massive exchange of land with Edward VI, 'sometime in the occupation of Thomas Rotsey and now of late in the tenure ... of John Field'.[44] The house may have been 'millerstenement', which it was suggested above stood on the Millwards grounds rather than next to the mill. Lord Clinton probably quickly sold the house and Millwards to the leaseholders, the Fields, who gathered together the former Rotsey holdings by acquiring the *Saracen's Head* from the bankrupt Thomas.

Whorwoods were to own the *Saracen's Head* to the very end of the 17th century but never lived there, and it appears that the last owner/occupiers of the house for some time to come were the Fields. A lease of 1639 confirms the link between the *Saracen's Head* and the land called Millwards. Broome Whorwood, son of William, leased to Bartholomew Kettle 'a mansion house … lying in the towne of Kings Norton adioyninge the Churchyarde … and all those landes … knowne by the name of Milwardes'. Millwards formed a compact piece of land on the east side of the road from King's Norton to Birmingham as it rose from King's Norton Mill (now a petrol station) up the hill to the centre of modern Cotteridge. The lower part of this land is occupied by the King's Norton Factory Centre.

CHURCH AND RELIGION

Reformation

The impact of the Reformation on King's Norton can be read in the wills made by local men and women between the 1530s and 1560s. Throughout the reign of Henry VIII bequests to the various altars of the medieval chantries still feature prominently in the wills of King's Norton's residents. When Isabel Norton lay dying in 1540 she left 10s. for a priest to sing masses for hers and all Christian souls. Gradually, as the Reformation progressed, the traditional commendation of the soul to God, the Blessed Virgin Mary, various named saints and 'the whole company of heaven' was replaced by a Protestant version which stressed the hope of salvation through Christ alone. While it is tempting to view these changes as the genuine growth of Protestantism, they may be more a pragmatic response to mounting government pressure. In some parishes wills reflect a reversion to Catholicism in Mary's reign as part of the

43 *Monument to Henry Field, owner of the* Saracen's Head *building in 1584, Queenhill church, south Worcestershire.*

63

Counter-reformation. In King's Norton the handful of surviving wills for the period 1553-8 repeated a simple formula which had already been established by the scribe in the late 1540s: 'I bequeath my soul to almighty God and my body to be buried in the churchyard of Kingsnorton'.

While people's true beliefs remained a private matter, physical changes to the fabric and fittings of the church were more obvious. The various national orders for the removal of lights, shrines, images and paintings form part of a complex chronology between the reigns of Henry VIII and Elizabeth I. There are no surviving accounts for King's Norton which might throw light on the process, but we can see the stark contrast between the pre-Reformation church, with its chantry chapels, multiple altars and spectacular tabernacle already described in the previous chapter, and the sparse furnishings listed in the Inventory of Church Goods for 1552.[45] By then the church possessed just four bells in the steeple, two silver chalices and patens, and three sets of old and worn vestments. It was noted that a sanctus bell (which had been rung at the elevation of the Host) and two brass candlesticks had been sold off since the last inventory was taken, allegedly for 'the reparacion of the churche'. Five years earlier Edward VI had ordered the dissolution of the chantries, the confiscation of their lands and income, and the removal from churches of physical attributes of the doctrine of purgatory and masses – the stripping of the altars.[46]

It is uncertain at what point the medieval rood screen was taken down. Its lower part was re-set between the chancel and the nave in one of the late 19th-century church restorations. Close examination of the screen shows that it had been richly painted. The spaces behind the tracery heads were once filled by panels, no doubt painted with saints. Such images, together with the Rood itself representing the great Crucifix, with Mary and John on either side, the rood beam supporting the Rood and the rood loft above the screen, would have fallen victim to the purging zeal of the Reformers. When the upper

44 *The rood screen in St Nicolas church was re-set in the 19th century. There is a vine trail upper rail and trefoil heads to the lower panels (missing) which would have contained images of the saints. Paint analysis has shown that the screen was painted red and green with water gilding.*

45 *The legs of the master's desk in the Old Grammar School are two cut-down moulded posts of medieval date which may have formed the upper section of the rood screen in St Nicolas church.*

part of the screen became separated from its base is unknown – it might well have survived into Elizabeth I's reign when arrangements were made throughout the country for the retention or substitution of this traditional division. However, a fragment of the upper part of the rood screen survives, not in the church but in the Old Grammar School, where it was re-used as legs to the master's desk. These supports are inverted medieval timbers which can only have come from the screen.

Something of the religious differences current in King's Norton during the Counter-reformation was captured in the complaint made during the reign of Philip and Mary by William Sparry, the Catholic owner of Monyhull Hall. He had recently erected a seat in the church for himself and his wife, but it was destroyed twice – first on Palm Sunday and then a week later on Easter Monday – by an ugly mob acting on behalf of the Protestant Rotsey family of the *Saracen's Head*.[47]

Recusants

Catholic families like the Middlemores of Hawkesley and the Fields of Weatheroak remained true to their faith throughout this period, but paid heavily through substantial fines for their recusancy. The first indication of the number of Catholics is provided by the Compton Census of 1676, which records 19 papists in the parish out of a total of 1,082 communicants.[48] The names of 'Popish recusants' are listed with regularity by the King's Norton churchwardens in the late 17th century, as they were required to report on those refusing to attend church.[49] John Field of Weatheroak Hill appears consistently. He lived in a large timber-framed house, now known as Hall Farm, Weatheroak. Within an early 19th-century brick skin are substantial remains of the original house which was a known Catholic refuge in the 16th and 17th centuries. A remarkable survival in the attic is a panelled but windowless room used as a secret chapel for Catholic worship. Less convincing however are the claims made for Masshouse Farm close to the village. The earliest spelling of the farm's name is Mash-house, which probably relates to a mash or brewhouse on the premises, rather than a place of worship. When the farm was demolished in 1933 panelling was transferred to Moundsley Hall, which in turn was removed to Harvington Hall in 1936 on the basis of a presumed Catholic connection. The panelling is marked F/WB and dated 1634. These are the initials of Frances (*née* Rotton) and William Bowater (died 1657). The Bowaters were firm Anglicans and the panelling commemorated their marriage which took place in 1634.[50]

Chantries and the Re-foundation of the Grammar School

When the Commissioners appointed to establish what possessions were owned by the chantries visited King's Norton they found three priests in office, which made it possible for one of them to 'always kepe a free Schole'. When there had been just one or two, the revenues from the chantry estates were used instead to maintain the bridges and highways and relieve the poor.[51] Henry Saunders, Master of Arts, aged 40, was the priest and schoolmaster in 1548. For the previous two years he had been assisted by John Peart, a 'well learned' but not ordained usher. The school was re-endowed at this time, but without any of the chantry lands, which were confiscated by the Crown. As partial compensation the Commissioners proposed that the Crown provide £10 per annum for the schoolmaster and £5 per annum for the usher. Among the confiscated property was the house of the three former chantry priests: the Soul Priest Chamber, the Lady Priest Chamber and the Trinity Priest Chamber. This building had become redundant at the Dissolution and it is possible that the new owners allowed Henry Saunders, the schoolmaster, to use the building as a school. In 1549 the King's Norton chantry lands, including the three priests' chambers, were sold by the Crown to Richard Field and Ralph Woodward.[52] Richard Field died in 1559 leaving 5s. for books for the scholars of King's Norton school and £2 to repair the school. This reference to the school is good evidence that it was in a separate building from the church, but not the converted priests' house. That the early school was close to the present one is also suggested by the field-name 'Schoolehouse close', first recorded in 1649 as part the former priory demesne fields lying immediately to the north of the churchyard.

In the subsequent history of the school the post of curate and schoolmaster was sometimes combined. The schoolmaster's salary was provided by the Crown from the income of the royal manor, and the Vicarage of Bromsgrove supported the living at King's Norton. In 1544 Henry Saunders replaced Thomas Baker as schoolmaster and the names of subsequent masters in the 16th and early 17th centuries are known: Mr Hamnett, Thomas Acton, Edmund Kettel, Mr Shuttleworth, Mr Ambrie, Henry and Samuel Kempster, and Tobias Gyles. The last was also the curate, but the neglect of his teaching caused a near riot when the villagers attempted to eject him from the school.[53] Kettel and Kempster had also been dismissed.

Thomas Hall's School

Matters changed significantly on the arrival in 1629 of a new master and puritan minister, Thomas Hall (1610-65). The school underwent a radical improvement as a teaching establishment, gained a national reputation as a centre for learning and prepared many students to go on to Oxford or Cambridge. The school was built in the form seen today and was a tribute to Thomas Hall as schoolmaster, pastor and benefactor of a library.

We are fortunate that Thomas Hall left an autobiography, written curiously in the third person.[54] In it he describes himself as 'a man of middle stature, his hair blackish, which he wore very short, scarce to cover his ears; his face pale and somewhat long'. In 1640, after service at Wythall and Moseley, he took over the curacy of King's Norton. The 'rude and ignorant people' of the parish soon became 'in the general tractable and teachable'.

Thomas Hall's reputation for his religious writings stretched well beyond King's Norton. He wrote a number of books that are regarded as influential in the development of Presbyterianism. In 1651 he published *The Pulpit Guarded*, which was followed a year later by a defence of infant baptism, *The Font Guarded*. Hall's writings have been described as 'an amalgam of populist and erudite writing, combining … mock trials with vigorous and punning Latin diatribes'.[55] In his *Beauty of Magistracy*, published in 1660, he demonstrated the interdependence of magistracy and ministry, using as his example the successful partnership he had enjoyed with Colonel Richard Grevis of Moseley, an 'active, prudent pious Justice'. At the Restoration he railed against the reintroduction of popular customs as well as the degeneracy caused by the fashion of painting body spots and displaying naked breasts. Revels and maypoles were condemned in *Funebria Florae, the Downfall of May Games* (1660). In this work he tells the reader that two maypoles had been set up in King's Norton – one had been stolen, the other given by a professed Papist. It has been generally assumed that one

46   *The Old Grammar School. Recent study of the structure demonstrated that the mid-15th-century upper floor was brought together with the brick and stone base in c.1662.*

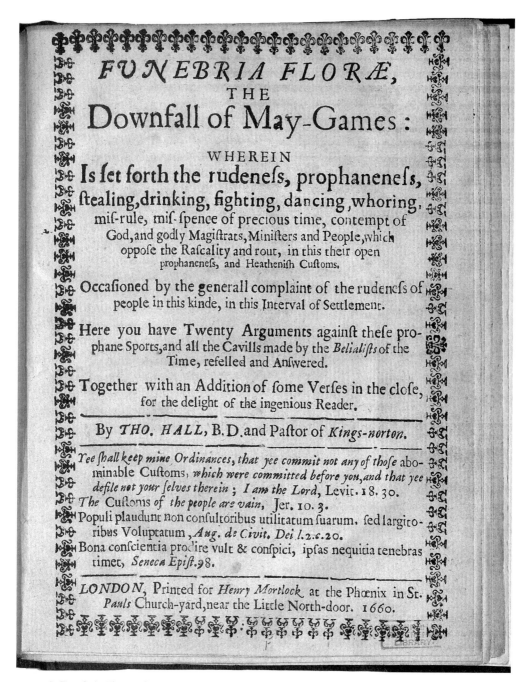

47 *In* Funebria Florae, the Downfall of May Games, *Thomas Hall refers to the two maypoles then existing in King's Norton and the unruly conduct they caused.*

of these was on The Green and another at what is today called 'The Maypole' on the city boundary with Worcestershire. Railing against popular entertainment can hardly have won Hall many friends in the local community, but it is also clear that many of his parishioners respected his dedication and successful mastership of the school.

Hall's collection of books, some of which are now lodged in Birmingham Central Library, would have distinguished King's Norton school from most others in the region, even the country. Late in his life Hall was troubled with ill health:

> [1662] ... for the Parishioners supposing that this might be his last
> sicknes, and understanding that he intended to bestow £200 worth of
> books for the good of the Parish, they undertook to build a library to put
> them in ... which now is completed, and is become as fine a monument for
> Church and schoole, as any in the county ...[56]

Around 1662 the grateful parishioners erected the Old Grammar School in the form we see today. Hall's reference above to the 'monument' suggests much more than the installation of library shelves and cupboards into an existing building. The building has a brick and stone mullioned lower storey, whose style belongs comfortably to the mid-17th century, upon which was raised portions of a medieval timber-framed building; this may have been a surviving part of the former chantry priests' house, already used as a school, but perhaps much dilapidated.

Thomas Hall was not to enjoy his monument for long and perhaps did not expect to do so, owing to his poor health. Some time in 1662, as a result of the Act of Uniformity, he was evicted for his nonconformism from both church and school, dying in poverty in King's Norton in 1665. His bequest of over 270 books to King's Norton, however, remained in their new accommodation.

THE CIVIL WAR

Worcestershire was the strategic centre of the Royalist forces during the Civil War, but even in a royal manor like King's Norton, where allegiances might have been assumed to lie with the Crown, war divided opinion. Old gentry families like the Middlemores of Hawkesley and Hazelwell were Royalists, whereas the Grevises of Moseley were Roundheads.[57] The head of the family, Colonel Richard Grevis, joined the Parliamentary army and served under the Earl of Essex throughout the war. More representative were men like William Collins of Wythall who belonged to a growing group of men whose sympathies lay with Parliament. Collins described himself as a gentleman; his fortune came from the leather trade and enabled him, in partnership with Edward Moore of Weatheroak Hill, to purchase the manor of King's Norton in 1650.[58] It is tempting to see the origins of opposition in the treatment tenants had received only a few years before during the Crown's attempted enclosure of Kingswood. William Collins and a small group of discontented men acted in concert, opposing the Queen's agents with a petition signed by 255 local inhabitants.

The Civil War in King's Norton was characterised by the movement of troops, royal visits, skirmishes, a siege and pillaging, all of which are, of course, best understood in the wider context of national events.[59] The location of most of the local events of the war years has been the subject of much debate by historians for over two centuries, but some clarity is now possible in establishing the main facts by revisiting contemporary sources.

Military manoeuvres brought the opposing armies through King's Norton on a number of occasions. The most celebrated was the visit of Queen Henrietta Maria in July 1643, but the town was clearly a well-established base for the royal army when on the move. On 17 October 1642, according to Thomas Hall, Prince Rupert 'with his followers Quartered in Kings-norton before he went to Edge-hill'.[60] Earlier that day Rupert's troops had been on the move between Stourbridge and King's Norton but 'two or three miles from Brumegem' they were attacked and defeated by the Parliamentary army under Lord Parham. The Parliamentary victory was soon dwarfed by the cataclysmic events at Edgehill on 23 October. Meanwhile, the Queen was sending arms and supplies to her husband from Holland. She returned to England in February 1643, landing at Bridlington from where she marched south raising troops and funds as she went. By the beginning of July she had reached the Midlands, moving in a south-westerly direction from Leicestershire into south Staffordshire. From Walsall she moved to King's Norton on 10 July before going on the next day to Stratford-upon-Avon and Kineton where she was reunited with the King. Sir William Dugdale recorded the outline of the journey in the barest details, but as an antiquary and Garter Herald to the King while the royal court was in Oxford he had reliable knowledge of contemporary events.[61]

Historians have speculated where the growing royal army of 3,000 foot soldiers and 30 companies of horse and dragoons was housed. In the 19th century it was claimed the district known as The Camp between King's Norton and Cotteridge (now remembered in Camp Lane) owes its origins to this event, but others regard the area as an encampment for gypsies or navvies. Most writers have, however, followed the tradition that the Queen spent the night of 10–11 July in the *Saracen's Head* on The Green. The early 19th-century antiquary William Hamper knew King's Norton well and was the editor of Dugdale's diary, published for the first time in 1827. Local residents had told Hamper of a royal visit to 'an ancient house, adjoining the Church Yard', but by then oral tradition had changed the story from Henrietta Maria to Elizabeth I.[62] Later in the 19th century locals claimed that a letter to or from Henrietta Maria had been discovered behind a fireplace in the *Saracen's Head* and that this proved the connection.[63] Unfortunately, if any letter was found it was never made available to any of King's Norton's Victorian chroniclers and the story of the Queen's visit must remain a tradition. Yet the *Saracen's Head* was certainly one of the most important houses in the village and its owners, the Whorwoods, would have been sympathetic to the Royalist cause and the Queen's Catholicism. It is certainly the most likely candidate for her reception.

The movement of troops and establishment of garrisons also brought the opposing sides into direct conflict, most famously in the siege of Hawkesley House (Great Hawkesley), Longbridge. Shortly after the outbreak of war the house, a known Royalist moated mansion, was taken by the Parliamentary army. It remained a Parliamentary garrison for the next three years. A valuable insight into its state within a year of its capture is provided by the inventory drawn up of its contents on the death of its absentee owner, John Middlemore, in December 1643. Middlemore had died in Worcester Castle where he had been imprisoned for debt several years previously. Now in the hands of enemy troops, his old home at King's Norton was clearly run down and only a shadow of its former glory. There were 17 rooms, and names like the Great Matted Chamber and the Great Wainscot Chamber are indicative of its once rich interior, but many of the contents were described as either old or broken, suggesting that damage and neglect had taken their toll. The entire contents of the mansion amounted to only £28 5s. 2d.[64] We might have expected them to have been worth at least ten times more. Middlemore had spent his last days imprisoned with only the barest of possessions – his clothes, bedding, a desk and just one book about earlier civil strife, Caesar's *Commentaries on the Gallic and on the Civil Wars.*

Hawkesley remained a Parliamentary garrison under its governor, Captain Gouge, until the summer of 1645 when it was recaptured by the Royalists en route to Naseby. In the meantime its defences had been strengthened by stonework brought from a local chapel demolished for the purpose. Richard Symonds, an ordinary trooper in the Mounted Lifeguards of the King, described the taking of Hawkesley as part of his contemporary account of the Marches of the Royal Army:

> Sunday, May 11, 1645. The King marched from Inkborough-Magna [Inkberrow] to the rendezvous of the whole army of foot; and his Majesty, with his own regiment of foot and horse-guards only, marched to Salt-wiche [Droitwich], in Worcestershire. The headquarters of the army this night was at Bromsgrove. His majesty stayed at Droitwich till Wednesday; in the meantime his highness, Prince Rupert, set down before Hawkesley House, belonging to one Mr Middlemore; Lord Astley's tertia of foot made the approaches which were left for us with a great deal of advantage; viz., banks, a lane, and trees. Captain Backster of the horse was killed here, and some foot soldiers and pioneers. On Wednesday, about two of the clock in the afternoon the King left Wiche and went with his guards to the leaguer before Hawkesley, and just as his Majestie appeared in view it was delivered unto the mercy of the King and the officers, and that they might be free from the insolence of the common soldiers. In this howse was a month's provision and ammunition, but the soldiers would not fight when they perceived it was the King's army. The son to Dr Gouge was the captain of foot, and governor, and Whichcott commanded the horse; there were 60 foot and

above 40 horse. After Lord Astley had pillaged the house, and taken the soldiers prisoners the house was set on fire. This night the King lay at Cofton-hall, two miles off.[65]

Local historians have long argued which of the two Hawkesleys, both moated farm-steads in King's Norton, was the site of the Civil War siege. Recent documentary research into the Middlemores has proved once and for all that the site was at Long-bridge.[66] It is therefore not surprising to learn that Civil War cannon balls and ammunition have been found nearby.

Worcestershire had an unenviable reputation during the Civil War for the extent of plundering by both sides. Armed bands of residents, known as Clubmen, were formed with the express purpose of protecting their own property from looters. They were, however, hardly a match for a concerted attack by hungry soldiers desperate for food. A Parliamentarian's view of the only known Royalist plundering of King's Norton town at the height of the pillaging is admittedly biased but does acknowledge that King's Norton had so far escaped throughout the war.[67] At midnight on 28 April 1645

48   *Pen and ink drawing by John Instan of St Nicolas church in 1826, clearly showing the mid-17th-century gables added to the south aisle.*

Colonel Guy Molesworth and 'his ragged regiment … plundered Kingsnorton seven times over'. They stole and consumed sheep from the commons, repeatedly plundered the place, and took 22 poor residents prisoner from the town, the rich having fled beforehand. Some writers have claimed that Parliamentary soldiers stripped lead from the roof of the church to make bullets, and others have surmised that the rebuilding of the aisle roofs in the late 1650s was part of the extensive repair required as a result of destruction a decade or so earlier. Whatever the cause, these changes produced a highly distinctive, almost domestic, appearance to the church, the addition of multiple gables to both aisles introducing a great deal of light. As these changes took place during the ministry of Thomas Hall it is tempting to see them as a puritan interpretation of what he regarded a church should be. In the Old Grammar School the 19th-century historian Brassington found the mid-17th-century 'orders for the removal of altars and images and there can be no doubt that Hall gladly carried out the behests of a Parliament with which he sympathised'.[68]

TRADE AND INDUSTRY

A substantial proportion of the population was engaged in trades providing for the basic necessities of life – food and drink, clothing and building. Manufacturing industry was still dominated by cloth and leather production, much of it still based in the countryside. Some specialisation is apparent in the emergence of nailmakers, locksmiths and bladesmiths.

The Cloth Trade

Inventories demonstrate the continued importance of the woollen cloth trade through the 16th and 17th centuries. They usually list one or more spinning wheels as well as quantities of wool and yarn, suggesting that spinning was still a domestic industry. Weaving required greater investment in a loom and space to accommodate it, thus leading to specialisation. Ground-floor weaving shops appear in inventories such as that of Robert Marson, who in 1585 had 'iii paire of weaver's lomes' in the shop attached to his two-roomed house. Edward Hunt, who died in 1575, had five weaver's looms with a warping bar and a trough for sizing warp, with all the gears or heddles, the wires through which the warp was passed. A century later Thomas Fewster had a draught loom, a garter loom and broadcloth loom, as well as other looms and gears 'in several places', hinting that he was employing outworkers. In his will he described himself as a weaver but his inventory, which includes his farmstock, called him a yeoman, emphasising the multi-faceted side of his enterprise. The woven cloth passed through the fulling process and was then ready for dyeing. This last process required large vats and furnaces which were built in a workhouse or dye-house, while finishing, pressing and cutting the cloth took place in the shop. Richard Cotterell's dye-house had two furnaces, while his shop contained a thousand teasels and their frames, used for raising the nap, and six pairs of dyer's shears used for cutting. The wealth that Cotterell had accumulated enabled him to act as a moneylender; his inventory records in detail debts amounting to over £660 owed by 32 people in King's Norton and surrounding parishes.

The Leather Trades – Tanning

The process of tanning hides to produce leather was concentrated in the south of the ancient parish at Wythall, where the place-name Tanners' Green is the most obvious indicator. Here in the 17th century lived the Collins family, who developed a tanning business that had roots in the late medieval period and relied on a plentiful supply of oak bark and water. It is significant that when a survey was made in 1591 of the woods in King's Norton the value of the bark amounted to about one third of the total value of all the growing trees – timber for building, firewood and bark.[69]

House Building

Timber was the favoured building material through the 16th and first half of the 17th centuries. It was also a material that was re-usable. When a new lease was made of the farm of Kingsuch in 1648 specific arrangements were made for 'taking down and erecting up again certain barns and other buildings upon the lands hereafter demised … for a dwelling house and barns'.[70] Careful woodland management and replanting programmes were maintained into the 17th century. When an owner wanted a new house he would enter into a contract with a carpenter who would normally find a suitable supply of timber. The details of such a contract exist for 1609 when John Spencer of King's Norton agreed to build a barn for a Warwickshire gentleman, Sir Richard Gryffyn, of Brome Court near Alcester. Spencer obtained his timber locally on land at Yardley Wood belonging to Daniel Sparry of Monyhull. He paid £72 for the timber, felled it 'and there made & squared a fframe of tymber which conteyned five Baye of Buyldine for the said Barne'. The prepared frame would have been transported twenty or so miles to Brome. The reason we know so much about the case is because Spencer reneged on his contract, sold most of the frame to someone else and the matter went to court.[71] Not all King's Norton carpenters acted as disreputably as John Spencer and some enjoyed employment on prestigious building projects. Thomas Bridgens and his brother William from Bromsgrove were employed from 1613-14 with John Pretty of Shawhurst, Wythall, as carpenters at Sir John Pakington's new house, Westwood Park near Droitwich. The brothers produced much of the woodwork and decorative detail at Westwood, showing a considerable level of specialisation. It is perhaps not surprising to find their descendants establishing a lucrative building business in early Georgian Birmingham a century later.[72]

Mills and Water Power

Trades carried on in King's Norton in this period were largely reliant on the muscle power of humans and animals. Water power was harnessed only for corn grinding and at one site for fulling. Most fulling or 'walking', however, probably continued to be carried out by literally walking or trampling the cloth in a tub of fullers' earth (a wool degreaser).

49 *Hawkesley Farm (Great Hawkesley), c.1895: looking across the moat to the 18th-century farmhouse on the island which replaced the timber-framed house and buildings damaged during the Civil War.*

50 *Lifford Hall north elevation. To the right is the grand 17th-century miller's residence; the 19th-century, two-storey crenellated bay window was built over the position of a water wheel and to the left is the surviving 17th-century mill, which contained a second water wheel.*

Two corn mills, King's Norton and Lifford, are known to have existed from the medieval period. King's Norton Mill, as the manorial corn mill, was probably the first to be established. It was situated on the corner of Pershore Road South and Camp Lane, the site of the present petrol station. Lifford Mill, about half a mile downstream, also began as a corn mill but only acquired the name Lifford in the late 18th century. The mill buildings still stand on Tunnel Lane, just off Lifford Lane, and are now known as Lifford Hall. There is nothing surviving above ground at the site of Wychall Mill, half a mile upstream of the manorial mill and below the dam of Wychall reservoir. It is first recorded in 1638 when it was sold as a redundant 'walk' or fulling mill, perhaps King's Norton's first industrial water mill; it was to be converted to a corn mill.[73] It is likely that the mill had been constructed on the Wychall estate sometime in the 16th century in order to take advantage of the local trade in weaving and selling of woollen cloth. By 1638 it appears that this trade had sufficiently declined for fulling by water power to be abandoned. Little else is known about this mill for the remainder of the century and its ownership follows the complications of the main estate.

King's Norton Mill is well documented from the late 15th century, and in the following century it was known as Hurst's mill, or Taylor's Mill, named after its tenants. A reference to two mills in 1608 does not imply two separate buildings, but two wheels or sets of machinery 'under one roof'. The mill was in the same ownership for most of the 17th century as the *Saracen's Head*. The Whorwoods sub-let the mill and twice in the century seem to have entirely released it – the cause of serious dispute. Matters erupted violently in 1628 when Thomas Whorwood and his followers attacked Edward Guest, the tenant, nearly slicing off his leg and killing a Richard Sugar.[74] In 1659-60 the Fowkes family claimed that the Whorwoods had promised to surrender the mill to them, after having spent over £300 around 1649 in constructing a new mill and water course. Bartholomew Kettle, leaseholder of the *Saracen's Head* from 1639, was tenant of the Fowkes family during this period.

Lifford Mill had been purchased in 1323 by the Hawkeslowe family of Great Hawkesley Farm, near Turves Green, and remained as a detached outlier of this estate until the beginning of the 17th century. By the 15th century it had acquired the name 'Hawkeslowe Mill', and a century later Great Hawkesley and its distant mill were owned by the Middlemore family. A deed records the sale of Lifford Mill by William Middlemore Esq. of Hawkeslow to John Turton of West Bromwich, yeoman, the nameless mill described as 'two water milnes called two Corne Milles'.[75] The mill eventually acquired the name Turton's Mill.[76] The Greves family of millers, who were tenants of both the Middlemores and the Turtons of West Bromwich, were part of a King's Norton clan as extensive as the Fields.

Lifford Mill is one of the three most important surviving water mills in Birmingham, the others being Sarehole Mill, Hall Green and New Hall Mill, Sutton Coldfield. The house at Lifford was once thought to have been a gentleman's residence of the 17th century, but detailed research has revealed that its history is of more interest and importance. The mill dwelling and mill alongside that can still be seen today

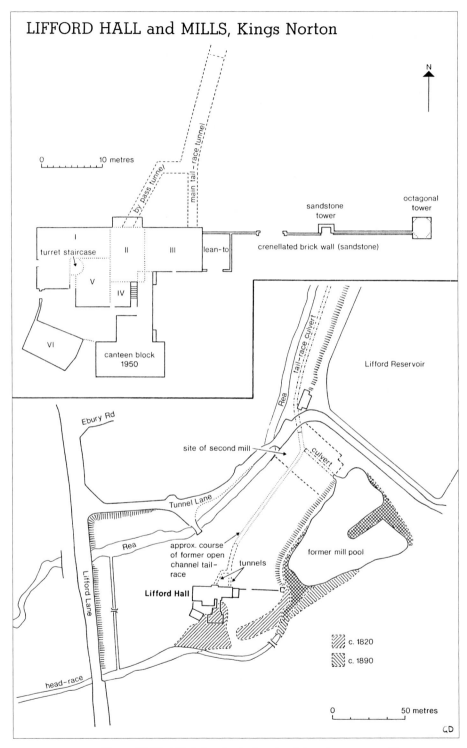

51 *Plans of Lifford Hall that clearly show it originated as a water mill.*

represent one of the earliest brick buildings in King's Norton. A timber in the roof has been tree-ring dated between 1672 and 1700. The evidence suggests the mill was built by the Turtons. Such a major investment in 'bricks and mortar' might explain why William Turton was much impoverished towards the end of his life. In 1682 he needed to mortgage his King's Norton estate to his kinsmen, Richard Turton and George Devenish, to provide for his family. It is clear from his son's accounts, compiled by John Turton before 1688, that a farmhouse built of brick, called the Redhouse, had already been erected on part of the estate to the north. Brick was still rare enough to be distinguished by name from the timber-framed buildings that were normal in the area at the time. It can be concluded, therefore, that a brick mill of some pretension and considerable expense had been constructed by William Turton in the 1670s to replace a timber-framed structure, perhaps medieval. In 1688 John Turton sold the mill and the Redhouse to John Bayley for £2,165 and the West Bromwich connection with a King's Norton mill was finally severed.

This remarkable survivor can be seen from the bridge to Lifford Hall in Tunnel Lane. On the right-hand side is the gabled house on an L-plan. The main door has been moved from the front to the side elevation, and the original stone mullioned windows have been changed to vertically sliding sashes, except on the rear. The mill itself lies to the left, and is unrecognisable as such: the right-hand part has had a two-storey crenellated bay window inserted in the 19th century, clearing out a mill floor entirely. One of the water wheels turned below the hall floor, the other was positioned at the end of the building on the extreme left, where there is still a stone-mullioned window in the gable. At the rear are later 18th- and 19th-century extensions.

Below the lawn in front of the building are two tunnels, which converge and run diagonally to the left. They are the tail-race culverts from the two water wheels, the mill pool having been situated at the rear (south side) of the house. There is no machinery surviving in the building. The transitional nature of building in brick in the 1670s can be seen in the timber-framed trusses within the gables in the interior, and a huge truss partition at first floor used to tie the front and rear brick elevations in case they would not be stable.

The new brick buildings of the late 17th century and the early industrial development at Lifford heralded the changes of the succeeding century, which were to transform the parish and set it on course for the cataclysmic development of the 19th and 20th centuries.

IV

Eighteenth-Century King's Norton

During the 18th century agriculture continued to dominate the economic life of King's Norton. Towards the end of the period, however, the area witnessed changes brought about by the influence of Birmingham. The industrial revolution had begun to transform the town that lay to the north. The canals constructed in the 1790s from Birmingham to Worcester and Stratford did not seek King's Norton in particular, but geography dictated that they pass through the manor. Once the cut had been made, however, the canalside in King's Norton would eventually attract industry. Local corn mills were the first to respond by converting to new industrial uses. The noise and din of Birmingham workshops must have seemed like a distant storm that would reach no closer, and few if any inhabitants of King's Norton village in this century could have imagined that Birmingham would eventually envelop the larger part of the manor.

The landscape remained distinctly rural, and the century was the last in which no part of the manor was encroached upon by the physical growth of Birmingham. In fact, the great size of King's Norton meant the study area around the village was not to be affected by urbanisation until well into the 19th century.

TENURE AND LANDOWNERSHIP

King's Norton remained a royal manor throughout the 18th century, but for much of the time it was held on lease from the Crown under the title of lord of the manor. From 1701 to 1702 Henry Parker, baronet, was the leaseholder.[1] From 1705 to 1716 Stephen Lilley and Constantine Phipps, a lawyer and Lord Chancellor of Ireland from 1710, were joint lords under William Aldworth, a royal auditor. Stephen Lilley's daughters succeeded until 1720 when Thomas Archer, uncle of Thomas, the 1st Lord Archer of Umberslade, took out a new lease. Thomas Archer is better known as a gentleman architect, his most famous building locally being St Philip's Cathedral in Birmingham (1710-15, tower 1725).[2] He was notable for 'having more in common with European baroque than that of any other English Architect'. King's Norton manor remained with Archer until his death in 1743, when the lease was eventually assigned under his will to his nephew, Henry, brother of Lord Thomas Archer. Henry died in 1768 and transferred the King's Norton lease to his nephew, Andrew, the 2nd Lord Archer of Umberslade, who died in 1778. Lady Sarah, his widow, held the manor until 1800, followed by her daughters until 1803, when the lease expired and it was returned to the Crown.[3] This ennobled branch of the Archer family had purchased the manor of Birmingham in 1746 and another connection between the Archers and Birmingham was created. Thomas Archer, the architect, acquired a considerable amount of King's Norton property including Kingsuch, Weatheroak Hall, West Heath Farm and *The Bell* in the village.[4] In 1804 King's Norton manor was sold to John Taylor for £7,568 17s. 6d. and the royal connection was finally severed. Norton could no longer claim the descriptor 'King's'.[5]

There were no significant changes to the system of tenure in the 18th century, with the vast majority of land continuing to be held freely. Likewise, the small number of customary tenures, the former escheat holdings, were renewed by presentation of new tenants (for all intents and purposes, freeholders) at the manorial court. Much of the land was actually farmed by sub-tenants, and, as in previous centuries, it is often not possible to distinguish whether the name recorded in the chief rentals is the owner or the sub-tenant. It is only in the late 18th century that owners and occupiers begin to be recorded side by side in official documents such as rate books and land tax lists.

POPULATION

The rising population of the 1690s reached a peak of an estimated 1,500 people around 1700 and looked set to continue its steady growth pattern. However, the years from 1727-30 marked a population crisis when the death rate soared and dramatically overtook the birth rate. Burials, which had averaged 26 per annum over the previous decade, more than doubled, tripling at the height of the crisis in 1729. Historians believe that a series of bad harvests led to shortages and high prices, leaving the population, especially the poor, vulnerable to epidemics of smallpox and influenza.

Following the crisis, recovery was initially slow, but the parish registers show that by the middle of the century the population was again increasing. By 1801, when the first census was taken, King's Norton's population numbered 2,807, an 87 per cent increase from 1700.

HOUSES AND HOMES

In contrast to King's Norton's legacy of medieval and Tudor/Stuart buildings, its Georgian architecture has not fared well. Hazelwell Hall and Bournbrook Hall have been demolished, and Monyhull Hall and Weatheroak Hall have been dramatically altered. Yet if we compare what did once exist here with Georgian buildings in neighbouring parishes, such as Alvechurch, Solihull and Tanworth, a stark contrast is noticeable. These parishes retain many examples of brick houses exhibiting the classically inspired polite architecture of pedimented doorcases and sash windows, as well as continuing the vernacular tradition of simple door surrounds and segmental heads over casement windows. King's Norton parish once contained examples of both styles, but it is also evident that the number of elegant 18th-century houses is less than might have been expected for a parish of its size, which raises questions about relative prosperity.

Contemporaries also believed that the inhabitants of King's Norton suffered financially more than most, and it is possible that this relative poverty in the 18th century may explain the dearth of good Georgian building. The parishioners pleaded poverty at every opportunity. When seeking the Crown's support for rebuilding work at St Nicolas church and at Wythall in 1774, they claimed they were 'not able to raise [funds] among themselves being most tenants at rack rents, and greatly burthened by the poor',[6] a claim that can in part be substantiated by examination of the costs of poor-relief. The Crown's right of heriot to take the best moveable possession of every deceased tenant was increasingly contentious. William Hutton, the Birmingham bookseller and historian (1723-1815), described it in 1783 as 'the detestable badge of ancient slavery'.[7] It was a far cry from earlier days when King's Norton tenants rejoiced in the advantages of being on a royal manor with the privileges of ancient demesne.

The 18th century saw the demise of some of the most affluent of King's Norton's families. The best documented is the fall of the house of Grevis.[8] The main branch of the family were lords of Moseley in the 17th century and had moved sometime in the early 18th century from the Elizabethan timber-framed manor house in Moseley village to a new site in the enlarged park. Richard Grevis Esquire was JP and a Deputy Lieutenant for Worcestershire. When he died in 1759 the contents of his 33-roomed mansion, Moseley Hall, had to be valued.[9] The Best Parlour had 'Two large looking glasses, one settee, two stools, two tables, a marble sideboard, one grate and fender, and fifteen pictures'. Most of the other principal rooms were equally elegant and hung with pictures, while the Best Staircase was a veritable gallery with 27 paintings. Outside was 'one charriott and one chaise'. Despite this apparent show of wealth the whole contents were worth only just over £300 and the debts were massive. The heir, Henshaw Grevis, was forced to sell the estate and, in a story of social decline that would be suitable for a novel, he earned a living digging gravel. Even then he was not able to make ends meet and in 1786 he appeared as defendant before Birmingham's Court of Requests which dealt with small debts. Its President, William Hutton, was shocked by the appearance of the penniless Grevis, a man who had once rode to his own pack of hounds. Grevis told Hutton that his ancestry could be traced back 'nearly from the Conquest', causing Hutton to reflect on the decline of the local squirearchy:

> One would think King's Norton fatal to greatness, for tradition tells us, that in the last age the parish could boast of the residence of five squires, who rolled in five carriages, but now the inhabitants themselves tell us they are a parish of paupers.[10]

The new owner of Moseley Hall was the successful Birmingham manufacturer John Taylor, who extensively rebuilt it. Although ransacked in the Birmingham Riots of 1791, much of the imposing 18th-century structure survives and epitomises the small Georgian country house with its pedimented wings added to the original five-bay frontage.

Another of King's Norton's great houses is Weatheroak Hall. Today it is the club house of King's Norton Golf Club and has the appearance of a Queen Anne revival mansion, having been extensively rebuilt in 1884.[11] However, embedded within the structure and detectable on the Victorian building plans is the core of the mansion owned by the architect Thomas Archer in the early 18th century. Archer had taken a lease of the manor of King's Norton from the Crown and, although his main residence was at Hale in Hampshire, Weatheroak was used as the family's Midlands base and was not far from his ennobled relatives at Umberslade Hall, Tanworth. The appearance of the old house at the end of the 18th century is shown in a painting within a painting. James Millar depicted Weatheroak's interior in 1797, when it was the home of the Birmingham surgeon Robert Mynors, and above the heads of the sitters he incorporated a painting of the house's main elevation.[12] It shows a three-storey main block with a classical pediment, lower side wings with Venetian windows and a long range of service rooms and stables.

Both Moseley Hall and Weatheroak Hall are beyond our study area but they represent an architectural benchmark to which others in King's Norton might aspire.

52 *Moseley Hall in an early 19th-century engraving. The 18th-century building is the central section which was burnt out during the Birmingham Riots of 1791. Classical pedimented wings were added either side in the rebuilding.*

53 *Robert Mynors, the surgeon, with his family, depicted by the artist James Millar inside Weatheroak Hall in 1797. The painting on the wall gives a view of the front of the hall with its side wings.*

The largest of the Georgian houses in the study area was Monyhull Hall. Much of the early 18th-century house survives despite considerable alterations in the 19th century but the earlier house is still visible in the roof space. It was built in the mid-1730s by John Arderne, gentleman and member of the Catholic community in Bromsgrove. Unusually, a farmhouse adjoined the western side of the mansion house and was occupied by Arderne's bailiff, Thomas Cotterell. In 1757 Monyhull was described as 'a very good modern-built house' consisting of seven main rooms on each floor with an entrance hall, three parlours – two of them panelled and a third hung with wallpaper. Upstairs all the rooms were papered and there were four cellars, a brewhouse, bakehouse, dairy, stable and barn. Surrounding the house was 40 acres of land, 'large gardens planted with wall-fruit and other trees, and several good Fish-Ponds'.[13] By 1782 Monyhull was owned by Gregory Hicks of Birmingham, and passed to his son William, a threadmaker of Digbeth. Both Gregory and William styled themselves gentlemen once they had acquired the hall.[14]

54 *Henry Pope's watercolour of Bell's Farm from the south in the late 19th century includes details of the square dovecote and garden walls that would have been familiar to 18th-century occupiers of the house.*

The histories of Moseley Hall and Monyhull Hall in the late 18th century are not isolated examples of the influence of new wealth in the town. Increasingly, local houses and small farms were leased or bought by Birmingham people in search of a rural retreat. One of the first signs of a process, which accelerated in the 19th century, can be seen in the sale of a 'genteel new built house' with 50 acres of land at Cotteridge which 'may answer a person in Trade that wants a House in the country'.[15]

Earlier houses continued to be adapted to changing needs. We catch a glimpse of one older timber-framed house, Bell's Farm, during the 18th century from newspaper advertisements and through inventories. When Edward Field, gentleman, died there in 1742 he had been occupying 12 rooms which still retained names such as hall and parlour which would not have been out of place a century earlier.[16] The Best Parlour had become a dining and sitting room with mahogany tables, leather seated chairs, a bureau and two armchairs. Eighteenth-century luxuries such as silver tea spoons, sugar tongs, a tea caddy, china and delftware were much in evidence. However, in layout the house was substantially as remodelled some eighty years earlier. Shortly afterwards, when Bell's Farm was advertised to let in 1764,[17] it was claimed the house and buildings were in good repair and, while some of the rooms were lined with old panelling, the rest was wallpapered. Four years later, when Bell's Farm was again on the market, the attraction of its immediate surroundings were promoted – 'a handsome Court in Front, walled in, and a large Pleasant Garden, well planted with a Variety of Fruit Trees, now in their Perfection, and a neat Summer House therein, as likewise a Kitchen garden adjoining to the same'.[18] It was marketed 'for a genteel private Family' and, as a slightly later advertisement for the house remarks, 'None need apply but Men of real Property.'[19]

By the end of the century the classic brick Georgian farmhouse, two and a half or three storeys high with a three bay symmetrical façade and one or more rear wings, had become a distinctive feature of the local landscape. The front range contained the parlour and dining room or kitchen either side of the central stair-hall, while the wings housed a back kitchen, other service rooms and a dairy. Eagle Farm (demolished 1947), wedged between the Redditch Road and Masshouse Lane, was another classic example. Until the 1960s similar farmhouses existed at Kingswood and the Maypole, while another particularly good example, Hollywood Farm, was needlessly demolished in the 1990s.

Timber building continued side by side with brick well into the 18th century but by then it was increasingly viewed as old-fashioned and, if used at all, was best concealed by plaster or used in the rear wings or lesser buildings. Encasing a timber house in brick sometimes provided a fashionable façade, but more often served as an affordable solution to the problem of a badly decaying frame. Examples of such brick skins added to medieval houses are Wychall Farm (demolished about 1953) and Primrose Hill Farm, where much of the external frame of the hall range was concealed. Similarly, in the 18th century the jettied front of the *Saracen's Head* facing The Green was replaced by brickwork.

If we read between the lines of auctioneers' advertisements in the 18th century it is possible to detect the two strands of polite and vernacular. When Warstock Farm was put up for

55 *Kingswood Farm, photographed in 1966, was a large symmetrical house of c.1800 whose windows had been enlarged in the early 19th century.*

sale in 1774 it was described as 'new-built, sashed and fronted two ways',[20] suggesting a degree of symmetry. Considerably grander was Newhouse Farm in Westhill Road, erected in 1792 when it was advertised as 'a large newly erected Mansion, genteelly fitted up, delightfully situated on an Eminence a few hundred yards from King's

56 *Wychall Farm in 1952. In the early 18th century the core of a late medieval house with an inserted 16th-century chimney was refronted in brick.*

Norton Church'.[21] In contrast were the more vernacular farmhouses which the agents described merely as 'substantial' or, as at Slade Pool Farm, Maypole in 1794, 'good and convenient'.[22] That 'good and convenient' brick farmhouse survives now as a pair of semi-detached houses almost hidden behind 1930s houses off a suburban street (58-60 Stotfold Road).

There is virtually nothing remaining of the parish's 18th-century brick cottages. A pair survived in Redhill Road until the 1970s and showed characteristic features, being 1½ storeys in height with gabled dormers and a plat band at first-floor level, suggesting they were 18th- rather than 19th-century.[23]

THE VILLAGE

The fair and market were held intermittently through the 18th century. By the 1770s the April fair had become in effect a market 'for all sorts of cattle', while the autumn fair took on the role of a mop or hiring fair.[24] Information on the physical layout of the village and on where its inhabitants lived is even more elusive than in previous centuries. The inns of the village, however, have proved to be an exception.

The Saracen's Head

Around the turn of the 18th century, Thomas Whorwood sold the *Saracen's Head* to Edward Lyndon. He sold it on quickly to John Hinckley, rector of Northfield,[25] who died within a year (1703), leaving the whole of the *Saracen's Head* complex to his brother, Henry Hinckley I of Harborne. John Hinckley had, however, provided for his sister, Mary Colles, to live for the remainder of her life in that part of the *Saracen's Head* which is now the site of the *Bull's Head* car park. In 1708 Mary Colles and her brother John Henry Hinckley sold this part to John Birch, vicar of King's Norton (1699-1717 and 1722-3).[26] The north range had no tenant at this time. It is clear from the documentary evidence that the whole complex was now divided into at least three dwellings and that Mary Colles was probably living in the central part. About this time, the wagon entrance that once formed the centre of the east range was filled in and a staircase constructed within it. A new but less elegant entry was created at the junction of the north and south ranges to gain access to the rear yard.

Mary Colles died in 1727 and her will and inventory give a detailed description of the contents of the 11 rooms she occupied, from the Hall, Scullery, Kitchen, Parlour, Pantry, Cellar and Brewhouse to the rooms above.[27] A good indicator of her relatively high social status is the listing of 'a Family Picture' in the Parlour, silver, window curtains and soft furnishings in most rooms.

Henry Hinckley I, Mary Colles' brother, died in 1732 leaving the *Saracen's Head* to his wife Elizabeth, for her life, and then to his son, Henry Hinckley II. At this time it consisted of three houses 'lying near the Church in Kingsnorton' in the possession of Ann Palmer, the elder, Ann Palmer the younger and William Hands Taylor. Elizabeth and her son were both alive, however, in 1756 when they leased all three parts to Mary Ward, already in occupation. She was a widow, who in the following year married a widower, Richard Lea, and it was probably during the Ward/Lea tenancy that the east range was converted into an inn, fronted in brick and its jetty underbuilt. The core of the building facing The Green had certainly become 'known by the sign of the *Saracen's Head* in Kings-Norton' by 1764, when an auction of property at Wythall was held there.[28] Next door to the south the Birch family had rented the former part of the *Saracen's Head* to Dr Collins, another vicar of King's Norton, and then sold it in 1764 to Mrs Ann Field of Moundsley Hall.

To be Sold to the best Bidder,

Upon Saturday the 14th Day of April, 1764, at the House of Richard Lea, known by the Sign of the Saracen's Head in King's-Norton, in the County of Worcester, subject to such Conditions as shall be then produced,

ALL that Freehold Estate, consisting of a well-accustom'd Publick House, with a Brewhouse, Barn, Stable, and other Conveniences thereto belonging, together with two Pieces of good Meadow or Pasture Ground thereto adjoining, which said Premisses are known by the Name of Drake's Cross, and are situate in the said Parish of King's-Norton, and now in the Occupation of John Townsend.

Further Particulars may be had of Mr. Whateley, Attorney, in Walsall.

57 *This advertisement in* Aris's Birmingham Gazette *is the first to mention the name* Saracen's Head *(14 April 1764).*

In 1777 Henry Hinckley II sold the *Saracen's Head* to Richard Lea. The building had been separated for perhaps a century by a different tenancy from Millwards, the compact block of land that lay to the east of the King's Norton Mill. This sale finally severed the ownership connection between the *Saracen's Head* and Millwards, established by the Rotseys over two centuries earlier. The Hinckley family had in fact constructed a new house on the summit of Millwards called High House in the early part of the 18th century and leased it to Thomas Roper of Broad Meadow.[29]

Richard Lea died in 1773. In his will he described himself as an innholder and left all his land, historically unconnected to the *Saracen's Head*, to his son Richard Lea II. Richard, maltster, also married a Mary, *née* Dudley, innholder, in King's Norton church in 1781.[30] He or his father was probably responsible for constructing a malthouse in the west end of the north range.

The Bull's Head

The *Bull's Head* once formed part of a long timber-framed 'terrace' connected to the *Saracen's Head* east range and projecting prominently into The Green; for this reason it may have may have been built by the Rotsey family in the late 15th century. At an unknown time this house in the village became attached to some land known as 'Brook Tenement' situated on the north side of Parsons Hill just east of the later Canal Bridge.[31] By 1742 Sandys Lyttleton, steward of the manor since 1720, was owner of 'Lett Brook', as it came to be known. Tradition has it that Sandys Lyttleton lived at the *Saracen's Head*, but this confusion with the *Bull's Head*, his actual home, is understandable in view of their proximity. It is likely that Sandys Lyttleton rebuilt part of the timber-framed house in a more fashionable style, using brick and prominent stone quoins and a dentilled cornice that show on early photographs. It was only to become an inn after Sandys vacated the house. He ceased to be steward in 1776, perhaps on his death aged 86. Humphrey Lyttleton, most likely his son, had inherited earlier and by 1782 had installed George Ken(d)rick as tenant.[32] In 1801 George Kendrick was paying tithe for the 'Bulls Head Inn' and the outlying land as tenant of Humphrey.[33]

The Old Bell

The *Old Bell* is first recorded in 1735, when Thomas Archer, lord of the manor and architect, leased 'the Bell' with additional land to John Field.[34] The lease is important, as it is clear that the building was under construction and Thomas Archer agreed to complete the work at a cost not exceeding £100. This was the first known house in the village to be rebuilt at this scale in this period. Old photographs show a tall brick building with sash windows surviving on the first floor with two plat bands – horizontal bands of brick above and below – and dentilled eaves. The ground floor had later bay windows. On style alone a date in the first half of the 18th century would seem reasonable. The gable bay of the timber building next door must also have formed part of the property at the time,

58 *The* Old Bell *inn on the south side of* The Green *was built in 1735. This photograph dates from* c.1895. *The inn was demolished* c.1964.

for the taller eaves and roof of the new construction were projected onto the roof slope of the older building in a most unusual way. In 1743 the 'Old Bell' formed part of the marriage settlement of Henry Archer, who had just inherited from his uncle Thomas. It was then in the tenure of Elizabeth Field. The land attached was located in the fields north of Wharf Road, stretching as far as Let Brook with its confluence with the Rea, now part of King's Norton playing fields. In 1772 the 'Sign of the Bell' was tenanted by Hannah Wheeler.[35]

Of shopkeepers round The Green we have only glimpses. William Shaw, one of the churchwardens, kept a grocer's shop and dealt in a wide range of goods, from sugar and coffee to raisins, currants and prunes. Adjoining the shop, which was said to be 'a very good one', was his own house. When he gave up the business in 1752 his stock was said to be worth between £300 and £400.[36] Other shopkeepers and traders are more elusive because the documents rarely give addresses, but we hear of a baker and a malster in the town.

A pair of three-storey brick houses, 16-17 The Green, may belong to the late 18th century (or very early 19th century). They have segmental heads to windows and doors. Others once existed round The Green but have all been demolished.

THE RURAL LANDSCAPE

Agriculture

As Birmingham grew from a town of 15,000 people in 1700 to 60,000 by the end of the century it exercised considerable influence on the agriculture of the surrounding rural parishes. Increasingly they became granaries and suppliers of meat, fowl and dairy produce to the town's new inhabitants. King's Norton had long enjoyed a tradition of mixed farming but the emphasis on milk, cheese and butter became important to the local economy with a ready local market just five miles away. Newspapers advertised grazing farms for sale and to let in King's Norton in the second half of the 18th century, and in doing so extolled their proximity to Birmingham. When a well-manured small farm of 21 acres of meadow and rich old pasture at Kingswood was offered in 1775 it was claimed each acre was 'capable of making a cow completely fat during the summer'.[37]

In the late 18th century government subsidies were available to farmers for growing flax. While flax had been significant in earlier centuries to encourage home industry among the rural poor, the initiatives of the 1770s were aimed at larger scale farmers. A number of King's Norton farmers took up the challenge, one of them being William Tay who farmed at Headley Heath; at Goodrest Farm and at King's Heath a field here and there was devoted to flax.[38] Some sold the crop on to flax dressers and their agents who organised its processing centrally, while others undertook the process themselves. After harvesting, the flax was 'retted' or rotted to separate the woody core of the stem from the fibre or filament. In King's Norton the decomposition process took place in retting pits, and then in adjacent buckhouses where the washing process was completed and the bark was stripped. Locally grown flax was woven into linen. When John Nichols, weaver, died at Kingswood in 1728 the workshop in his home contained two looms, the chamber over it was used for the storage of flax and hurds, and the finished linen was stored elsewhere in the house.[39] Flax also supplied the wick yarn business situated in the 18th century at Wythall and Headley Heath.

Enclosure of the Commons

The place-names of Birmingham's southern suburbs, King's Heath, Balsall Heath, Highter's Heath, West Heath and Walker's Heath, are all indicators of the survival into the 18th century of King's Norton's commons and wastes. When enclosure came between 1772-4 the place-names with the 'heath' element were so well known that they persisted. Of the heaths and wastes to be enclosed the largest was King's Heath, which stretched from the present railway line near Queensbridge Road in a southerly direction to Alcester Lanes End, and from Millpool Hill to the Maypole, stretching from Kingswood on the west to Highter's Heath and Hollywood on the east. Running south from Birmingham across the largest of these open tracts of waste and heathland was the highway to Alcester. Before it was turnpiked in 1767 it was described as 'narrow, incommodious and dangerous to travellers'.[40] A 19th-century tradition maintained that the finger posts on the eponymous Maypole were added by a grateful traveller who had lost his way. In the winter time King's Norton's commons could also be hazardous for locals well acquainted with the landscape. When the labourer Jacob Greathead was returning to his family in January 1772 he lost his way in the snow and was found dead the following day.[41] Of more importance to landowners was the need to consolidate their holdings and take advantage of the improvements taking place in farming methods at the time. Accordingly, King's Norton's remaining commons were finally divided and enclosed as farmland after a private Act of Parliament was obtained in 1772.[42]

59   *The Maypole* c.*1900 showing the great height of the pole above the signpost.*

As a preliminary in May 1772 the proprietors entitled to rights of common in King's Norton rode the boundaries of the commons to establish the limits of the manorial waste. Between King's Norton and Yardley was an area known as 'No Man's Land' where the boundary was very unclear. It was finally resolved that this land be divided equally between the two parishes. On 15 June 1772 the first meeting of the Commissioners for the enclosure of King's Norton's wastes and commons was held at the *Bell* inn on The Green. One of their first tasks was to appoint surveyors to map the remaining unenclosed land in the parish.[43] Their work showed that it totalled just over 2,000 acres, or one sixth of the total parish, and the principal commons, wastes and heathland were at King's Wood, King's Heath, Wythall Heath and West Heath, while smaller areas were to be found at Balsall Heath, Moseley Wake Green, Headley Heath and Walker's Heath.

The first element in the enclosure process was to stake out the lines of public and private roads. The Act stipulated that these were to be at least sixty feet wide between the fences and ditches, allowing wide verges for roadside grazing, passing places for wagons and the avoidance of pot-holes. By September 1773 the roads had been marked out.[44] The next stage was to settle disputes about the proposed allocation of allotments.[45] Once this was done the heaths and wastes were cleared of gorse and undergrowth, the soil was broken using a breast plough, and any trees were removed by the lord of the manor, if he so wished to exercise his right, within a year. The land was then burnt and horse-ploughed.[46] Perimeter fences were erected and planted with hawthorn to create hedgerows. The new land was then subdivided at the proprietor's expense to form fields.

The result was the creation of a network of largely long and straight highways and uniformly square or rectangular fields. In comparison to the earlier fields these enclosure allotments have remarkably straight edges because they were laid out using surveying equipment, such as chains and sextants, at one point in time. The Tithe Map of the Walker's Heath area shows the irregularly shaped old enclosures around Bell's Farm contrasting with the symmetry of the new enclosures to the west.

The new enclosures were divided among 200 landowners who had been entitled to rights of common.[47] The largest allocation – 217 acres at Hollywood – was to the Dean and Chapter of Worcester Cathedral in respect of glebe land and the Great Tithes. The Crown, as lord of the manor, received 142 acres in the Higher's Heath area as well as the squatter cottages and encroachments which had been taken out of the waste. The majority of allocations were far more modest, being less than two acres, and wherever possible these allotments were sited contiguous with an owner's existing lands.

60 *Extract from the Tithe Map east of Walker's Heath (1840) showing the contrast between the irregularly shaped fields of old enclosure around Bell's Farm and the straight-edged fields of parliamentary enclosure at Walker's Heath.*

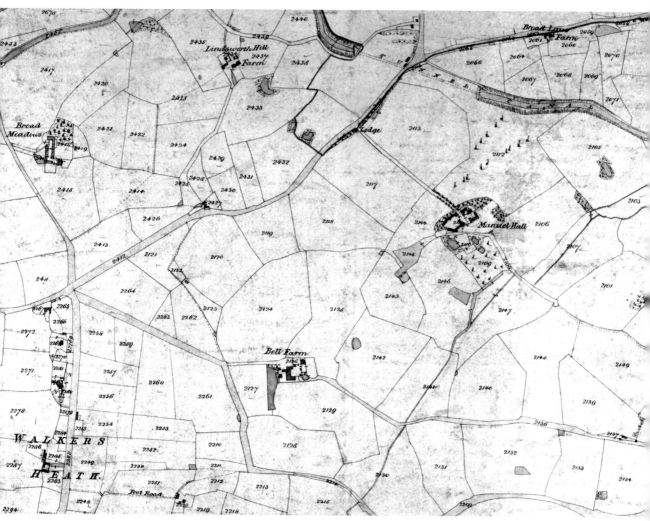

THE POOR

The hardship caused to the poor by enclosure is one of the recurrent themes of 18th-century social, economic and agrarian history. In open field parishes many became landless and were unable to sustain themselves and their families because of the loss of what had in effect been smallholdings. Measuring the impact in a parish like King's Norton, where the enclosure was entirely of common land, is more difficult, especially because the sources are so slight. Those allotted new enclosures were existing landowners or proprietors entitled to the right of common. They numbered 200 people, but since we know the parish contained 450 families at the time, more than half the population must have been deprived of any access to the commons, even though their use of it may not have been legal. With high grain prices leading to the rising cost of bread, poverty levels increased in the second half of the 18th century. The burden of responsibility fell squarely on the parish to fund the care of the poor from levies or rates on its householders.

Until 1803, when a workhouse was opened in the village, the poor of King's Norton were supported directly from the parish levies through 'outdoor' relief. There were two principal categories of payments: monthly payments which provided basic income and, secondly, necessities which met needs.

The survival of 18th-century documents relating to care of the poor in King's Norton is disappointingly thin, and of the few that remain access is restricted because of their fragile condition.[48] From the overseers' accounts that are available we can begin to build a picture of the types of outdoor relief provided and of the growing costs. The aim of the overseers of the poor, the parish officials responsible, was to contain costs by keeping the poor in work. Payments were therefore made for the supply of tools – a scythe to an agricultural labourer, an anvil and bellows to two nailers at Rednal, and repairs to spinning wheels for two women in the village. Help was also provided for those unable to help themselves. A man was paid for digging and planting widow Blun's garden, and potatoes were supplied to widow Wickitt for her to plant. Clothing was provided to the sick and the most needy, usually consisting of single allocations of shoes, a shift or a shirt, but Richard Pittaway was clearly a more deserving case and he received a new shirt, a pair of leather breeches and 'a round frock' or loose-fitting coat. Payments were made for washing the sick and, when absolutely necessary, medical help was summoned by fetching Charles Kidman, the surgeon from Birmingham. Those unable to look after themselves in their own homes were boarded out as in the case of widow Bissell, who was placed in Nell Tovey's house. Long periods of sickness meant that paupers were unable to pay their rents, so a substantial proportion of the monies spent was consumed in compensating landlords.

It was the responsibility of the overseers to ensure that only those eligible for help received it. Thus anyone claiming relief who was not officially settled in King's Norton could be removed and returned to their home parish. Despite the claims made in 1765 by the labourer, John Woodhouse, that he had been hired at King's

Norton mop by a local farmer and had rented part of a farm in the parish for the last 19 years his name did not appear in the rate books and the Justices of the Peace agreed with the overseers that he should be returned to Yardley where he was officially settled.[49] In their determination to keep down expenses the overseers could occasionally be tempted to break the law. In 1777 Thomas Mainwaring and Durant Kidson, overseers of King's Norton, were charged with bribing an Ipsley man, Daniel White, to marry the pauper, Ann Parker, whom they described as 'a helpless and miserable wretch greatly burthensome to the parish of King's Norton', and thus relieve them of responsibility.[50]

In 1798 expenditure in Moundsley Yield amounted to just under £400, and if that figure is multiplied by five for all the yields we arrive at an estimate of £2,000 for the whole parish. That the cost of poor relief was rising dramatically in the last thirty years of the century is well attested nationally and local evidence demonstrates the same upward trend. King's Norton parish spent £730 in 1776; this had risen to £1,200 by the 1780s and by 1803 had topped £3,000. By then King's Norton's expenditure on poor relief was only exceeded in the whole of Halfshire Hundred by Bromsgrove where £3,600 was spent.[51] But Bromsgrove was a town of 14,500 inhabitants so the cost could be more equably shared, whereas King's Norton was about a fifth of the size with a population of 2,800. Perhaps it is not surprising that contemporaries bemoaned the spiralling cost of the poor rates in King's Norton and the burden it placed on the parish in general and the ratepayers in particular.

CHURCH AND RELIGION

For much of the 18th century the physical state of the parish church was a recurrent cause for concern. Deterioration had set in and the churchwardens struggled to raise the necessary funds to repair the structure. In 1712 two of them, John Roper and Daniel Well, left their names on the flying stone buttresses they built within the north aisle to support it.[52] It must have been a practical if inelegant solution to the problem. Outside, the north wall was propped up by two stone and brick buttresses built in the churchyard. By 1774 the tower and spire, together with other parts of the church, were in such a state that 'the Parishioners cannot assemble therein for divine worship without bodily danger'.[53] Matters had deteriorated even further at Wythall where the 'ancient chapel' was ruinous and 'must be taken down'. Together the costs of repairs to these two churches amounted to over £1,000, a considerable sum for the parishioners who were not slow to point out that they were 'mostly tenants at rack rents and greatly burthened by the poor'.

That repairs and rebuilding were undertaken is shown a decade later when the reply to Bishop Hurd's survey of the state of the diocese in 1782 confirmed the church and chancel were once again in good repair.[54] At some point in the 18th century a gallery was erected at the western end of the nave which provided a dedicated space during services for the pupils of the school.

Dissent and Riots

During the 18th century Protestant nonconformity became established in the parish. By 1782, three out of 460 families within King's Norton were Roman Catholics, two were Quakers and 17 Presbyterians, the last having established a dedicated Unitarian chapel known as Kingswood Meeting House at the beginning of the century.[55] The Toleration Act of 1689 had given congregations the right to worship in licensed meeting houses. In 1708 such a licence was granted to Edward Hawkes of King's Norton to use a house which had been built on a small plot of land in Dark Lane half a mile west of the Alcester Road at Hollywood as a meeting.[56] Its founders and original trustees were men from King's Norton and Birmingham who, conscious of intolerance shown to nonconformists at the time, wanted a suitably secluded but accessible site. But during the Sacheverell riots in 1715 an attempt was made to burn down the chapel. One of the rioters, named Dollax, was executed at Worcester and had the dubious distinction of being the first offender to be executed under the Riot Act of 1715.[57] As a result the Kingswood Meeting gained the alternative name of Dollax's Chapel, or St Dollax. It survived on its Dark Lane site until 1791 when it was totally destroyed during the Birmingham Riots.

The Birmingham Riots of 1791

When riots broke out in Birmingham on 14 July 1791 following a dinner commemorating the second anniversary of the storming of the Bastille, they must have seemed remote from King's Norton. However, four days of rioting followed which saw four meeting houses and 27 private houses attacked in an area stretching from Birmingham town centre well into the surrounding countryside. Those targeted were mainly Dissenters or sympathisers with the radical cause. Of these the most celebrated was the scientist, philosopher and preacher Dr Joseph Priestley, whose house and valuable laboratory at Fairhill, Sparkbrook were fired. The mob regarded such men as threatening the stability of the Established Church and the State, and the alternative names are the Church and King Riots or the Priestley Riots. How far the authorities were in collusion will never be known but the delay in sending troops to quell the rioters suggests those in power were not averse to demonstrating the dangers of radicalism.

King's Norton parish saw considerable destruction, especially in the Moseley and Balsall Heath area where Moseley Hall itself and several mansions were looted and set alight. On the fourth day the trail of destruction pushed south as far as King's Heath and Warstock where the homes of at least two nonconformists were razed. In a letter written a few days after the events the attorney Thomas Lee described how he managed to escape the mob as it moved south. He avoided King's Heath by going via Moor Green where he was shocked to see the destruction of Thomas Russell's house. From here he made his way to King's Norton town and then to the *Maypole* where he heard the shouts of the rioters attacking Mr Cox's house at Warstock.[58]

A prime target was the Unitarian Meeting at Kingswood, which was destroyed in the early hours of Sunday 17 July together with the nearby house of its minister.

61 *Kingswood Meeting was rebuilt on a new site in Packhorse Lane, Hollywood in 1792 after its predecessor in nearby Dark Lane was destroyed in the Birmingham Riots of 1791. On the left is the memorial to James Baldwin, the Victorian owner of Lifford Paper Mill.*

William Hutton, the Birmingham bookseller and historian, left a near contemporary account of the riots. As he suffered considerable loss of property and possessions in the riots it is a partisan account, but his remarks on King's Norton offer a reason why the rioters then turned back to Birmingham:

> Perhaps they found the parish of King's Norton too barren to support a mob in affluence; for they returned towards Birmingham, which, though dreadfully sacked, yet was better furnished with money, strong liquors, and various other property. King's Norton is an extensive manor belonging to the king, whose name they were advancing upon the walls, whose honour they were augmenting by burning three places of worship in his manor, and by destroying nine houses, the property of his peaceable tenants.[59]

Within two years Kingswood Meeting was rebuilt on a new site in Packhorse Lane, Wythall at a cost of £461. Bricks on the south-eastern corner are incised with the date 1792 and the building was opened in the following year. Claims for damage from owners of destroyed or ransacked property in the combined parishes of King's Norton and Yardley amounted to nearly £8,000, a sum that was eventually reduced to £5,500.[60] The irony is that the taxpayers of the whole of Halfshire Hundred were then faced with further subsidies to cover these costs.

Shortly after the Birmingham Riots the King's Norton Association for the Prosecution of Felons had substantially increased the rewards it offered for the arrest of culprits. A series of armed burglaries in the neighbourhood in December 1796 prompted the inhabitants of King's Norton to form 'an armed association for the protection of persons and property'.[61]

THE SCHOOL

Little is known of King's Norton's school in the 18th century. It continued to occupy the stone and timber-framed building constructed by the parishioners for the Rev. Thomas Hall in the mid-17th century. The names of the clerics who performed the dual role of clergyman and schoolmaster are known for the early 18th century. John Birch had taken over as master in 1694 and remained in post until his death in 1727. He was succeeded by the Rev. Joseph Benton, by John Hancox from 1731 and from 1734 by Samuel Middlemore. In 1757 the post of schoolmaster was advertised, the incumbent perhaps no longer willing to teach. For a salary of just £15 per annum the new master must be 'duly qualified to teach Latin, Writing and Arithmetic and well recommended for Virtue, Sobriety and Discretion'.[62]

TRADE AND INDUSTRY

King's Norton Mill

One of the three mills converted to industrial use (Lifford), while Wychall and King's Norton Mills continued to grind corn. The latter remained a customary holding, in effect the manorial mill. All changes of ownership were still declared at the manorial court (the three-weekly Court Baron) but very often this was a delayed affair, a rubber stamping of private sales that had taken place long before. In 1694 one of the last property transactions of the Whorwoods in King's Norton was to lease the mill to Daniel Lyndon, miller. Four years later it was sold with the *Saracen's Head* to a relation, Edward Lyndon, who in turn quickly sold to John Hinckley, a member of a Harborne family. The Lyndons remained as tenants of the Hinckleys. In about 1768 the mill and High House were sold by Henry Hinckley II to William Guest the younger of 'The Cotteridge'; this was about ten years before Henry disposed of the *Saracen's Head*. In 1792 Thomas Hooper, a miller of Aston, purchased the mill and High House. A plan of his newly acquired land[63] makes it clear that tanning had once taken place opposite the mill below High House on the land formerly called Millwards (Tanners Close and Meadow).

Turton's Mill/Bayley's Mill/Bird's Mill/Lifford Mill

John Bayley of Coventry, who had bought Turton's Mill in 1688, died in 1717 and his son of the same name inherited.[64] It is unlikely that the Bayleys actually worked the mill at this time, particularly since Thomas II was MP for Derby before 1727, but their tenants are unknown. Thomas II died in 1730, leaving his estates in trust to his wife Bridget to provide portions for several young children.[65] Apart from the mill these included the 'Brickhouse' (later Redhouse Farm) in King's Norton and lands in Warwickshire and Derbyshire. The mill was still known as Turton's in 1739, in recognition of the builders of such a distinctive brick structure about sixty years before. After a long Chancery dispute the mill and the 'Brickhouse' were sold in 1752.[66] On the purchase of the mill by James Hewitt, a lawyer of Coventry, we discover that a Job Bird was miller, but it is not known how long he had worked the mill.[67] James Hewitt was responsible for renaming 'Bird's Mill', as it became known. In 1767 he became Lord High Chancellor of Ireland and was elevated to the peerage in the following year as Baron Lifford, advancing to the viscountcy in 1781.[68] In celebration of these events the mill was named after a small town in County Donegal and the name has stuck.

More significant events were unfolding at the mill through Lord Lifford's new tenant, Thomas Dobbs. He arrived sometime in the late 1760s and in 1770 married Cordelia Wyatt, daughter of the inventor, John Wyatt. He was not destined to be a small-time corn miller and soon set about a major conversion of the mill into rolling of metal. This was the first mill in the King's Norton area to industrialise, and by 1773 Dobbs was receiving orders from the Soho Manufactory for rolled plated metal and copper to be shipped abroad.[69] He was also a customer of Soho, not paying his bills promptly and began making steel buttons around 1777 to the consternation of Matthew Boulton, who possibly feared the competition.[70] In 1780 the button-making partnership that had been formed just a few years before between Dobbs and John Whateley, a Birmingham gunmaker, was dissolved.[71]

Five years later this remarkable entrepreneur enquired of the infant Boulton and Watt firm about the cost of a pumping engine that could return water to the top of his water wheel and of their newly developed rotary engine, to replace one of his 10ft diameter wheels.[72] Dobbs finally chose a sun-and-planet rotary engine, the first to be installed in the greater Birmingham area. John Southern, one of Boulton & Watt's principal engineers, surveyed the site in June 1785 and during the visit he made the acquaintance of Dobbs' eldest daughter Cordelia, whom he eventually married in 1793. Southern produced a drawing of the rolling mill before the installation of the 10hp, 18-inch cylinder engine.[73] It shows two separate water wheels, one at each end of the mill, powering two sets of metal rolls, and confirms that these positions link directly to the two tail-race tunnels that today lead north from the former mill. The drawings reveal that the engine was to connect to one of the water wheels rather than

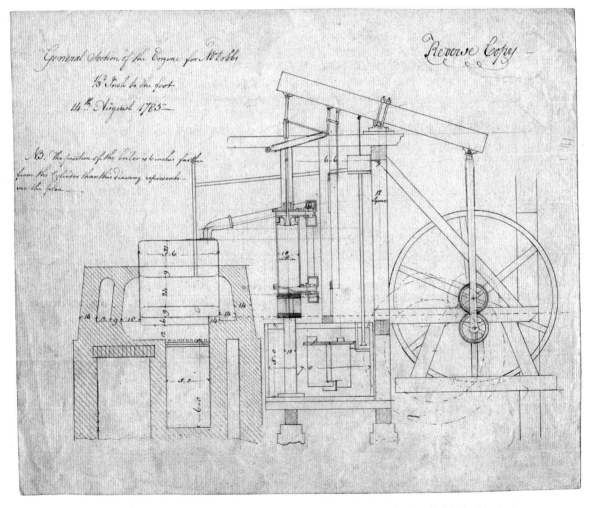

62 *Elevation of Boulton & Watt steam engine at Lifford, 1785, one of the few installed in the Birmingham area in the late 18th century. It was located at the end of the 17th-century mill (extreme left Fig. 50).*

replace it, enabling the wheel to work at low water. The steam engine house was built at the western end of the mill, on the site of the present caretaker's accommodation. The engine was manufactured in 1786 and installed in 1787 or thereabouts, but there seem to have been delays in bringing it into proper operation. In 1790 Boulton & Watt agreed to allow Dobbs to use the engine for four months without paying the premium that was the normal requirement.[74] By December 1792 they had received no payment at all and threatened legal action. Dobbs offered to return the engine and in August the following year claimed the engine had 'been a very great loss' to him 'from a sudden change of business', but that it was 'little impaired' from the little work it had done for him. In 1794 the engine was sold to a Mr Holloway of Leeds.[75]

This first application of rotary steam power a mile from the village could not be considered a success. Undeterred, Dobbs diversified, always looking for a new opportunity through his contacts in the metal trade. In the 1790s he became manager of the Garston Oil of Vitriol (sulphuric acid) works near Liverpool, built by Thomas Williams, the 'Copper King' and owner of the Parys copper mine in Anglesey. It is not known how time was divided between Garston and Lifford, but it is likely the Garston works were neglected in view of Dobbs' other commercial ventures; the works were not profitable and closed down in 1799.[76] By 1799 Thomas Dobbs had established his own Aqua Fortis Works on land he acquired immediately to the north of his leasehold estate. It was located on the west bank of the Worcester & Birmingham Canal, newly constructed two years earlier.[77] In the same year he sold sulphuric acid to Matthew Boulton.[78] Thomas faced the turn of the new century with undiminished energy and endeavour, and through his efforts Lifford became the focus of the first canal-side manufactory in King's Norton, but it took a considerable time for others to follow suit.

Wychall Mill

Wychall Mill ground corn throughout the century and remained part of Wychall Farm but was held on a separate tenancy. It was the smallest of the local mills with only one water wheel. In 1723 the mill and dwelling was leased to Richard Rostons for 99 years.[79] The lease was eventually transferred from the Roston family to William and then Francis Lindon, both millers. Under his 1781 will Francis left the lease of the mill to his grandson Henry Palmer. After this it was twice put up for sale (1787, 1795) but its days as a corn mill were soon to come to an end.

TRANSPORT AND COMMUNICATIONS

Highways and Turnpikes

Although the turnpiking of roads began in the 17th century, the creation of toll roads did not begin in earnest until the following century. Goods needed to move quickly and cheaply. By 1750, 400 turnpike trusts had been set up to improve existing roads and build new sections. The local network converged on Birmingham but King's Norton did not lie on a principal arterial route, such as the Bristol Road, Stratford

Road or Coventry Road, which were turnpiked early (1720s to 1740s). The first local road turnpiked was the route to Alcester in 1767 via Balsall Heath, Moseley, King's Heath, Millpool Hill, the Maypole, Wythall and Inkford. The turnpike trust was to take advantage in 1772 of the enclosure of the King's Norton commons, when wide straight sections were laid out across Balsall Heath, King's Heath, Highter's Heath, Bateman's Green and Headley Heath.

Two other turnpikes passed through the parish. The Northfield Turnpike skirted the study area, leaving the Alcester Road at Inkford to Weatheroak Hill and Forhill, and so on to West Heath via Redhill Lane. The second road was the short-lived western end of the Hatton Turnpike which operated as such from 1767-89. The route from Frankley to Hatton by Warwick entered King's Norton parish at Rubery. At Longbridge it followed Tessal Lane to West Heath and then headed via Rednal Road and a place called Foul Lake through King's Norton village. It then proceeded up Parson's Hill to Hill Top, and over Walker's Heath to the Maypole via Bell's Lane. Prior to being turnpiked, the road had followed the northern line of Bell's Lane 'through Mr Field's yard' at Bell's Farm, as the route was described in the 1720s.[80] A southern diversion, Druid's Lane, now took traffic away from the farm. At the Maypole the Warwick Turnpike followed the Alcester Turnpike to Hollywood and then via Hollywood Lane and Lea Green Lane to Grimes Hill and the Warwickshire boundary at Low Brook.

The road from King's Norton village to Birmingham was a minor rural track until it reached the Alcester road at King's Heath. There was no Pershore Road from Stirchley to Birmingham, for this was not constructed until 1825 as a completely new road, causing significant changes in and around the village which will be dealt with in the next chapter.

Canals

After many years of lobbying, the promoters of the Worcester & Birmingham Canal Company finally obtained their Act of Parliament in 1791.[81] The canal eventually created a short cut from Birmingham to the Severn and Bristol, avoiding the longer route past Wolverhampton to the Aldersley junction with the Staffordshire and Worcester Canal. Its construction, however, was a long and protracted affair, taking 23 years to complete. Disputes with landowners over compensation took time to resolve, and there was much opposition from the owners of mills concerned about the potential loss of water from streams. Labour and supplies needed to be sourced and barracks erected for workmen.[82] Work began at the Birmingham end, and by summer 1796 had reached the junction with the new Stratford Canal, just to the west of Lifford Mill.

It was a major undertaking then to drive a tunnel through the Cole/Arrow watershed at West Hill. Work began at the end of July 1794 and over ten million bricks were required. Brick kilns were established in the locality – one at King's Norton wharf was known as kiln no. 4 and others were sited either end of the tunnel, but these were insufficient to meet the demand, and substantial quantities were imported from Selly Oak and Tipton.[83]

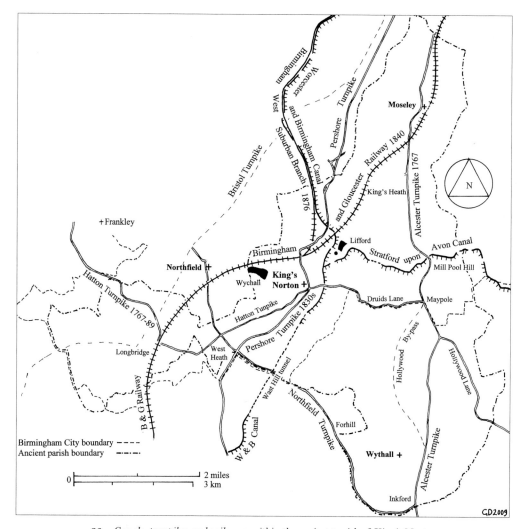

63 *Canals, turnpikes and railways within the ancient parish of King's Norton.*

Wast Hill Tunnel was completed to Hopwood in February 1797 and when opened on 27 March 1797 was immediately hailed as a triumph of engineering. 'The extent of the tunnel is upwards of a mile and a half, and yet so straight that it may be seen from one end to the other', proclaimed one newspaper account. It was not long before Wast Hill Tunnel had become one of the sights which readers of guidebooks to the county should not miss. The new wharf at Hopwood would bring great economic benefits:

> The country that will be supplied from this wharf is extremely populous and very extensive: the towns of Alvechurch, Feckenham, Redditch, with the large parishes of Beoley, Studley, &c, &c, will be furnished with coal, &c, by this grand communication; and the farmers will find a very ready and cheap conveyance for their grain to the very populous town of Birmingham.[84]

Dogged by funding crises, completion of the canal to Worcester would take another 18 years. In the meantime work had got underway in another direction. The Stratford Canal Company obtained its Act in 1793,[85] after the Dudley Canal decided to extend to the Worcester & Birmingham Canal. Supplies in Stratford could be obtained via both the Birmingham and the Dudley Canal, guaranteeing lower prices.

By a combination of commercial forces and geography, the junction of the Worcester and Stratford came to be constructed one mile east of the village. A tollhouse was built on the west bank of the Worcester & Birmingham Canal facing towards the Stratford Canal. Now known as Junction House, it is a fine example of a Georgian tollhouse with the windows of the canted central bay giving the tollkeeper views of oncoming traffic. A rainwater head at the back confirms the date known from the canal company records – 1796. The Stratford company had intended to build its own tollhouse at the junction, but agreed to share the costs of one building. Later, another tollhouse was erected at Bridge no. 1 where a guillotine stop-lock was installed. The gates are raised by a hand winch on the north bank of the canal, while the counterweight on the other bank helps with lifting.

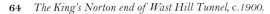

64   *The King's Norton end of Wast Hill Tunnel,* c.1900.

65 *Guillotine lock, today symbolically marking the boundary but formerly dividing the Stratford-upon-Avon Canal from the Worcester & Birmingham Canal.*

66   *The tollhouse known as Junction House was built in 1796 and controlled traffic where the Worcester &*
Birmingham and the Stratford Canals met.

The tight angle of the junction entrapped Lifford Mill as if in watery jaws. The
transformation of the local landscape here by the exploitation of water was carried
a stage further with the construction of Lifford Reservoir in the following century.
Thomas Dobbs knew by the early 1790s that the Worcester and Stratford canals
were intended to join very close to his mill and negotiated hard with the Worcester &
Birmingham Canal Company to get as high a price as possible for his freehold land that
was to be crossed. He had purchased it at £25 per acre and was demanding £120 per
acre; agreement was finally reached at £75.[86] In 1799 Dobbs offered Matthew Boulton
marl that was to be removed in making a tow-path along the Worcester & Birmingham
Canal.[87] He claimed he had 'cut about 3 miles of the Stratford Canal' and 'was pretty well
acquainted with the business'. Little did he know that his canal construction endeavours
were ultimately to aid the process by which Birmingham overwhelmed King's Norton.

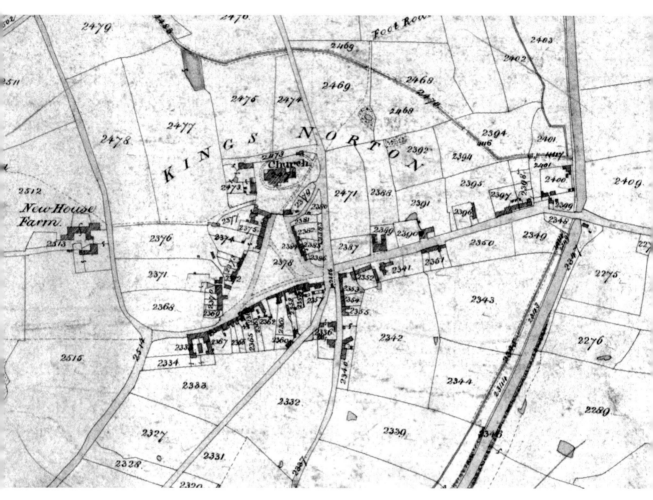

67 *Extract from the King's Norton Tithe Map (1840) showing the village.*

V

Nineteenth-Century King's Norton

he growth of Birmingham in the 19th century from a population of 73,670 in 1801 to 522,204 in 1901 was reflected in an expansion of the built-up area from Deritend to Cotteridge, a distance of approximately five miles. The northern fringes of the study area had been reached and this century was the last in which the rural landscape predominated. Even so, the influence of Birmingham on all aspects of the life of the parish, from landownership and employment to architecture and agriculture, was formidable.

TENURE AND LANDOWNERSHIP

In 1804 King's Norton was sold to John Taylor II for £7,568, and the royal connection was finally severed.[1] The Taylors epitomised the growing influence of Birmingham on local affairs as John's father, John Taylor I (d. 1775) had amassed a fortune in the town making buttons and japanned and gilt snuff boxes, and in 1765 co-founded the bank, Taylor and Lloyds, still trading today as Lloyds. In 1767 he had purchased from the Grevis family Moseley Hall and other farms in King's Norton, as well as extensive parts of the neighbouring manor of Yardley.[2] The acquisition of the manor of King's Norton by John II did not bring with it much land. Its income was derived mostly from court fees, the ancient chief and customary rents and rents from cottages and plecks (small enclosed fields) that had been established on the king's waste in the previous two centuries. Over 140 cottages and plecks located on only 120 acres of land generated over 40 per cent of the manorial income.

The Tithe Survey of 1838-40 provides the first accurate and mapped record of ownership and tenancy across the whole manor. James Taylor was the largest landowner and lord of the manor, but most of his estate lay to the north of the study area in the enlarged Moseley Yield, which had absorbed part of Lea Yield soon after 1804. Altogether nearly 600 owners of land in the manor shared a larger number of tenants and the Tithe Survey reveals how little land was owner-occupied. Twenty-four of these owned over 100 acres, the most being James Taylor's (938 acres), followed by Robert Mynors (582 acres), who had acquired much of the Archer estate, and George Attwood, owner of the old Rotsey estate at Colmers Farm and King's Norton Mill. There were 32 owners with 51-99 acres and 83 owners with 11-50 acres, leaving about 450, over three-quarters of the total, possessing 10 acres or fewer. King's Norton had never been a manor with great estates, and during the next century landownership was set to fragment into a myriad of pieces as streets replaced fields.

King's Norton became an increasingly attractive area in which to invest in land, as Birmingham crept ever nearer. Successful businessmen aspired to owning rural property, even if they were not to live there. The richest, such as the Taylors and the Lanes of Moundsley, could afford a country retreat. Most of the larger farms were worked by tenants, e.g. Cotteridge, New House (Kingsuch), Bell's Farm, Lindsworth, Little Hawkesley, Goodrest and Headley Heath Farm. Eagle Farm, immediately south of the village, was one of the few exceptions, Daniel Pritchett being the owner-farmer in 1838.

The ancient copyhold or customary tenures, which included King's Norton Mill, were 'enfranchised' or extinguished between the 1860s and 1880 and converted into freeholds in exchange for a single one-off payment well over 100 times the old rent.[3] The chief rents that had been paid since the medieval period were redeemed in the early 1890s for a payment equivalent to twenty years rent.[4] The manorial court had been in long decline, dealing mainly with copyhold tenures. Once these had been enfranchised the court ceased to operate and last met in 1876.[5] By this time national legislation was creating new types of local administration which, in view of the continuing growth of Birmingham, turned out to be short-lived.

Administration

Under the Public Health Act of 1848 a Rural Sanitary Board was established for King's Norton. It was given additional powers as King's Norton Rural Sanitary Authority under the Public Health Act of 1872, which controlled the building of new houses and streets through bye-laws. The Sanitary Authority developed into King's Norton Rural District Council in 1895, and in turn became King's Norton & Northfield Urban District Council in 1898 until its absorption into Birmingham in 1911. The short-lived King's Norton Parish Council existed between 1895 and 1898.

Even by the time of the Tithe Survey a small part of King's Norton manor at Balsall Heath was urbanised – where Birmingham had spread from Bordesley along the main road towards Moseley. By the 1860s the built-up area had reached Moseley and in 1862 a Local Board of Health for Balsall Heath was set up, followed by an Urban Sanitary District by 1872. In 1891 Balsall Heath was taken into Birmingham, the first absorption of a part of King's Norton manor by the city.[6]

POPULATION

With the national decennial census introduced in 1801 it is at last possible to present accurate population figures for the parish, rather than rely on source material such

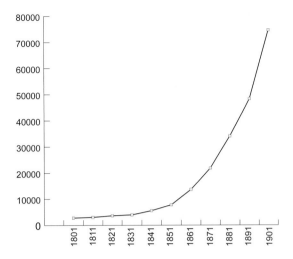

as parish registers and taxation lists that were not designed to give such data. The figures enable us to chart the growth of King's Norton from just under 3,000 in 1801 to nearly 75,000 a century later. In the first thirty years of the 19th century the population increased by a third. In the next twenty years it nearly doubled to 7,759. In the decade 1851-61 it doubled again, a remarkable rise, and continued to increase sharply through every succeeding decade.

These significant increases were largely contained in the extreme north of the old parish and it was not until the 1890s that Cotteridge expanded from a couple of farms to take on its new role as a late Victorian suburb. Nineteenth-century building development began at Balsall Heath in the 1830s and 1840s and started the process of urbanisation from the very edge of Birmingham southwards. By 1881 Balsall Heath alone had reached a total of 22,497 people, leaving about 10,000 other residents of King's Norton still spread quite thinly across the rest of the old parish. When Balsall Heath was incorporated in the city of Birmingham in 1891 its population had reached 30,000.

The census returns enable comparison to be made between various districts at specific points in the 19th century. In 1841 the district that contained King's Norton village stretched from Cotteridge to Walker's Heath and westwards to West Heath. It housed 721 people in 141 houses. Thirty-six per cent of the population was engaged directly in agriculture or its service industries. Around The Green there was a concentration of agricultural labourers while others lived within their employers' households in outlying farmhouses. The village supported a wide variety of shopkeepers and other retail traders – a butcher, two bakers, a coal dealer, saddler, publican, innkeeper and two malsters. There was also a basketmaker and tinplate worker, two tailors and nine shoemakers. The number employed in newer trades, such as metal rolling, was very modest, but the signs of change were beginning to show themselves: three houses were in the course of construction when the census was taken and the building trade involved 15 per cent of the workforce.

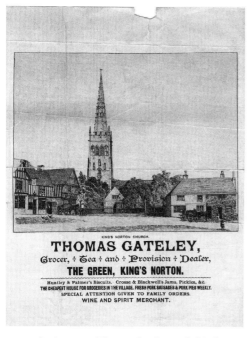

THOMAS GATELEY,
Grocer, ✛ Tea ✛ and ✛ Provision ✛ Dealer,
THE GREEN, KING'S NORTON.

Huntley & Palmer's Biscuits, Crosse & Blackwell's Jams, Pickles, &c.
THE CHEAPEST HOUSE FOR GROCERIES IN THE VILLAGE. FRESH PORK SAUSAGES & PORK PIES WEEKLY.
SPECIAL ATTENTION GIVEN TO FAMILY ORDERS.
WINE AND SPIRIT MERCHANT.

68 *In the 1890s Thomas Gateley used this classic image of the north end of The Green to promote his stores, which were based at Oakford House (now part of the Post Office).*

The 1901 census paints a rather different picture. The agricultural labourers have totally disappeared from The Green, and the village supported a wide variety of workers, some of them following traditional trades but many now employed in industry and on the railway. There were more shops covering a wider range of goods: besides a butcher and baker there was now a bookseller, stationer and post office, as well as four grocers. Of the last, Thomas Gateley combined his grocery business with that of draper, hosier, haberdasher and ironmonger from his new premises at Oakford House next to the Square on the western side of The Green. Gateley's offered the latest in wringers and mangling machines, while Mortiboys on the corner of Redditch Road advertised 'Home-fed ham and bacon', Huntley & Palmer's biscuits, Pattison's pure sweets and Cadbury's chocolate.

THE CHANGING LANDSCAPE

Urbanisation

The construction of the Pershore Turnpike in the 1820s and 1830s encouraged the growth of Birmingham in a two-pronged direction towards King's Norton village, firstly via Moseley and King's Heath and secondly through Selly Park, Ten Acres/Dogpool and Stirchley Street. The former route along the ancient Alcester Road developed more quickly. By the 1880s middle-class housing was developing in Selly Park, which contrasted with the artisan dwellings farther out in the new settlements of Ten Acres and Stirchley Street along Pershore Road. All were separated by open countryside and Cotteridge was still the name of a farm rather than a district.

The first major phase of suburban development in King's Norton came with the building of middle-class villa residences in Middleton Hall Road. The new road was cut in 1868 through the ancient moated site of Cotteridge, making a more direct route between Northfield and King's Norton station.[7] The station opened in 1849 but in 1876 Birmingham West Suburban Railway introduced a greatly improved service to Birmingham.[8] For Birmingham merchants and professional classes in search of fresh air and space, commuting became an attractive option. The first houses were built on the south side of the road, enjoying extensive views south over the Rea valley to the church of St Nicolas, with generous gardens sloping down to the railway

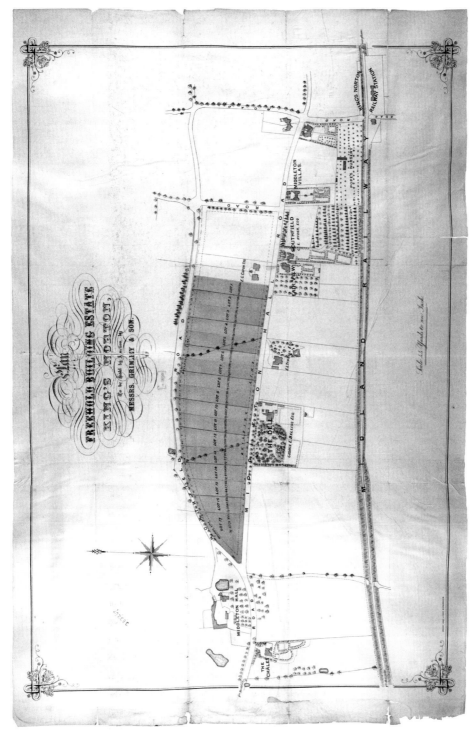

69 *A number of large villa residences and substantial semi-detached houses had already been built along Middleton Hall Road by c.1875 when these 17 building plots on the north side of the road were auctioned.*

cutting. Building development was underway in the 1870s, but it was to be a long and protracted process. Over sixty houses were built in Middleton Hall Road between the 1870s and 1901.[9] The Pope family, who owned and operated Row Heath nursery, saw the opportunities and started to develop some of their land. They engaged local builder, Frederick Clulee, to erect one of the first houses but went on to build a further eight villas in the 1880s, by which time they had engaged the services of a professional architect, W. S. Peckmore of Small Heath.[10] Other developers supported by the Birmingham Freehold Land Society used a wide range of Birmingham architects. The list reads like a roll-call of the profession at the time: Ewen Harper, George Gadd, F. W. Baker, Crouch & Butler, Hipkiss & Stephens, Newton & Cheadle, Wood & Kendrick, Yeoville Thomason and William Hale. Hale's practice is better known today for its work designing central Birmingham pubs, but he designed the new school buildings in the village and oversaw the restoration of the Old Grammar School in the 1890s. He was well placed to get involved since he lived nearby at The Rookery, a house he built for himself in 1875 just west of Cotteridge Farm on the Pershore Road.[11] As the railway later cut across his garden, Hale too moved to Middleton Hall Road.[12]

The pattern had been set for the development of Cotteridge with middle-class housing along Middleton Hall Road to the west and artisan houses along Pershore Road towards Lifford Lane and Breedon Cross to the east. The last decade of the 19th century, and particularly the last five years, witnessed an explosion of growth that brought Birmingham in all but name to the doorstep of the village. Rows of tunnel-back terraces were built on the former Cotteridge Farm and New House (Millwards) (Midland Road, Holly Road, Laurel Road, Cotteridge Road, Frances Road). In 1892 about a hundred people lived in twenty houses in the district, but by 1902 there were 868 houses with a population of 4,300.[13] With the housing came industry and the establishment of the largest factory in King's Norton at the time, the King's Norton Metal Company (c.1890), which took more of the New House estate but was separated from workers' housing in Cotteridge by the railway.[14] The rapid expansion of Cotteridge contributed to the doubling of population over the whole of King's Norton (less Balsall Heath) from 17,750 in 1891 to 35,750 to 1901. As this increase had been mostly accommodated in Moseley, King's Heath and Stirchley Street, over 90 per cent of the study area remained rural and its landscape relatively unchanged. The agricultural appearance of these areas, however, masked a transformation that had taken place in the occupation of many of the rural dwellers.

Agriculture

The principal sources for understanding the agrarian landscape of King's Norton in the early 19th century are the records produced by the Tithe Commissioners, which required the detailed mapping of land and the recording of what tithe payments were due. There are four maps made in 1840 for the whole parish in its four yields, the Tithe Apportionment or Award Book of 1838, and a Tithe File containing reports, correspondence and drafts.[15] Taken together, these provide an overview of King's Norton's farming at one point in time. Two thirds of the parish was either meadow or pasture, supporting 2,000 sheep and 800 cows. The remaining third was arable. Near the village the stiff nature of the soil was particularly well suited to the growing of wheat and beans, and a four-crop rotation of turnips, barley, seeds and wheat was in place, as well as permutations of fallow. The grassland in the neighbourhood of the village was well known as being 'luxuriantly rich and, from its vicinity to Birmingham, lets at a high rent, chiefly for pasturing milch-cows'.[16] The difference in annual rent values between King's Norton's arable at 21s. per acre and its pasture, which commanded 35s. per acre, is striking and helps to explain the emphasis on milk production and the village's special position in relation to the demands of an expanding town on its doorstep.

An insight into the life of one local farmer is provided by the diaries of Richard Pountney (1804–1891).[17] The diaries begin in 1836 when Richard was working for his uncle, William Pountney, who rented Goodrest Farm on Icknield Street from the Lea family. They record the daily tasks undertaken by Richard and the two farm labourers. One extract, for Friday 8 January 1836, will give a flavour of them:

> Winnowed 1 bag of oats and ½ a strike for the pig. We plowing in the Big Piece [one of the fields]. I took the share [part of a plough] to be pointed and 2 traces [part of the harness] to be mended. Flower had the bellyache. I gave her 2 spoonfull of spirit of turpentine. Did her good.

The diaries enable us to piece together the cycle of the farming year, which began with ploughing fallow and muck spreading, followed by harvesting, threshing and winnowing, through to autumn ploughing and sowing. Butter, eggs and cheese supplied the market on a weekly basis. Two local women were paid on a casual basis for gathering stones from any newly ploughed fields, the stones then used to repair potholes in the public highways. Goodrest was a 90-acre mixed farm and, unusually for King's Norton, showed a high concentration of arable production. In 1836 Pountney was growing considerable quantities of wheat, clover, peas and oats, leaving other land fallow. In addition he grew potatoes in a roadside pleck opposite the farm and vegetables in his garden. He sold surplus hay and straw in Birmingham and grain was sent to the Albion Flour Mill there. The government protected the price of corn from cheaper imported grain through the Corn Laws, but by 1840 it was clear the farm was

70 *Goodrest Farm photographed in 1966. By the time that Richard Pountney was farming here in the early 19th century the original timber-framed house had been clad in a brick skin.*

losing money, despite Richard's best efforts to supplement income as a land surveyor, tithe and tax collector. He gave up the farm and became a schoolteacher, helping with the erection of the new school at Wythall where he taught for the rest of his life.

At the time Richard Pountney abandoned farming agriculture was the dominant occupation, and it was still a major 'industry' by the end of the century, with 90 farmers listed in local directories. But farming was by then geared to supplying the city's need for milk, butter, hay and straw. Of the farmland, 86 per cent was pasture or meadow and only 14 per cent arable. The 1901 census records the existence of many small farmers living cheek by jowl with workers employed in industry. It also demonstrates that some of the smaller farms had been taken by horse breakers, hay dealers and market gardeners serving an increasingly urban market.

A graphic picture of late Victorian rural life in King's Norton is provided by the writings of John Bridges. He was a gentleman farmer who lived at Hawkesley Hall (Little Hawkesley) for twenty years from about 1870. He witnessed King's Norton's transformation from a rural to a suburban locality and between 1889 and 1910 wrote three books describing the changes he witnessed which eventually led him to abandon farming.[18]

> I was a good deal younger when I first came here. The village now so populous was then really what it now only apes, a country village, with real country folk for its inhabitants. The change has been so gradual that I have hardly noticed it …

Bridges described the old-fashioned country ways of an older generation, which was being subsumed by the new inhabitants. In the changing landscape men like the farmer 'old Barton' were just managing to make a living from what was clearly prime land for development, where farm buildings were badly maintained and the labour was as old-fashioned as the machinery. Bridges rued the loss of character and compared the old miller to the new one with his smart modern ways and a growing fortune tied to the processing of American grain imported through Liverpool. He gives us snapshots of people like Joey, with his 30 or 40 acre grass farm and an enormous number of hayricks, and of the hay tyers who worked up the ricks for market, selling them on behalf of the farmers. He admits there were advantages to be had from being so close to an urban market – he sold one crop of useless hay as packing to a Birmingham bedstead manufacturer. However, in the summer the proximity to the built-up area brought unwelcome influxes of sparrows, rooks and starlings, all of which damaged the crops. The deciding factor for Bridges came with the new housing development of Cotteridge:

> A few days ago, looking towards the hill, which is almost a mile off, I noticed a new feature in the landscape. Some red brick buildings were creeping over the top of the hill. The day was very clear, and I could see, I thought, that they were one end of a row, or rather a street, of cottages which were being

pushed into the country ... The bright red object was suggestive of an advance guard. A thin red line. The outposts of an enemy before whom I in my capacity of farmer should be unable to stand. I recognised it was time to go ...

The neighbourhood of a large town is all very well, and supplies a ready market; but when it comes to diving about for your hay at the back of villa residences, and mowing round big posts supporting notices whereby passers-by ... are informed that Messrs. So and So are prepared to let the land on building lease, the 'pursuit of agriculture' becomes slightly wearisome. So my friends, who mostly lived in places earlier affected than mine by the advance-guard, found out some time. One genial good fellow went to New-Zealand. I hope he does not regret it, but I have sometimes thought that he may have pushed his protest too far. The others are too far removed to make our old daily intercourse possible. The quaint old houses in which their calm and peaceful lives were passed are stuccoed over and provided with bow windows. The farm-buildings are being allowed gradually to go to ruin. The land has been taken by little jobbing hay-dealing farmers. Where these live it is impossible to say ... One great reason for giving up suburban farming is the dearth of agricultural labourers. The few survivals are on their last legs, and are dropping off one by one. The young men will not take to farming, and small blame to them. They prefer to go to the 'Works', of which there are already three large ones in the parish.[19]

HOUSES AND HOMES

Newcomers arrived in increasing quantities in the parish with money they had made in Birmingham. Initially the wealthiest sought country retreats, but as their numbers expanded smaller villas catered for creeping suburbia.

Rural Housing

At Gay Hill Farm a new frontage was built forward of the late medieval timber-framed house. With its neat symmetrical façade and pedimented doorcase it is Georgian in character, but its window lintels help us place it firmly in the first half of the 19th century. Encasing an old house in Victorian brick took place at Masshouse Farm, where the outward appearance gave no hint to the much earlier house with its panelled room that lay inside. More modest were the changes to the front windows at Kingswood Farm, itself a late 18th-century farmhouse. A terrace of four early 19th-century brick cottages was built on the west side of the *Bell* inn on The Green in 1830 and conformed to the usual pattern: it was two storeys high, each floor containing two rooms, and displayed dentilled brick eaves, segmental headed windows and doorways.[20]

71 *Gay Hill Farm. A new brick frontage in a late Georgian style was added to the medieval farmhouse in the mid-19th century. The gable end of the earlier house is visible at the back.*

72 *Moundsley Hall, c.1895-1900. In the mid-19th century the Lane family rebuilt the hall by encasing the Jacobean house in brick and extending it. (Compare with Fig. 40.)*

116

Squires and Merchants

The Taylor family, who acquired the manor of King's Norton at the beginning of the 19th century, resided for a comparatively short time in Moseley, preferring to live at Strensham Hall in south Worcestershire. The lord of the manor's place in King's Norton was therefore filled by lesser squires, many of whose fortunes were based, like that of the Taylor family in the previous century, on successful Birmingham businesses. Some stayed comparatively short periods of time, seeing the parish as a staging post before going further into the country, while others, like three generations of the Lanes of Moundsley, stayed for nearly a century. James Baldwin was a self-made man who moved his paper manufactory out of Birmingham in the late 1840s and was content to live at Breedon House close to his works, employing a farm bailiff and labourers to run his farm at Broad Meadow. The lodge to Baldwin's small estate survives as no. 1653 Pershore Road South.

The first of the Lane family to settle in King's Norton was Thomas Lane, a Birmingham merchant and bullion dealer who moved from Moseley to King's Norton in the early 1850s. The old timbered house at Moundsley was deemed unsuitable by its new owners but, rather than demolishing it, they had it encased in brick and extended on a grand scale. The family was attended by five resident servants – groom, butler, cook, housemaid and kitchen maid, while in the lodge, which still stands and bears the Lane family crest, lived a farm worker and his wife, who acted as gate keeper. Thomas Lane was succeeded in the late 1870s by his son Charles Pelham Lane (1851-1936) who was known as 'Squire Lane'. He became a pillar of the local community, a county councillor and magistrate. Older residents of King's Norton recalled him driving his high dog cart in the early 20th century, while his wife preferred a one-horse monogrammed brougham, even in the days of the motor car.

Substantial rebuilding took place at Monyhull Hall when it was bought by the successful Birmingham gunmaker Ezra Millward in 1862. Millward raised the height of the building and added extensions, thus transforming the early Georgian house into

73 *The external appearance of Monyhull Hall owes much to Ezra Millward, who soon after 1862 added another storey to the early Georgian house.*

what we see today. The Millwards had been living relatively modestly at Erdington, but Ezra's new position at Monyhull, described in the 1871 census as 'manufacturer and landowner', meant that he now needed six domestic servants as well as a gardener, coachman and lodge keeper on his new estate. No wonder that by 1881 the census enumerator gave his occupation as 'gentleman'.

At Hawkesley Hall (Little Hawkesley) we can trace the transformation of a substantial farmhouse into a gentleman's residence suitable for a Birmingham merchant. The old moated house, with 150 acres of land, had been farmed until the early 1850s by Thomas Vincent with the help of his sons and two cowmen. About 1855 the old house was pulled down, leaving only the stone cellars, and a new brick house with distinctive Dutch gables reminiscent of Aston Hall was erected on the site. The square moat, which lay close to the house, was filled in and a new one created among ornamental ponds and gardens a little further away. The new moat was old enough by the 1880s to confuse the Ordnance Survey, who marked it on the 1st edition 6-inch map in Gothic letters. Hawkesley 'Farm' now became Hawkesley 'Hall', and as such was ready for its new residents Benjamin Goode and his family. Goode was a highly successful Birmingham jeweller who had pioneered the production of gold chain. With the business booming the family moved to Hawkesley from Selly Hill, but by 1871 were to move deeper into the countryside to an even bigger house at Packwood, Warwickshire. In the meantime Hawkesley provided convenient access to Birmingham and a rural lifestyle.

If Hawkesley provides a good example of a modest antiquarian rebuilding, then Lifford Hall shows what could be achieved with determination and architectural knowledge. The house and mill at Lifford had passed in the mid-19th century to Charles

74 *Hawkesley Hall photographed in the 1960s. The farmhouse and its outbuildings were rebuilt in the 1850s by Benjamin Goode, a Birmingham jeweller, as a residence and model farm.*

75 *Octagonal tower and crenellated wall, Lifford Hall. These structures have given rise to stories of monastic origins, but they are merely Victorian follies designed by the owner of Lifford Hall, Charles Wyatt Orford.*

Wyatt Orford, a great grandson of Thomas Dobbs. As a civil engineer and architect practising between the 1840s and 1860s, Orford is the likely designer and instigator of the crenellated wall and octagonal tower that later gave rise to legends of monastic origins.[21] They are in fact Victorian Gothic follies. Half of the long-redundant original mill was gutted and a 'medieval' hall was created, open into a new higher roof and fronted by a tall crenellated bay window. It is not certain when Orford executed this work, as John Nash tenanted the house between 1850 and 1860 before purchasing the *Saracen's Head*. Charles Wyatt Orford reoccupied the house from at least 1863 until his death in 1867, after which his widow continued to live there for a few years.[22]

Suburban Villas

The houses built in Middleton Hall Road between *c.*1870 and 1900 provide a good example of the new villas that marked the start of suburbanisation. They belong to two main groups – impressive detached homes with extensive grounds, and groups of semi-detached villas which became increasingly popular as the century wore on. Their brickwork was relieved by the use of gables, bay windows, porches, decorative chimneys, terracotta and timber-framing, and an occasional corner turret if space allowed. Standing apart from this assembly of architectural elements was Montfield, a stuccoed Italianate villa designed in 1874 in the office of celebrated architect Yeoville Thomason.

All the houses had names. Some of them, like Hill Crest, Fairview, The Hollies and The Firs, were descriptive of their plots and immediate surroundings, while others proclaimed the aspirations of their owners – Claremont, Kingston and Tudor Lodges. Inglenook, The Cottage and The Nest hint at a rural idyll. Some took rural place-

76 *The Dell was one of the first and certainly the largest house in Middleton Road. From the 1870s it was the home of the Belliss family.*

names like Eastnor, Martley and Padstow, and others created their own sylvan arcadia in Fernlea, Oakhurst and Woodleigh. The largest and earliest of them, The Dell, was so called after 'its charming ivy-clad dell'. It was built *c.*1870 close to the Northfield boundary and boasted extensive gardens, greenhouses and 14 acres of land and its own 'farmery'.

The Dell was built for George Belliss, co-partner of the firm Belliss & Morcom, manufacturers of steam engines and boilers. Montfield was the home of John Sherwood, the owner of an electro-plating business in Lichfield Street, Birmingham. Other Birmingham industrialists attracted to Middleton Hall Road were Hyld Elkington and Arthur Spurrier (electro-platers), James Restall (jeweller and silversmith), Albert Hughes (gun maker) and Jenkin Evans (a die-sinker, whose works in the Jewellery Quarter have recently been purchased by English Heritage). The road also housed solicitors, commercial travellers and those living on independent means. It was attractive, too, to a handful of local residents whose fortunes were rising. By 1901 the miller Aaron Jones (d. 1912) had moved his family into Bradwardine, having succeeded in his local business of importing American grain and grinding it at King's Norton Mill.

Almost every household in Middleton Hall Road was supported by two servants, usually a cook and maid, who were accommodated in attic bedrooms. At The Dell the comfortable lifestyle of the Bellisses was serviced by no fewer than 10 resident staff – a cook, lady's maid, parlour maid, two housemaids, a serving maid, kitchen maid, a coachman or groom and two gardeners.

THE VILLAGE

The Buildings

The tithe survey of 1840 provides the first accurate plan of the village. It can be seen to consist of two parts: 1) The Green and 2) the road descending eastwards to the Worcester & Birmingham Canal (later Wharf Road). The Pershore turnpike, constructed in 1827, created a by-pass to the village on the east side and split it in two. The Green was relatively densely built-up on all three sides of the distinctive triangle of open land. At the north end, the view of the church was restricted by a house that stood east of the present lych-gate (The Malthouse). The range of buildings from the *Bull's Head* to the *Saracen's Head* projected well beyond the other houses and shops on the west side. In all there were about seventy houses around The Green and illustrations show these were both timber-framed and brick.

Earlier 19th-century maps show that the road from Cotteridge and Birmingham originally ascended the steep hill from the river Rea directly to the church, turned sharp east past the Old Grammar School and entered The Green via the modern Back Lane. The route was abandoned with the construction of the Pershore Turnpike and Birmingham traffic henceforth mainly entered and left The Green from the east.

77   *The west side of The Green from the old* Bull's Head *to the* Saracen's Head *in 1900. The roof line of the* Saracen's Head *extends as far as the* Bull's Head *where it steps, indicating a join in this great range of late medieval building. A year later the* Bull's Head *was rebuilt in brick and terracotta.*

The village was less densely built-up along Wharf Road, giving the impression this is a later development, influenced by the arrival of the Worcester & Birmingham Canal. In fact this part of the village already existed in the early 16th century, lined with houses at a density similar to that of the 19th century. By 1838 a short terrace of houses had been built from the corner with Wharf Road along Masshouse Lane towards the farm of the same name. According to the Tithe Survey there were about 33 houses in this part of the village, making a total for the whole settlement of just over a hundred houses and a population of about five hundred.

The physical layout of the village appears not to have changed significantly between 1838 and the first edition of the Ordnance Survey 1:2500 map published in 1884. The line of the lost 'Schoters' Lane survived as a field footpath running from the *Navigation* inn northwards and parallel to the Pershore turnpike. In 1878 a Board School had been constructed between the footpath and the turnpike and new detached and semi-detached houses lined the turnpike road as it left the village in a south-westerly direction (now Redditch Road). These houses were of suburban 'villa' character and very different to the vernacular dwellings around The Green. Suburbia had visited the village for the first time, although it was a gentle embrace at this stage.

The Saracen's Head

The Tithe Survey confirms that the *Saracen's Head* was owned by the Lea family. Richard Lea II had died in 1840 leaving the property to his daughter Mary Frances Lea. She occupied the east range,

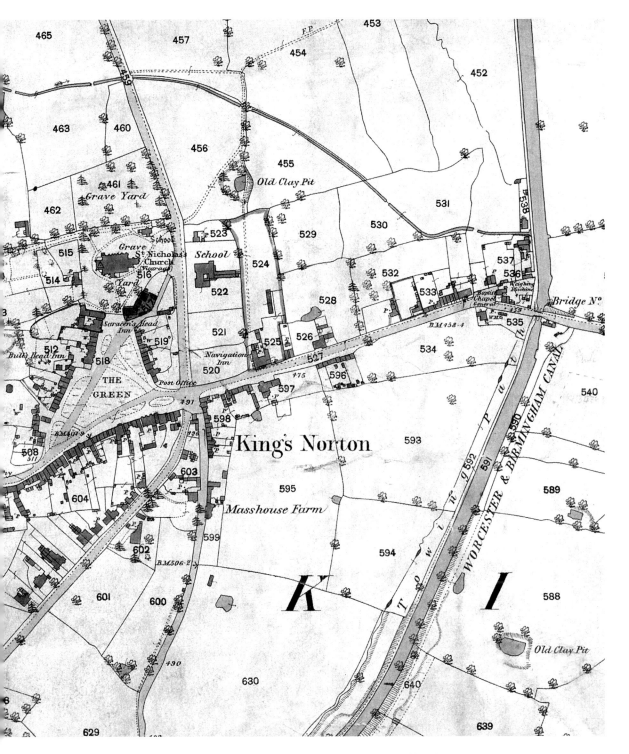

78   *1st edition OS 1:2500 map, surveyed 1882, published 1884.*

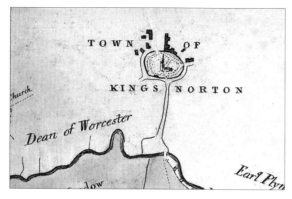

79 *Extract from a plan of High House, 1817, showing how the road from Birmingham ran up the hill directly towards the church before it was diverted by turnpiking in the mid-1830s.*

the only part at the time functioning as an inn, while Richard Brittle Lea, her nephew, lived in the north range. In 1860 Mary Frances Lea sold the whole complex to John Nash, who had previously been a tenant of Lifford Hall. He may have been responsible for constructing the brick gable that covered the former carriage entrance. In 1866 Thomas Rudge became the new owner, running the public house in the east range while letting out the north range. The main parlour of the north wing was converted into a shop between 1874 and 1888. William Rudge, son of Thomas, sold all the buildings to William Osborn Atkinson in 1887, and in 1888 building plans were approved to construct a new south range with mock framing. In 1890 the brothers William and Frederick Atkinson conveyed the buildings

80 *The* Saracen's Head *inn when Benjamin Mutlow was the licensee between 1896 and 1900. At this date the false 'framing' was painted on the brickwork.*

124

to Atkinson's Ltd, who installed William Harris as the licensee while allowing other tenants to run a grocery business in the north range. In 1901 Richard Beach was 'hotel keeper' with Eliza Bluck in the grocer's shop next door. This division of function and occupancy continued into the next century.[23]

The Bull's Head

The Kendrick family, publicans since at least 1782, continued to run the *Bull's Head* until well into the 19th century. Humphrey Lyttleton, the owner, died about 1801 and the inn may have passed to Richard Frances, perhaps a relative by marriage. He was owner at the time of the Tithe Survey and his tenant was George Kendrick. In about 1872 the Rev. Richard Sandys Lyttleton Francis, the owner, died and the *Bull's Head* was auctioned. The tenant at the time was Edwin Tongue, also a blacksmith, who had run the pub since at least 1851.[24] By 1881 Thomas Chaplin, a Leicestershire man, had taken over. John Bridges described how he frequented this unpretentious pub in the 1880s, praising the quality of the landlord's home-brewed

81 *The south side of the* Bull's Head *inn photographed between 1860-79 when Edward Tongue was the landlord. Next door was the wheelwright's shop operated by the Shephard family before their move to the Alpha Farm in Wharf Road.*

ale but bemoaning the fact that it was then the last of the houses in the village still brewing its own. The large breweries had taken over all the other pubs and were supplying them with beer that tasted uniformly poor![25]

Other Public Houses in the Village

The *Bell* had been one of King's Norton's principal inns in the 18th century, but lost its prominence in the 19th century. It was run for much of the latter part of the century by the Foster family, described variously as beer retailers and cordwainers. The *Plumbers' Arms* was built in the middle of the south side of The Green in the early 19th century. It was run successively by the Hobbis and Kimberley families until 1930 when it was de-licensed. The name of the *Navigation* near the top of Wharf Road eloquently reveals its origins in the era of canal building, although it was rebuilt in its present form in 1906. The *Boat* (now 1-3 Canalside) was a hostelry much frequented by those who worked the canals.

82 *The old* Navigation *inn in Wharf Road in the 1870s when it was run by Mary Rogers and her son Henry, who brewed the beer.*

The Workhouse

A workhouse was built on the western edge of the south side of The Green between 1801-03.[26] It was substantially rebuilt and extended between 1837-9 to designs by Birmingham architect John Fallows.[27] In 1841 it housed 102 men and women paupers under the control of the governor William Phillips and his wife Louisa, the matron. Twenty years later, when Robert and Mary Ann Layton were master and matron, there were 114 inmates, only identified in the census by their initials, their age and their former occupations. In 1872, when a new workhouse was completed at Selly Oak, the 150 inmates were transferred from King's Norton and the old workhouse on The Green was used temporarily between 1876-8 as the Village Board School and thereafter for housing, under the new name of West End Buildings.[28]

The Mop Fair

The Mop Fair continued to be held on The Green through the 19th century, although arguments over its future in the 1890s opened social and cultural divisions, which reflected the changes taking place in the village. By the late 1860s the Mop had largely lost its role as a statute or hiring fair where rural workers had stood for employment carrying traditional emblems of their trades. In 1867 the lines of wagoners, shepherds, cowherds and domestic servants which had once lined both sides of The Green had dwindled to 'a ragged few' who stood by the entrance to the churchyard.[29] The Mop was becoming a pleasure fair with an ox roast, rides and sideshows, whose wagons and vans occupied most of The Green. As such it attracted large numbers of visitors from Birmingham, who year by year extended their merrymaking at King's Norton over several days.

When the writer George Augustus Sala visited the Mop in October 1872 he was disappointed to find it had lost its distinctiveness and was a pale imitation of the Birmingham Onion Fair. A decade later the Mop had deteriorated further:

The King's Norton saturnalia is growing worse. Hardly a man or woman with any pretensions to self-respect could be seen at the 'Mop' last Monday, and the thousands there were composed of shouting hobbledehoys, screaming girls, drunken men, and shouting women. They swarmed from the station in hundreds during the day, and as night drew on the crushing, the shouting, the swearing created an indescribable confusion. A great mass of people stood round the roasting ox, which had been frizzling all night before a huge fire, and was then cut up for the delectation of the crowd. A basket of slices of bread stood near, and two or three hot, red-faced men with carving knives sliced away at the haunches, the ribs, and the

83   *Union Buildings in 1935. The core of this complex on the south-western edge of The Green comprised the four-storey workhouse opened in 1803 (middle distance) and extended towards the camera in 1837-9.*

84 *In this view of the Mop Fair in the 1890s the showmen's vans, tents, sideshows and swings have taken over the whole of The Green.*

shoulders, putting a slice of meat between two slices of bread, and selling the tasty morsels at fourpence a piece. Dozens of hands were held out at a time during the busy part of the day, and two carcasses could have been sold had they been cooked. The public houses were packed, and customers had to fight their way in and out, treading on floors wet with slopped beer. Some disgraceful scenes took place in one part or another of the vicinity during the day and night. The general proceedings offered a spectacle of debauchery, drunkenness, noise and blasphemy, in strong contrast to the ordinary quiet life of King's Norton.[30]

By the 1890s the autumn influx of what were called 'Birmingham roughs', together with fears of 'grievous immorality' during the Mop, were uppermost in the minds of the Parish Council and the increasing number of middle-class residents. The Mop was seen as 'a terrible nuisance to quiet residence and an insuperable obstacle to the wishes of the Parish Council to improve and ornament the Village Green'.[31]

In the spring of 1895 the opponents of the Mop engaged the support of the King's Norton Rural District Council, who in turn sought police help and the involvement of the Home Secretary. An attempt was made by the Rural District Council to abolish the fair, which caused a storm of protest from local people who lived on The

Green. They were incensed that a keenly awaited and popular event should be swept aside. The two sides submitted petitions to the Home Secretary. Only two of the 60 signatories opposing the Mop lived on The Green itself and a high proportion lived some distance away in the recently built houses in Middleton Hall Road. The counter-petition of 74 names was made up predominantly of labourers, builders, papermakers and metal rollers who lived on The Green or in the immediate vicinity.

The Home Secretary was faced with a difficult decision. The civil servants' briefing notes reveal an unexpected compassion:[32]

> The Petition against Abolition is in. The persons signing it are not beer retailers or tradesmen for the most part, they are workmen & labourers; it is true most of them live on the Green; but persons living on the Green are those most likely to be annoyed and best able to judge of the character of the Fair. On the other hand the Rural District Council is the principal Local Authority and they act on the request of the Parish Council of King's Norton in their unanimous wish that the Fair should be abolished. The question is a difficult one to decide, Secretary of State must either deprive the lower classes of the village of a recreation which they value, or he must override the strongly expressed desire of the constituted authorities.
>
> The matter is one in which Secretary of State should have regard to the rights of minorities. If the villagers wish to retain the fair I do not think it should be abolished because the presence of couples from Birmingham causes some annoyance to residents who can afford a different class of amusements. That would be a reason for abolishing most race meetings and all bank holidays.
>
> These village pleasure fairs are in many cases all that remains of the engagements which used to distinguish village life. They are no doubt enjoyments not cared for by 'villa' residents but they are appreciated by the humbler classers, especially by children & young people who look forward throughout the year to the advent of the 'Fair'.

The Home Secretary took the advice and refused the request to abolish the Mop in 1896.

CHURCH AND RELIGION

The church of St Nicolas, which had been a chapelry of Bromsgrove, achieved ecclesiastical parish status in 1846. But nonconformity was spreading fast throughout the parish, and by the middle of the century the Church of England no longer held dominance over the religious life of the parish.

A snapshot of the spiritual life of the parish is provided by the Census of Religious Worship taken on Sunday 30 March 1851.[33] It shows a high level of nonconformity, which had grown considerably since the turn of the century, and a low attendance at the parish church. Across the whole parish there were now 13 churches and chapels, three of them Church of England (St Nicolas; St Mary, Moseley; St Mary, Wythall), while the other 10 were made up of Dissenters. The 13 places of worship drew 1,975 attendances, or 25 per cent of the population. This is a surprisingly low figure but equates with the lower attendance noted in the north-eastern corner of Worcestershire when compared with the rest of the county. In 1851 there was no Roman Catholic church in the parish so any worshippers had to travel to either Birmingham or Bromsgrove.

The episcopal hierarchy of the Established Church was opposed to the compilation of the census, perhaps realising that it was fast losing pre-eminence. The census provided the statistical evidence to confirm this and local Anglican clergy, keen to explain the situation, blamed poor attendance on the fact that the day the census was taken was Mothering Sunday. Nationally 49 per cent of attendances were in Anglican churches and 51 per cent in other denominations. Across Worcestershire as a whole nearly 57 per cent of worshippers were Church of England, making it 'a good deal more inclined to Anglicanism than the nation'.[34] However, on the borders of Birmingham the census revealed a very different situation and the data from King's Norton, where only 46 per cent of worshippers were Anglican and 54 per cent belonged to other denominations, is typical.

These other denominations were represented by the Baptist Chapel in Wharf Road, established in 1815, the Providence Primitive Methodist Chapel on the corner of Masshouse Lane and Redditch Road, built in 1838, and, a little further away, the Unitarian Meeting House at Kingswood.[35]

The parish church had seats for 800 people, but filled only 32 per cent of them in 1851. It is not surprising that the large gallery inserted into the western end of the nave in the 18th century was no longer needed and was removed in the major restoration of 1870.

Higher attendances were recorded in the non-Anglican chapels and meetings. The diminutive Providence Chapel of the Primitive Methodists measured internally just 19ft long by 13ft 7in wide and had sittings for 20 people. In 1851 it must have been bursting at the seams with double its capacity attending.

As suburbs spread across the northern part of the parish many new churches were established, but it was to be the last decade of the 19th century before any real impact was made on the study area. In 1903 a writer described the growth of Cotteridge and the need for more churches, comforting himself in the belief that:

> It is indeed a wonderful change of scene that has brought about this need at King's Norton. The purely agricultural aspect which was the main feature of the locality a decade ago has quite disappeared. Corn has been swept away by manufactories, and acres of pasture land have been blotted out by the builder. In 1892 the population was 4,084, and three clergy with one

85 *The junction of five roads where Wharf Road joins the Redditch Road became known as Five Ways. On the narrow plot between Masshouse Lane and Redditch Road the Primitive Methodists erected the minuscule Providence Chapel in 1838.*

church, and a mission room, were adequate for the spiritual requirements of the residents. Now the population has trebled, while, in the meantime, the church facilities have been only doubled, and that solely through the great energy of the Rev. C.W. Barnard and his coadjutors.[36]

Church Restoration

By the middle of the 19th century St Nicolas church had fallen into a serious state of disrepair. Photographs taken in the 1860s show the extent of the deterioration, with ivy spreading over walls and roofs, decaying stonework and a heavily buttressed north aisle which was also supported internally by a flying buttress to prevent the collapse of the nave roof. Some repair work had been done earlier in the century and the spire had been repaired in 1840, but in the late 1850s the architect Dudley Male was brought in to advise on a substantial programme of 'improvements', including the design of a new pulpit and railings.[37] It was with the arrival of the energetic vicar, the Rev. John Meredith Lawrence Aston, in 1859 that a new era began in the life of the parish. Major changes took place not only in educational provision, but also to the fabric of the parish church and the accommodation of the clergy. Between 1860 and 1872 the church underwent a series of major restorations, while a new vicarage, replacing one at Hill Top on Parson's Hill, was built close to the church in 1861.

Within a very short space of time of his arrival in King's Norton the Rev. Aston had thrown himself into a fundraising campaign. One of the most successful events was his lecture given in 1866 on 'The Antiquities of King's Norton', which was later published as a booklet to raise more money.[38] With these new funds the first phase of church restoration began in the 1860s under Ewan Christian (1814-95), architect to the Ecclesiastical Commissioners and responsible for hundreds of church restorations. Christian concentrated his efforts on the chancel, where he renewed the roof. No sooner had this been achieved than the Diocesan architect, William Jeffrey Hopkins of Worcester (1821-1901), was engaged to work on an even larger restoration scheme undertaken between 1870 and 1872. This resulted in the creation of the interior we see today. The works included the removal of the medieval roof over the nave and its replacement by a new one of hammer-beam form, rebuilding and re-roofing the north aisle and the removal of its 17th-century stone gables. New tiled floors were laid, plaster was stripped from the internal walls, church monuments were shuffled, and a new organ, pulpit and reredos built. Stained glass windows were installed as well as life-sized figures of the Saviour, the Virgin Mary and St John in the niches of the tower. The work cost over £3,000 and was funded by subscription.

86 *Demolition of the 17th-century gables on the north aisle of St Nicolas church was about to begin in 1870 when the Birmingham Archaeological Society recorded the scene.*

87 *Interior of St Nicolas church. The roof and the corbels supporting it are part of the 1870s restoration, when the walls were stripped of plaster. Many of the pews are 18th-century or earlier and were cut down and re-arranged in the 19th century.*

However impressive the efforts of the vicar and parish were in raising funds to undertake the work, the restoration was not without criticism. A small but influential group of concerned architects and historians monitored the work and deplored the loss of the church's original fabric in the name of restoration. Their philosophy was one of repair rather than replacement and restoration, a principle that was soon to be embodied in the Society for the Protection of Ancient Buildings founded by William Morris in 1877. The exchanges between the restorers, led by the vicar, and the repairers, represented by J.R. Holliday and A.E. Everitt of the Birmingham Archaeological Society, were particularly heated.[39] The philosophy of the 'scrapers' and restorers resulted in the removal of most of the historic plaster from inside the church, including the Doom painting over the chancel arch, and the rebuilding of the north aisle to an assumed medieval form by the removal of the 17th-century gables. The same arguments, based on differing philosophies of restoration and conservation, would be repeated again over the fate of the Old Grammar School in the 1890s.

One of the late 19th-century churchwardens, John Bridges of Hawkesley Hall, has left us a description of the challenge faced by King's Norton's Victorian clergy as the social structure of the parish changed. He described the situation:

> The old rector had been there forty years, and when he was young his was a purely agricultural parish. Things gradually altered as the manufacturing town spread, and he had to change with the times. When villas sprang up and farmhouses were changed into 'mansions', he had the good sense to restore the church. When fine ladies rustled up the nave, and swept into seats from which shabby old farmers had been swept out one by one, the rector ceased to preach in his black gown, and put a stone cross and pair of brass candlesticks on what he had up to this time called the table.[40]

The new residents were clearly worth cultivating and, as the lists of donors and sponsors testify, their financial support for the various restoration schemes and the subsequent acquisition of fittings, from stained glass to an organ case, were essential. The incumbent needed to court the new inhabitants without offending his older congregation, who were not necessarily as enthusiastic about change as either he or his architect.

EDUCATION

In 1806 John Taylor, as the new lord of the manor, appointed James Cox as master of the Grammar School, informing the bishop that this was his prerogative as the manor had traditionally paid the annual salary. Cox was neither a graduate nor ordained. It appears that from this time new masters were sought from within the pupils of the school. By 1833 the upper room, which still housed Thomas Hall's library, was being used as a girls' Sunday School, while the boys were taught in the room below. Access to the upper floor was via a winder stair in the porch. According to the Charity Commissioners' Report of 1833, instruction was given to 'about 15 or 16 boys, children of such persons in the parish as are unable to pay for their schooling', who were taught 'reading, writing and accounts without any charge. They provide their own books and stationery. A few children of the neighbouring farmers, who pay for their instruction, are also received at the school.'[41]

Shortly afterwards Thomas Simpson was appointed master, combining this post with that of sub-postmaster, while for a time Mrs Simpson taught girls in the upper room. Under their instruction there were 'about 50 boys and 50 girls in the parochial schools, and 40 boys and 60 girls in the Sunday school'.[42] On the arrival of the Rev. Aston in 1859 matters came to a head with the Simpsons, whose teaching skills were considered deficient. The vicar wanted to establish a National School for girls in the upper room, but this clashed with the Simpsons' determination to increase the number of fee-paying boys. The situation was resolved surprisingly quickly for within a year the vicar was able to get his own way and Thomas Simpson resigned. Teaching from now on was to be in the hands of the curate. The separation between boys and girls was achieved when an external staircase was built in 1861 on the west gable and the original porch entrance was re-opened.

88   *The atmosphere of the upper school of the Grammar School, with its iron-framed desks and benches, is captured in this watercolour of c.1870 by the artist A.E. Everitt (1824-82).*

An inspection in 1867 revealed:

> History, geography, and English grammar are taught, as well as the elementary subjects. One boy learns Latin, and it is hoped that mathematics and French will in time follow. The classes meet in the lower room of the old grammar school building, in size about 31 feet by 15 feet 9½, not well ventilated or furnished, but much improved, as I was assured, within the last year or two. In the room above, approached by an external stair, the National school for girls and infants has been accommodated since 1861 … The building stands on the edge of the churchyard, nor is there any other playground.[43]

Clearly conditions were still unsatisfactory, and with increasing educational standards nationally, the school was gradually falling behind. For those able to afford it, alternatives to the village school were available: 'The sons of the richer people in the neighbourhood, if they do not go to boarding schools go daily to Birmingham grammar school by railway, so that the need for a classical school is but slight.'

In the late 1870s teaching came to an end at the Old Grammar School. The new School Board established schools on a different site for boys and girls. The boys were moved in 1876 first to the old workhouse while the girls remained temporarily in the rest of the Old Grammar School. Two years later purpose-built schools for both sexes were completed on a new site on the east side of the main road, together with a master's house (288 Pershore Road South). These were all designed by architect William Hale.

After closure the Old Grammar School continued to be used for multiple purposes. Upstairs was Thomas Hall's library and it was here that Mothers' Meetings and other parish groups met. It was a valued space and large enough to accommodate the Vestry meeting, but the building was clearly deteriorating. There was a long argument over who was responsible for the structure, but by the middle of the 1880s the Charity Commissioners agreed the parish could use the building for its own purposes and apply some of the endowed funds for repairs. By then the building was so unsafe that meetings could no longer be held in it and the cost had spiralled. In 1891 William Hale was appointed architect and an appeal was launched for £250. This figure was raised from local landowners and residents in a remarkably short space of time and work was soon ready to be put in hand. But the debate between restoration and conservation, which had proved so heated at St Nicolas church twenty years before, re-ignited. Jethro Cossins and Oliver Baker, representing the Birmingham Archaeological Society, championed the cause of repair and minimum interference with the original structure, while the vicar and his architect, through their successful fundraising campaign, had raised considerably more than was required. They now had reserves they felt should be spent. Fortunately Cossins managed to persuade the vicar that nothing could be done without the consent of the Society for the Protection of Ancient Buildings and he offered help in preparing an outline specification for the architect who was more used to designing modern buildings. His help, on this occasion, was accepted and by 1892, when work was completed, it was generally agreed the restoration had not been excessive. Twenty years later the process would begin again when far more of the historic structure would be removed.

Thomas Hall's library was still in place although regarded as an irrelevance. In the 1860s the Rev. Aston had wanted to sell it and use the funds partly to repair the building but also to start a parish library of modern books that would be 'instructive to the working classes'. Attempts to sell the library faltered though its historical value to the nation was demonstrated when William Salt Brassington of Moseley drew attention to it in lectures to the Library Association and elsewhere.[44] It was finally rescued in 1892 and transferred to Birmingham Reference Library, where it remains.

TRADE AND INDUSTRY

Industry, which had been confined to water-powered sites, domestic production and the processing of agricultural products, was now inexorably transformed with the arrival of recognisable factories or manufactories. Although King's Norton's hand-made nail trade persisted well into the second half of the century, it could not compete with factories producing machine-made nails. The Lifford area developed quickly with its advantages of canal and railway communications and Wychall Mill was converted to metal rolling. The ancient manorial corn mill was not immune to new industrial processes. Early guides and directories extolled the new industries and the advantages they gave King's Norton's expanding population. The higher wages offered by the new manufactories encouraged immigration, but they also caused labour shortages in local agriculture, to such an extent that farmers were sometimes forced to pay their labourers more than the going rate simply to retain them. Factories closer to Birmingham, such as Cadbury's, exerted their influence and made commuters of King's Nortonians. They also stimulated the growth of Stirchley and Cotteridge for workers' housing. By 1871 King's Norton as a whole employed 11,000 workers, but this total would have included Balsall Heath, which was by then in effect a dormitory for those working in Birmingham.[45]

Nailmaking

In the early 19th century King's Norton was well known for its nailmaking. The parish formed the north-eastern edge of an area based on Bromsgrove, which was the centre of the trade in Worcestershire. In 1831 there were 97 nailers in King's Norton while Northfield, a much smaller parish, had slightly more (122) and Bromsgrove a massive 1,169. In King's Norton the main centre of production was Rednal village, in effect an outlier of the Bromsgrove trade, but there were also significant concentrations at West Heath and Red Hill, and scatters at the Maypole, Wythall and in King's Norton village. The trade was organised by nail masters who supplied rod iron and coals to the nailers, as well as overseeing collection.

Nailmaking was an arduous and hugely repetitive process, but it required relatively little equipment and was well suited to a domestic industry in which husbands, wives and older children played their part. As well as a hearth, the nailer needed a bellows, a small anvil, hammer and block and a few cutting and sharpening tools. Rod iron was heated in the hearth and fashioned into a great variety of sizes and shapes of nail with the aid of an oliver. The latter had been introduced into the region in the early 19th century and consisted of a treadle-operated hammer used in conjunction with dies set into a block or base.

All the equipment could be housed in a small forge near the operator's own home. Sometimes it was a brick addition to the back or side of the nailer's cottage; alternatively it was built a few feet away either as a detached building or in a terrace or block of forges shared by neighbours. All three types of nailshop were in use in King's Norton parish during the early 19th century. However, two drawings of a nailer's workshop on Millpool Hill by the artist Henry Martin Pope (1843-1908) show a rather different type of structure, a timber building of post-hole construction built on a roughly square plan with a thatched roof and a chimney set at the back. It is a striking reminder of what was probably the norm, rather than the brick nailshops which were robust enough to survive into the 20th century.[46]

The highwater mark of the nail trade in King's Norton was the middle of the 19th century. In 1851 the number of nailers in the parish was 178 but by 1881 this had dropped dramatically to just thirty-two. By then machine nails were gaining ground, and although the hand-made trade carried on well into the early 20th century

89 *Late 19th-century etching by Henry Pope (1843-1908) of a timber nailshop on Millpool Hill. This type of workshop leaves little archaeological evidence apart from four postholes at the corners and the base of the hearth.*

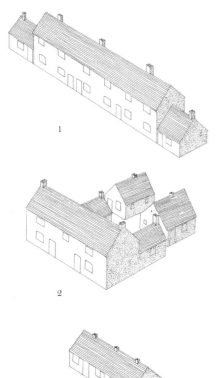

in Bromsgrove, it had virtually disappeared in King's Norton. In 1901 a sole worker, 64-year-old Thomas Melley, was recorded as a nailer in the parish, living in West Heath Road. The forges in the old centres of nailing at Rednal, Red Hill and the Maypole were all now silent.

Lifford Mills and Chemical Works
In 1807 Thomas Dobbs purchased Lifford Mill from the five grandchildren of the 1st Lord Lifford.[47] About the same time he became involved in protracted negotiations with Worcester & Birmingham Canal Company for the land that would be required for the reservoir immediately below the mill.[48] This was one of three that had been agreed under the Canal Act to

90 *Three types of brick nailers' workshop found in King's Norton: (1) terrace with nailshops at the ends (2) detached nailshops behind the cottages (3) multiple nailshops in separate blocks.*

compensate mill owners for loss of water caused by the construction of the canal. The other two were at Wychall Mill in King's Norton and Harborne Mill on the Bourne Brook. Dobbs asked a high price for the land required for the reservoir and the matter was not resolved until 1810 after adjudication. The reservoir took nine acres of land and was a major civil engineering undertaking, diverting both the river Rea and the tail race from Dobb's Mill.[49] It was constructed between 1812-13 and, owing to soft ground, the tail race had to be culverted between the river and the reservoir. Thomas Dobbs planned to move his rolling mill from beside his house but this expensive project was not carried out until about 1820. A plan shows the mill in its new position, below the larger part of the mill pool and nearer the reservoir (Fig. 92).[50] Dobbs died in 1827 and the mill and estate passed to his two sons and two daughters.[51] They attempted to sell the mill, but were still owners at the time of the Tithe Survey, although soon after they managed to lease the mill to Samuel Davis.[52]

The re-sited mill only operated as a rolling mill for a few decades into the 1850s and was converted in about 1862 to making vulcanised rubber. A series of firms occupied the buildings, including the British Ebontine Co., George Wilson and Co., the Imperial Rubber Company and Edward Capon. Edward himself married Lilly Mary Orford, a daughter of Charles Wyatt Orford, and by 1883 he had entered into partnership with Harry Heaton.[53] Capon-Heaton and Co. manufactured india-rubber at Lifford until the mid-1890s when the firm moved to Hazelwell, the next mill downstream. The mill at Lifford appears then to have been left vacant for many years.

91 *Lifford reservoir was constructed by the Worcester & Birmingham Canal Company in about 1810 to compensate Thomas Dobbs, the owner of Lifford Mill, for the loss of water; its use is now entirely recreational.*

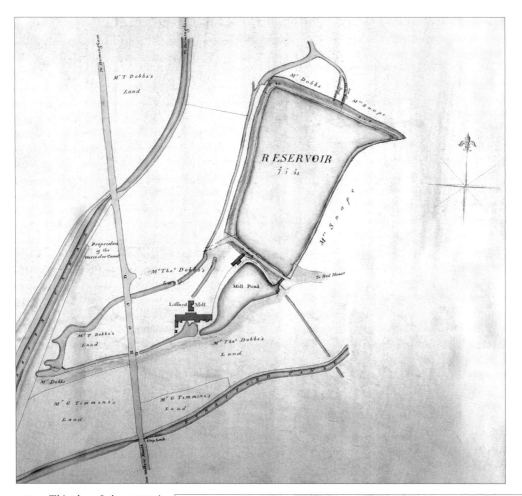

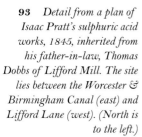

92 *This plan of about 1820 is the only one that shows both the old Lifford Mill (attached to the house) and new mill (untitled) between the mill pond and the reservoir.*

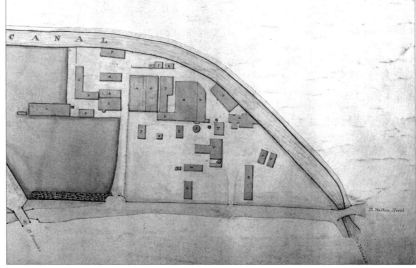

93 *Detail from a plan of Isaac Pratt's sulphuric acid works, 1845, inherited from his father-in-law, Thomas Dobbs of Lifford Mill. The site lies between the Worcester & Birmingham Canal (east) and Lifford Lane (west). (North is to the left.)*

By 1799 Thomas Dobbs had acquired some land on the east side of Lifford Lane beside the Worcester & Birmingham Canal and established his Aqua Fortis Works (nitric acid). He was also manufacturing sulphuric acid on the site and in his will of 1827 described himself as an oil of vitriol maker.[54] The alkali works passed to his son-in-law, Isaac Pratt, and became known as Pratt's Works. The pollution 'must have been offensive in some ways to the feelings of mankind if not the vegetation' and it appears the works were eventually abandoned as a result of litigation with farmers in the neighbourhood, who obtained heavy compensation for damage done to their crops.[55] A rare detailed plan of 1845 has survived (Fig. 93) and also a view; the tall chimney, erected in 1836, was visible for miles.[56] It is not known when the works were eventually demolished, but the Birmingham West Suburban Branch Railway was constructed across the site in 1876.

Baldwin's Paper Mill, Lifford Lane

The pool on the west side of Lifford Lane is sometimes regarded as a water mill site. It is in fact a reservoir to supply water for paper making and was constructed in the 1850s by James Baldwin as part of a steam-driven paper making works.[57] The field in which it was built had formed part of the ancient Broad Meadow estate, which Baldwin had acquired. In 1851 he lived in the farmhouse itself, and may have purchased the estate with the intention of constructing the new works, which he called Sherborne Mill (after the original Sherborne Street works in Birmingham) but which became known as Baldwin's Mill.[58] His paper making business had outgrown the Sherborne Street site just off Broad Street. Broad Meadow Farm provided an ideal location at the junction of the Stratford and Worcester canals, which offered an easy supply of coal and raw materials, as

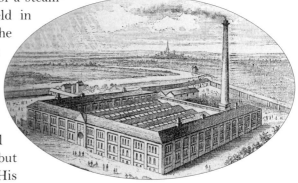

94 *Perspective view of Baldwin's paper mill and steam engine chimney, 1881, with the junction of the Stratford-upon-Avon Canal and the Worcester & Birmingham Canal at the rear and King's Norton church on the horizon.*

well as easy distribution of the finished paper.[59] In addition to the normal rags, the mill also used waste paper, an early example of recycling. About 400 tons of waste paper a year were sorted by hand and the end product, for which the mill was best known, was brown paper for wrapping and blue paper for bags. It also made gun wadding. By the 1880s James Baldwin and Sons was heavily mechanised, using 20 steam engines. Some 30,000 gallons of water were needed per hour, which passed through settling tanks and filters after use to be discharged into the river Rea. This water was nearly as clean as that received, pumped mainly from below ground. Pollution did not cause the closure of the paper making works, the fate of the alkali works across the road, and it continued to operate well into the 20th century.

James Baldwin was an active campaigner for the abolition of the heavy excise duty of £15 a ton on paper. Tradition has it that two excise tax collectors, one for the night and the other for the day shift, lived in cottages close by the mill. Baldwin was Mayor of Birmingham in 1853 and was able to persuade William Gladstone, then Chancellor, to visit him at Broad Meadow and hear the case against the crippling tax. Gladstone eventually repealed the excise duty in 1862, helping to convert paper from a luxury item to a more day-to-day commodity.

Wychall Mill

Wychall mill had been grinding corn for well over a century and a half when it was converted to wire drawing a short time before 1808.[60] By this time it appears that the compensation reservoir at Wychall had been constructed by the Worcester & Birmingham Canal Company, its 17 acres being the largest body of water in King's Norton parish.[61] Plans made in 1804, which are the earliest to show the mill, indicate it was at this time a modest sized building. The existing head race running to a small pool determined the shape of reservoir, as its north bank was constructed following the contour of this older channel. In 1814 Wychall Farm and mill were sold to William Shorthouse and he became involved in negotiations with the canal company, which

95 *Burman and Son's Wychall Mill in the late 1940s showing the steam engine (middle distance, to the left of the dividing wall) and the water wheel on the extreme right.*

wished to extend the reservoir to well over 100 acres, creating a vast lake that would have stretched upstream almost as far as Northfield Mill.[62] This extraordinary scheme was abandoned, presumably due to cost and practicalities, and about 1821 a canal feeder from Wychall reservoir was constructed to the canal near Wharf Lane.[63] It can be seen today crossing King's Norton Park and Playing Fields.

In 1822 Wychall was described as a rolling mill and it is possible it had been converted after 1814 by William Shorthouse's tenant, Joseph Merry.[64] By 1838 the mill was in the tenure of Charles Emery and the Tithe Map shows the buildings had grown considerably since 1804. Between 1820 and 1840 a beam engine was connected to the water wheel to provide extra power and this engine, unlike the Boulton & Watt engine at Lifford Mill II, remained in the building until after the Second World War. It is now preserved in Millennium Point after many years on display in the old Science Museum in Newhall Street. The engine was later coupled with another smaller beam engine.[65] By 1855 Charles Ellis and Sons were in occupation, continuing in the metal rolling trade. During the Franco-Prussian war of 1870-1 the firm supplied metal cartridges for rifles; they also made buttons and badges.[66] Charles Ellis and Son expanded the premises during the late 19th century to the size of a small factory, but the site remained isolated from other industry until the 20th century.

King's Norton Corn Mill

King's Norton mill continued to grind corn, as it had for many centuries. In the early 1800s it was acquired from Thomas Hooper by the Worcester & Birmingham Canal Company. By 1812 the building and associated structures were in poor condition and the company agreed to spend £250 on repairs.[67] Although 'in part newly erected' in 1817, the mill, containing two pairs of stones, was sold by the canal company to Matthias Attwood. We cannot be sure of the appearance of the mill at this time, as there are no contemporary views. According to the Tithe Apportionment (1838) it was still in the ownership of the Attwood family with a tenant, Thomas Oliver. More investment had been necessary and in 1852 the water wheel and machinery were described as new and capable of running three pairs of stones.[68]

The Jones family appear as tenants for the first time in 1857 and were to be associated with the mill until well into the 20th century. William Jones had arrived from Tanworth, where he had run the flour mill, and by 1864 his son Aaron had taken over the business.[69] In the following year the mill was put up for sale after the failure of Attwood's Bank, and it was purchased in 1866 at a good price by Aaron, who also paid for the enfranchisement, extinguishing the ancient copyhold tenure and converting it to freehold.[70] Aaron, a young man in his late twenties, represented a new breed of miller: he pulled down the old mill in 1868, installed five pairs of stones, and only four years later, in 1872, doubled its size and put in three more pairs of stones.[71] His nephew, Robert Summers from Tanworth, supplied the machinery.[72] Restless in the pursuit of improvements to his production of flour, Aaron removed the water wheel around 1879 and replaced it with a turbine, which did not perform satisfactorily. He reintroduced a

96 *King's Norton mill from the west c.1940, looking towards Aaron Jones's large mill building constructed in the latter half of the 19th century. The mill pool and Camp Lane are hidden by the buildings on the left-hand side which are built against the dam. Only the part visible through the shed on the right still stands. This is probably the oldest mill site in King's Norton.*

water wheel, but an all-iron ventilated version. Although it was the latest model, the wheel was taken out in 1887 for 'cutting-edge' flour milling technology. Abandoning stones, the corn was to be ground in rollers powered by a steam engine and a turbine, all supplied by Henry Simon of Manchester.[73] Roller mills were able to grind the hard American grains and they were mostly sited at ports where the grain entered the country. A railway station was situated just a short distance up the hill and the American grain could be transported to King's Norton to be ground at a rate never witnessed before at the ancient manorial site. All this needed a new building and photographs show an enormous barn-like structure built of brick, four storeys high and 13 bays long, with a wide span. It was all very far removed from 'the picturesque tumble-down brick and timber' mill recalled by John Bridges, who described the changes brought about by the new miller in his new building, with hardly a speck of flour on his shiny black coat.[74]

Nettlefold and Chamberlain

In 1861-2 James and Son constructed a screw factory about halfway between Lifford Mill and the Cadbury's factory in the triangle of land created by the Worcester & Birmingham Canal and the turnpiked Roman road. In 1865 the two-year-old firm,

James, Son and Avery, was taken over by Nettlefold and Chamberlain, ambitious to dominate the Birmingham market in woodscrews. John Sutton Nettlefold had begun making screws in Birmingham in 1834 in a steam-powered factory off Broad Street.[75] In 1854 he entered into a partnership with Joseph Chamberlain, his brother-in-law, to buy an American patent to manufacture a revolutionary woodscrew with a pointed end. Joseph Chamberlain sent his son, the more famous Joseph Chamberlain, to look after the investment. By the late 1860s Nettlefold and Chamberlain were producing nearly 70 per cent of the screws made in the Birmingham area.

In 1874 the Chamberlains left the firm in the hands of Joseph Henry Nettlefold, son of John Sutton. The firm, incorporated as Nettlefolds Ltd in 1880, had expanded vigorously, absorbing other small firms to become the leading manufacturer of wood screws in the country by the 1880s.[76] This necessitated considerable expansion of the King's Norton site with a new foundry, and dressing, annealing and carpenters' shops. Two beam engines drove the main shafting and the chimney dominated the local scene.[77] Apart from screws, the factory also produced screw-eyes and hooks, skewers and scissors and box-making machinery that was sold to Cadbury's and the Birds' factory in Deritend.

In the last decade of the 19th century considerable expansion took place, almost doubling the factory's size.[78] In 1895 a large recreation ground providing for tennis, bowls and cricket was laid out on the north side of the factory, effectively preventing any future development in this direction.[79]

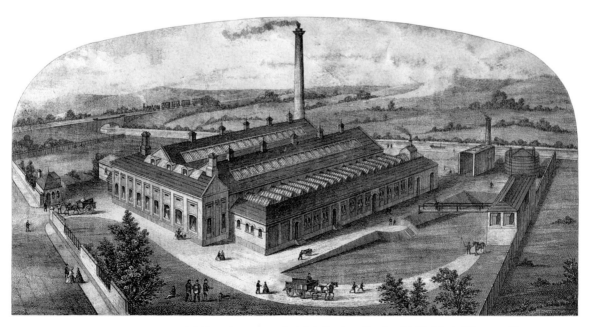

97 *Perspective view of Nettlefolds Ltd, 1881. To the left is Pershore Road and behind is the Worcester & Birmingham Canal, with the Gloucester railway crossing it by a bridge. Most of the main block of buildings still stands today.*

The King's Norton Metal Company

In about 1889 T. R. Bayliss (1838-1914) established the King's Norton Metal Company at Lifford to make ammunition, wire, rivets, strip and sheet. He had been a managing director of the Birmingham Small Arms' (B.S.A) Adderley Park Rolling Mills.[80] The 27-acre site chosen, halfway between Nettlefolds and Lifford Mill, was as attractive as it was spacious, and adjacent to both the Worcester & Birmingham Canal and the Birmingham West Suburban Branch Railway, which linked to the main Birmingham to Bristol line. The major improvement of the BWSB in 1883-5 for use as a goods line must have been an influencing factor.[81] Metal ingots for the rolling mills and coal for the steam engines could be transported easily to the site. By 1900 another 30 acres had been added and the size of the works doubled. The metal components produced at King's Norton were sent to the newly acquired Abbey Wood site near the Woolwich Arsenal for assembly, thereby avoiding the handling of explosives at the Lifford site.[82]

Cadbury's

The removal of George Cadbury's factory to Bournville in 1879 not only led to the creation of the famous garden suburb, but also encouraged the development of Stirchley and Cotteridge. As a major employer in the district, Cadbury's also widened the job opportunities for local women and girls in King's Norton itself.

In June 1878 Richard and George Cadbury bought 14½ acres of land at Bournbrook on the border between King's Norton and Northfield parishes. This enabled them in 1879 to move their chocolate and cocoa factory from Bridge Street in the overcrowded centre of Birmingham to the countryside. The site chosen lay adjacent to the canal and railway. Originally to be called Bournbrook, the new name derived its first element from the local stream while 'ville' hinted at a link with France, then home of the best chocolate.

When the factory moved out of Birmingham the new works employed about 300 people; a decade later this had risen to 1,200 and by 1899 it had soared to 2,685, of whom about two thirds were women. Initially just 16 semi-detached cottages were built near the factory for foremen and senior employees, leaving most of the workforce to travel by train from Birmingham to Stirchley Street (now Bournville) Station. Only later did Cadbury's visionary development of the model village enable workers to live close by. In the meantime housing development for those who wanted to live near to the works took off, first at Stirchley and from the 1890s at Cotteridge.

For those living farther south, in the area of King's Norton village, the arrival of Cadbury's was to offer further opportunities. The story of local people queuing for employment at the new works has often been told, and we can see in the census returns of 1881 how the impact of this large employer was felt. The streets of Stirchley were inhabited by many Cadbury workers – chocolate box makers, cream makers, wrappers, coverers, packers and cocoa essence weighers – but the firm's impact on the old village was less pronounced and only two men, a chocolate moulder and chocolate maker, are listed in the immediate area. By 1901 the situation was very different, with many young women between the ages of 15-20 then working at Bournville.

The potential dangers for women of travelling to work through open countryside, especially after dark, was of concern to the Cadburys and this is just one example of the paternalism shown to their employees:

> The problem of the girls from the surrounding villages was the easiest of settlement. There was no danger in their coming across fields early in the morning, even in the dark, but in the evenings there might well be undesirable characters about, and therefore it was arranged that women workers should be escorted home, at night, by men carrying lanterns.[83]

The census returns for 1901 also demonstrate that the majority of those in the village area who were not engaged in agriculture or its service industries worked in the immediate locality – at the metal works, the paper mill and the brickworks. It was the sons and especially the daughters of these workers who travelled further for their jobs to Cadbury's, or into Birmingham. For the well-to-do, professional men and merchants who moved into Middleton Hall Road, commuting by train into the city was the norm and made life at King's Norton with its many attractions both desirable and feasible.

TRANSPORT AND COMMUNICATION

Birmingham's emergence as a major centre of population and industry in the 19th century ensured the town would extend its transport tentacles in all directions and over greater distances. The construction of turnpikes and canals had initiated the process and railways would intensify the centripetal forces focusing on Birmingham. It was inevitable some of these new transport links would pass through King's Norton on their way elsewhere, but a consequence was that the ancient manor was being brought ever closer to the growing city.

Pershore Turnpike

Before the construction of the Pershore Turnpike the route from Birmingham to King's Norton followed the Alcester Turnpike via Moseley and the King's Heath, then a heath rather than a suburb. At this point there was a choice, to travel along the present Vicarage Road to Stirchley and enter King's Norton from the north or to use the present Grove Road and Brandwood Park Road and arrive at the village from the east.

The Pershore Turnpike, authorised under an Act of 1825, eventually provided a direct route from Birmingham to King's Norton. A new road ran from the edge of the town near Smithfield Market, via Pebble Mill, to the Bourne stream crossing, south of Ten Acres (near the junction with the present Cartland Road).[84] It then joined the old Roman road running almost due south to Breedon Cross, cutting out a large bend (the old and new road are akin to a curved bow and string respectively and form the current one-way traffic system). From Breedon Cross the turnpike used the old road to the present double traffic island in the centre of Cotteridge. From this point a new road was constructed direct to King's Norton Mill, abandoning the former route, which later became Station Road. After cutting out another small bend the turnpike crossed the river and pivoted eastwards onto a new route, by-passing The Green on the east side. It formed a new crossroads with Wharf Road and another section of new road was squeezed between Masshouse Lane and the houses on the south side of The Green. The road then headed in a straight line to Grange Farm where it joined an existing lane to West Heath.

The Ordnance Survey one-inch map, revised in 1831-2, shows only certain sections of the road completed, the most significant lengths missing being the village by-pass and Pebble Mill to Dog Pool Mill in Northfield parish. It is clear that old sections of road were being used by the turnpike trust. It was not until December 1834 that the new road around the village was authorised, although the longer length running south-westwards towards Grange Farm was constructed about 1827 (Redditch Road).[85] A map of 1835 shows that the the trust short-cuts at Ten Acres and Stirchley Street had not yet been constructed, but on a map produced in the following year the first is drawn as completed.[86] Subsequent competition from railways bankrupted most turnpikes and the Pershore Road was disturnpiked in 1879 and the Alcester Road in 1874.[87]

Canals

The completion of the Worcester & Birmingham Canal to the river Severn at Worcester was a protracted affair. Construction was delayed by spiralling costs during the Napoleonic Wars, the shortage of labour during the canal-building age, and the cost of having to

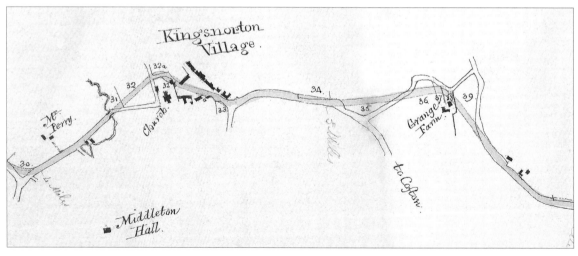

98 *Extract from the Pershore turnpike map (c.1825). The original idea was to abandon the old line of the road from Birmingham, but enter The Green as normal. The actual road by-passed the village completely, entering The Green from the east. (North is to the left.)*

build reservoirs to placate the owners of mills, whose livelihoods were threatened by the changes to drainage and water supply. In the end the Worcester & Birmingham proved to be one of the most expensive canals to construct, with a final bill of over £600,000 and a cost per mile of £20,000.

Once open to Worcester, in 1815, the canal's full potential in the movement of coal, timber and agricultural produce could be realised. In the 1830s additional cargoes to and from the newly established salt and alkali works at Stoke Prior and the limestone quarries at Dunhampstead gave a further boost to trade. But just as this traffic was getting established a new threat appeared in the shape of the railway from Birmingham to Gloucester in the late 1830s. Further expansion of the railway network meant the Worcester & Birmingham Canal struggled to survive through the 1840s and 1850s. The company went into liquidation in 1868 and was eventually taken over by the Gloucester & Berkeley Canal Company in 1874, becoming the Sharpness New Docks Company.

In 1876 steam tugs replaced the need to leg boats through Wast Hill Tunnel, a change which necessitated additional ventilation via the sinking of two new shafts. Accommodation was provided for the tugmen and their families in cottages at both ends of the tunnel, the two pairs built at the King's Norton end near the junction of Primrose Hill and Masshouse Lane being little altered today.

The 1871 census recorded six boats which had moored overnight on 2 April near the guillotine lock at King's Norton. Three of them, the *Neptune, William* and the *Seven Stars*, were each carrying between 23-8 tons of Droitwich salt. A fourth, the *Elizabeth*, was loaded with 21 tons of limestone, the *Emma Moore* had seven tons of hay and straw, and an unnamed boat held 20 tons of coal. The crews were mainly husband and wife teams with help from children. There were two men in charge of the limestone boat – John Lea and his helper, Thomas Dale. All but one of the 16 people on these six boats was born in the Midlands, the exception being boat boy Eli West, the 12-year-old son of John and Eliza West on the *Neptune*. Eli was born in London, his father in Stoke Bruerne, Northamptonshire on the Grand Union Canal and his mother in Droitwich. The social contacts had clearly been made through the canal network between the Midlands and the capital.

The Birmingham and Gloucester Railway

The Birmingham and Gloucester Railway formed part of a major link to Bristol and was started from Gloucester, with the section through King's Norton completed between September and December 1840.[88] It was not until August 1841 that the connection to the London and Birmingham line was made that enabled trains to run to Curzon Street Station. Lifford and Moseley (strictly speaking King's Heath) were the only stations in King's Norton opened in this phase, Lifford to serve the growing industrial zone, and King's Heath, the infant suburb. King's Norton station was not built until 1849. Initially 'only limited accommodation was provided consisting of a small, brick-built ticket office and a waiting room, all that was required for a relatively

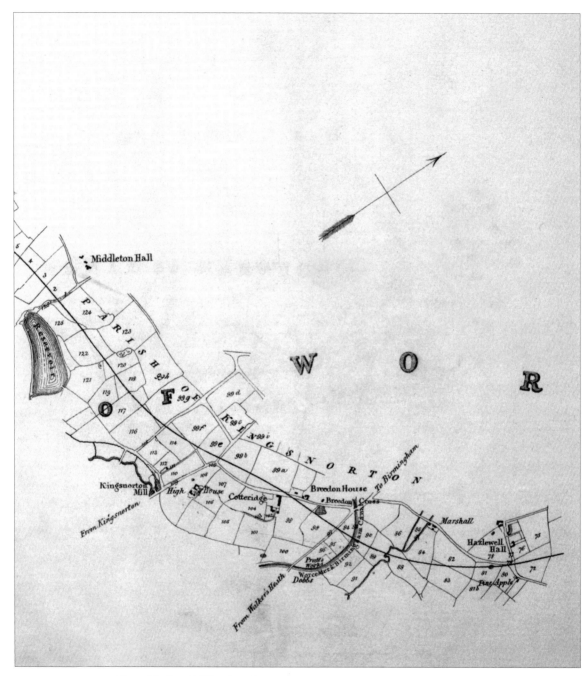

99 *Plan of the intended line through King's Norton of the Birmingham to Gloucester railway.*

unimportant stopping place'.[89] In 1867-8 new station buildings were erected at King's Norton to designs by John M. Sanders.[90] The main building was an impressive brick block, in the middle of which was a large waiting hall with an office, lamp room, coal store and urinals on one side and ladies' and gentlemen's waiting rooms on the other. More modest was the open-fronted brick waiting shed designed at the same time for the platform opposite. The station with its improved facilities was instrumental in attracting middle-class housing into the area around Middleton Hall Road. The construction of the Birmingham West Suburban Branch in 1876 joined the Gloucester (Midland Railway) line at Lifford and services terminated at King's Norton station. Lifford Station was moved south onto the Birmingham West Suburban Branch line. It only returned to the original line when the latter was upgraded in 1883-5, but in this third move was positioned on the east side of Lifford Lane. The Birmingham West Suburban line became more important than the old Gloucester line via Camp Hill, due to its shorter distance to New Street station.

The Gloucester line is topographically prominent as it crosses the river Rea on the high embankment near Fordhouse Lane and Brandwood Park Road. The embankment begins at Lifford Lane where the line is carried over the road on a bridge. Westwards of this point the railway follows the north side of the Rea valley in a relatively shallow cutting to King's Norton Station and emerges at the surface again at Pope's Lane.

'The improved train service,' declared an auctioneer's sale particulars in 1889 for building plots in Westhill Road, within a few minutes walk of the station, 'has made King's Norton the most accessible suburb of Birmingham, and greatly increased the demand for Residences.'[91] Trams, motor buses and cars would arrive in the following century to make King's Norton even more accessible to the city.

VI

The Twentieth Century

In the 20th century King's Norton ceased to be a rural settlement and became a suburb of the second largest city in the United Kingdom. About two-thirds of the ancient manor and parish was incorporated in 1911 into a much enlarged Birmingham City Council area. This left the area around Wythall within Worcestershire (today Bromsgrove District Council), and as a result this part of King's Norton has remained mainly rural to the present day. The northern part of rural Wythall between Redhill Road and the Hollywood By-pass forms part of the ecclesiastical parish of King's Norton and therefore lies within our study area.

TENURE AND LANDOWNDERSHIP

During this century the pattern of landownership that can be traced back to the medieval period was destroyed. Farms were sold wholesale or piecemeal by their owners for building land and landownership fragmented. Only when Birmingham Council began to develop municipal housing after the Second World War were large areas assembled under a single owner. The policy of council house sales has significantly broken up these great municipal estates. Ancient property boundaries, however, can still be detected in the shape of housing estates, streets and garden boundaries as new roads were squeezed into the fields made available for purchase. Land was developed piecemeal and new houses could look over open fields for several decades before these fields in turn succumbed to development.

POPULATION

In 1911 King's Norton (the ancient parish less Balsall Heath) had a population of 49,160, a rise of 38 per cent from 1901 (35,750). The pace of growth had in fact slowed in comparison with the decade 1891-1901. After the annexation of King's Norton by Birmingham in 1911 population figures are not easily available for the area of the ancient manor nor for our study area. It is worth emphasising that Greater Birmingham, created in 1911, contained a population of about 840,000; this total increased to just over a million in 1931 and 1.1 million in 1951. The physical expansion of Birmingham into rural areas such as King's Norton was not accompanied by the growth rates experienced in the 19th century. During the 20th century, and particularly after the Second World War, the densely built up slums of the inner areas were cleared and overspill estates constructed at much lower density in the suburbs. The inner city area of Balsall Heath, for example, was itself redeveloped at lower density than the previously crowded courts and terraces. The net effect of this movement of population from the inner city to new suburbs was to maintain Birmingham's population at around one million throughout most of the 20th century, even with the absorption of Sutton Coldfield in 1974. The population dipped to 977,087 in 2001 and rose to 1,006,500 in 2006.[1]

GREATER BIRMINGHAM

King's Norton and Northfield Urban District Council was only eight years old when the question of incorporation was seriously considered 'in view of the phenomenal growth of the urban portion of the Council's area'.[2] The Council Clerk completed a report in January 1907 which accepted that subdivision of the district was inevitable but that purely agricultural areas should be excluded, except those likely to be developed in the future. Incorporation for the Council did not mean absorption by Birmingham, but the creation of an independent municipal borough headed by a mayor. The Urban District Council was therefore comfortable with dividing its area in half, Rednal, Rubery, Wythall, Bartley Green and Beoley being excluded from the new municipality.

For the Boundaries Committee, publishing its report in February 1909, incorporation was a synonym for absorption, a necessary step in the plan for a greater Birmingham. It proposed that King's Norton and Northfield Urban District Council, together with the Borough of Aston Manor, Erdington and Handsworth Urban District Councils, and Yardley Rural District Council be annexed to the city.[3] It is not surprising that Birmingham Council accepted its findings unanimously. The authorities to be incorporated resisted the proposals, despite the fact that they were unable to cope with the administration of the populous districts, already effectively parts of Greater Birmingham, that fell into their areas. King's Norton and Northfield Urban District Council had no natural centre: its clerk's office was in Newhall Street in the centre of Birmingham, its workhouse in Selly Oak and other departments were housed in separate and widely scattered buildings. The ratepayers in King's Norton were more uncertain in their attitude, but only 38 per cent voted in a poll held on 6 December 1909, the anti-annexionists gaining twice the pro-unification vote (3,638 to 1,764).[4] The District Councils allied with the anti-annexionists against those ratepayers who organised unification committees. Worcestershire County Council, responsible for upkeep of the highways and the provision of education, also agreed 'to strenuously oppose' Birmingham's unification with King's Norton and Northfield Urban District Council.[5] A considerable amount of the rateable value in the county was located in areas contiguous with Birmingham.

A propaganda war broke out, with posters printed by both sides. A pro-unification poster exhorted ratepayers to vote for Greater Birmingham for 'Lower Rates, Lower

Rents, Lower Water Charges'.[6] A printed fact sheet listed 20 advantages, including a cheap and plentiful supply of electricity, something which had not yet reached King's Norton. Notwithstanding all these advantages the document concludes bluntly that it is time to choose between ancient parochial allegiances and the fact that the communities are 'in truth, if not at present in name, "Birmingham"'. For anyone who stood in the graveyard of St Nicolas and looked north across the valley towards the advancing Cotteridge, it was indeed difficult to deny this assertion

A Local Government Board of Inquiry into Birmingham's claims took place in December 1909. J.S. Nettlefold (1860-1930), grandson of the John Sutton Nettlefold who founded the screw manufacturing firm with its factory at Breedon Cross, was an active supporter of amalgamation and was unable to attend owing to illness.[7] John Baldwin, owner of the paper mill to the south on Lifford Lane, appeared as a witness. When pressed he admitted to supporting incorporation, including the Lifford area, which he considered to be 'on the borders of the great city'. He suggested that the boundary could be drawn to the south of his mill, leaving out that part of Lifford Lane still in the countryside and also the village of King's Norton for its 'old associations'. It was not to be: the inquiry inspector submitted a confidential report to the Local Government Board favourable to Birmingham's claims. On 26 May 1910 the Board issued a Provisional Order supporting the Greater Birmingham scheme in almost all detail. In October 1910 King's Norton and Northfield Urban District Council agreed not to object, soothed by negotiating a lower rate for the first 10 years. This was much to the dismay of Worcestershire County Council who were informed by the Urban District Council in December that it was to make terms, but not what they were.[8]

The Bill to incorporate most of King's Norton, together with Handsworth, Aston, Erdington and Yardley, and the other independent councils, was passed by the House of Lords on 19 May 1911. Birmingham gained control of an area three times the size of Glasgow and twice the size of Manchester, Liverpool or Belfast. The neighbouring authorities still contained large areas of open countryside, but Birmingham did not want these rural acres in order to preserve them. Nearly a hundred years has passed since the Greater Birmingham Act and the process of urbanising extensive rural tracts has been accomplished. Most if not all of the inhabitants would consider themselves inhabitants of a large city, and the negative attitude of those who saw themselves being overwhelmed by Birmingham is now a distant memory.

MAKING THE SUBURBAN LANDSCAPE

At the beginning of the century Cotteridge and the village of King's Norton faced each other across the river valley, like two opposing armies holding high ground. Despite the patchiness of the physical growth of Birmingham to the north, the forces on the south side were destined to lose. Cotteridge was not attached to the huge reserves of the city, but formed an isolated island of development. Only at the Nettlefold screw works did it touch the next suburb to the north, one focused on the Bournville chocolate works and Stirchley. There were still gaps of open countryside

100 *Pro-unification poster setting out the advantages of joining Birmingham and separating from Worcestershire, c.1910.*

to Selly Oak, Ten Acres and King's Heath. The vast majority of nearly 3,000 houses that were built in the ancient parish of King's Norton between 1902 and 1909 were in Moseley and King's Heath.[9] Cotteridge filled in a little more along new streets such as Franklin Road and Ashmore Road and along existing lanes renamed Selly Oak Road and Northfield Road that ran beside the ancient boundary with Northfield manor. From 1906 most of these roads were developed by Bournville Tenants Ltd, which leased 20 acres of land from the Bournville Village Trust, and the Trust architect, W.A. Harvey, designed the houses.[10] Linden Road had not yet been constructed as a direct link to Bournville and Selly Oak.

A few years before incorporation two new roads were laid to the west of the village on the former Kingsuch estate (Newhouse Farm) for middle-class housing, both semi-detached and detached. Beaks Hill Road and Meadow Hill Road formed a sinuous 'Y' shape, its arms clasping a 19th-century pool on the estate, by then atttractively tree-lined. The ancient highways of Westhill Road and Wychall Lane were also being loosely developed. By 1914 only about fifty houses had been constructed, leaving large areas of open land and the Newhouse Farm still standing. By contrast, terraced houses were built east of the village on Wharf Road and Parson's Hill earlier in the century, presumably to serve the new brick and tile works; they were separated from Parson's Hill by a new road, Cyril Road, which also contained a row of houses.[11] By 1914 more terraces had been built on the opposite side of Parson's Hill at the beginning of Baldwin Road.

The First World War brought a halt to house building so that by the end of the decade the requirement for houses in the city had risen from 2,500 to 12,000 new houses per year.[12] Birmingham Council was determined to solve the crisis by instigating from scratch the largest programme of municipal housing in the country. This began in 1919 and continued through the 1920s and 1930s. The main impetus of private house building was felt in the 1930s, eventually overtaking the council programme. By the outbreak of the Second World War over 110,000 houses had been constructed in the city, of which just under half were council-built.

Demand for housing was encapsulated in the 'Homes for Heroes' campaign. A group of six houses, known as the 'Mail' houses, was built rapidly within eight weeks in Pershore Road South just below the station. The land was bought by Sir Charles Hyde, the owner of the Post and Mail Company, and the houses were erected by Grant's of King's Norton.[13] Despite this initiative relatively few houses were built in the 1920s and early 1930s and the area to the south and east of the village remained decidedly rural. In the latter half of the 1930s private house building suddenly exploded and continued at a phenomenal rate for a few years until interrupted by the war. As a consequence the village was finally embraced by suburban Birmingham.

King's Norton was unusual in being an area where few council estates were constructed. A small estate of 35 acres containing 319 houses was laid out in the mid-1930s on the west side of Broad Meadow Lane within the ancient Broad Meadow Farm landholding. The roads included Elderfield Road, Woodmeadow Road and the

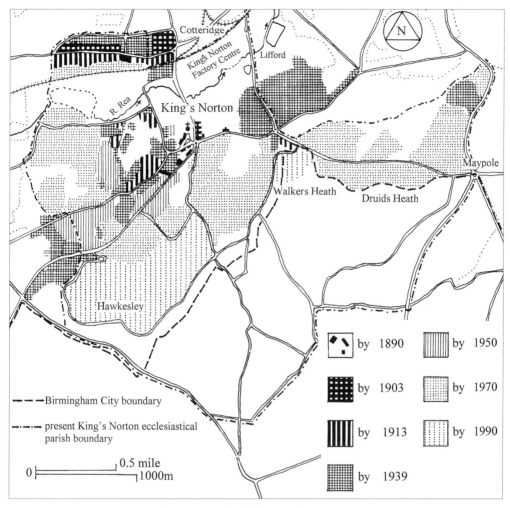

Cotteridge

King's Norton Factory Centre

Lifford

R. Rea

King's Norton

Maypole

Walkers Heath   Druids Heath

Hawkesley

◆ ◗ by 1890 ||||| by 1950

▓▓▓ by 1903   ░░░ by 1970

|||| by 1913   ┊┊┊ by 1990

▦▦ by 1939

– – – Birmingham City boundary

–·–·– present King's Norton ecclesiastical
        parish boundary

0 ┝━━━━━━━┥ 0.5 mile
  ┝━━━━━━━┥ 1000m

101   *The growth of King's Norton in the 20th century.*

continuation of Baldwin Road. The new tenants came from the Hurst Street slum clearance in central Birmingham and by all accounts were not happy with their new facilities, hankering after a corner shop and the rag market.[14] Broad Meadow Farm itself was not immediately demolished and for a time separated the council estate from the private houses that were being developed from the mid- to late 1930s on the ancient Lindsworth estate to the east (Lindsworth Road and Approach, Midhurst Road, Sheringham Road). Lindsworth Farm itself was eventually removed to make way for Bradstock Road. Houses were built along the north side of Monyhull Road opposite Monyhull Colony. The Monyhull estate had been acquired in 1905 by the Guardians of the Poor for Birmingham, Aston and King's Norton for an experimental mental hospital.[15] The male patients were intended to work the farmland so there was a need to retain both Bell's Farm and Kingswood Farm as part of the estate; the hospital's policy changed in the 1960s. New houses along Brandwood Road and Broad Lane finally joined King's Norton to King's Heath, and the link was consolidated by the laying out of the Brandwood Park Estate in 1937-9 along Brandwood Park Road, Yarnindale Road and Kernthorpe Road, among others. The developers were Birmingham Housing Industries and The Model Building Company using two firms of architects, L.E. Hewitt & Meredith and Nicklin & Bull.[16] King's Heath was also spreading southwards along the Alcester Road (South) so that at the eastern extremity of our study area, at Millpool Hill, Matthews & Baker and L. and F. Baker laid out an estate based on Marsham Road, Meadowfoot Road and Camford Grove.

In the mid-1930s the fields in the triangle immediately south-east of the village stretching to the Worcester & Birmingham Canal were filled with new roads of private houses (High Meadow Road, Old Oak Road and Lanchester Road). Some of this land had belonged to the ancient Masshouse estate and the farm itself was demolished to make way for houses on Masshouse Lane. West of the village, Meadow Hill Road and Beaks Hill Road had gradually filled during the 1920s and 1930s and Grange Hill Road was cut around 1920 to continue the line of Beaks Hill Road to Redditch Road.[17] Kingshill Drive forms a typical 1930s cul-de-sac off Westhill Road with its terminal turning circle; it was on the site of Kingsuch (Newhouse Farm). Development continued along both Redditch Road and Rednal Road, but in

102 *Redditch Road, 1939, looking north towards King's Norton. The houses in Aversley Road (left) were nearing completion when this photograph was taken and sit in front of 18th-century Grange Farm, which survived until the 1960s.*

103 *Aerial view of ribbon development along the Redditch Road south of King's Norton, c.1939. Suburban sprawl was already beginning to link Redditch Road with Rednal Road.*

the typically interrupted linear sprawl of the 1930s. So there was a gap at the former Cistercian Grange Farm and the relatively new Burford House before new houses began again in Aversley Road, Alborn Crescent, Greenacres Road and Glenwood Road on the fringes of West Heath. The builders, Bull & Tewkesbury, employing architects Nicklin & Bull, laid out Aversley Road just before the war. The most expensive house was the 'Rutland,' a detached house with a garage selling at £575. On the other side of Rednal Road Bertram S. White managed to start a small estate off Beaks Hill Road, based on Grassmoor Road, Hazelbank and Fairmead Rise.

Once more a world war interrupted the momentum of house building. The devastation inflicted by the conflict was responsible for the introduction of a novel type of house, the prefabricated bungalow or prefab. These were intended as a temporary measure to house people made homeless by air raids. Ironically they became popular with their residents, who were reluctant to give them up, and it took many post-war

159

104 *Aerial photograph of prefabs on the Bell's Lane Estate in 1950 with Bell's Farm in lower left-hand corner.*

decades to clear them finally. One of the largest prefab estates in Birmingham was constructed between Druid's Lane and Bell's Lane.

The war had severely crippled Britain financially and it was not until the late 1940s that a much needed house building programme was restarted. New homes were required by those displaced by the war, and to replace the many thousands of unfit houses in the inner city area. In contrast to the late 1930s, council house building in the late 1940s and 1950s far outstripped the efforts of the private sector. King's Norton witnessed the construction of large municipal estates in all available directions, a process which continued into the 1980s. The pressure led developers to build fast and high, but some of the methods of rapid construction using prefabricated units did not stand the test of time. Furthermore, tower blocks did not prove popular. The first estate was constructed in 1952-5 at Wychall Farm, mostly outside historic King's Norton, Pope's Lane being the parish boundary. The farm itself was demolished for housing on Pope's Lane. A footpath continued the line of the boundary southwards from Wychall Lane, along which six blocks of flats were constructed, the first in

160

this part of Birmingham (Chaddesley Road). About 500 houses were erected using prefabricated reinforced concrete (Smiths Construction) but both flats and houses lasted barely half a century before being demolished around 2005. The estate has been entirely redeveloped by Bromford Housing Association at a cost of £40 million. In the early 1950s another 500 houses were built at the north end of Pope's Lane (Bunbury Road, Kipling Road and Longfellow Road). The blocks of flats on Longfellow Road were demolished a few years ago.

In the mid- to late 1950s the council developed the Pool Farm estate to the south-east of the village, with houses, maisonettes and three blocks of flats on Walker's Heath Road. Built on the land of other historic farms such as Masshouse, the new roads included Sisefield Road and The Fold (names based on field-names), Hillmead Road and Heathside Drive. For a while the ancient lane, Primrose Hill, formed the boundary of the built-up area of the city. In the late 1960s the council developed another estate along the south-east side of Redditch Road bounded by an ancient lane, Green Road (Lane), and new roads, Shannon Road and Foyle Road. It was named the Primrose (Hill) estate after the farm (formerly Hole Farm) that had survived in open land between the two council estates. The council had to persuade Cadbury's, who had purchased the land with Hawkesley Hall and Moundsley Hall and gifted it to the city in 1937 as 'a reservation of green areas', to remove the restrictive covenant and allow part to be developed.[18] The houses were laid out in the fashionable Radburn style, a street being lined with back gardens on one side and the fronts of homes on

105 *Meadowsweet Avenue was cut in 1972 and the side roads followed soon after this photograph was taken, encircling Primrose Hill Farm and its outbuildings.*

161

106   *Aerial photograph of the Hawkesley estate, 1966*

the other. Not surprisingly this confusing and insecure street scene eventually fell out of favour, but not before it was used elsewhere in King's Norton. Seven blocks of flats were also erected. Finally, in the late 1970s and early 1980s, the largest of the council estates, Hawkesley, was laid out according to a plan prepared in 1972.[19] It resulted in the demolition of Hawkesley Hall, whose approach avenue of lime trees survives along with an open space on its former site. Again, the estate reflected contemporary ideas on housing layouts and most of the homes were low-rise houses in short culs-de-sac linking to spine roads such as Longdales Road, Edgewood Road, Meadowsweet Avenue and the continuation of Shannon Road. More effort was made to incorporate green space, create a network of new footpaths and preserve ancient lanes and footpaths.

Half a century after the Pool Farm estate appeared in the fields beyond the Worcester & Birmingham Canal it had become notorious as one of the most deprived areas of the city. In 2001 the city council was awarded £50 million under the New Deal for Communities scheme to regenerate not only Pool Farm but the Primrose and Hawkesley estates, under a project called 'The 3 Estates'.[20] Most of the Primrose estate is to be demolished, along with large parts of Pool Farm. One tower block was removed in 2004.[21] Currently the project is sagging under the weight of a confusing medley of plans, already completed or still to be written.

In the area east of the village from Walker's Heath Road to the Maypole the council predominated. Development began with the demolition of the 1940s pre-fabs between Druid's Lane and Bell's Lane. In the mid-1960s Bryant and Son Ltd secured the contract to build nearly 2,000 homes on the site, consisting of houses, maisonettes and flats. A mix of traditional construction, pre-cast concrete from the Bryant factory in Handsworth, and the Bison Wall Frame system for 16 blocks of flats was used.[22] In the late 1960s another large estate was constructed north of Bell's Lane and west of Alcester Road South, with 10 tower blocks, based upon Manningford Road and Baverstock Road. In the 1970s attention focused on the north side of Bell's Lane and two estates, separated by the Chinn Brook, were developed based upon Brockworth Road and Pennyacre Road. The former partly enveloped the timber-framed Bell's

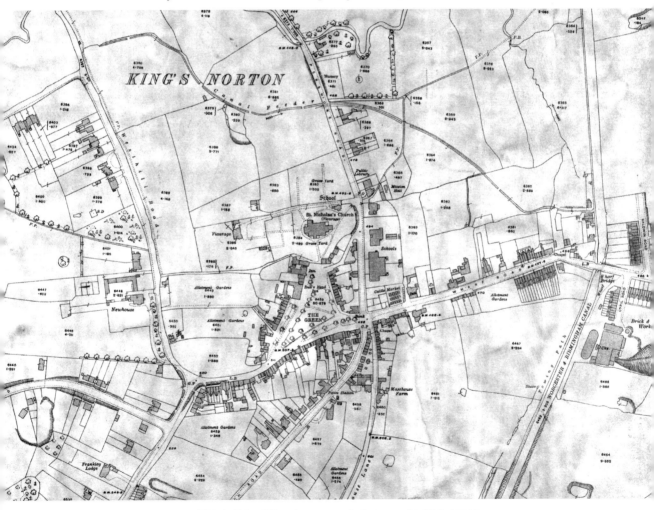

107   *Third edition OS 1:2500 map, revised 1914 and published 1916.*

Farm. In the same decade the last remaining open land west of the village, used as a golf course, was lost to development. The spine roads, The Parkway and Vardon Way, were built on the land of the former Kingsuch (Newhouse Farm) Farm and West Heath Farm respectively, and an ancient footpath was preserved, continuing the line of Pope's Lane farther south. The footpath had acted as the ancient boundary between the two farms.

Private house building in King's Norton after the war was insignificant, restricted to a few infill culs-de-sac, such as Wychall Park Grove off Wychall Lane (late 1950s), St Nicolas Gardens off Westhill Road (early 1970s), and Millpool Gardens off Alcester Road South (late 1970s). Peplins Way off Lindsworth Road caused the removal of Broad Meadow Farm sometime in the 1940s. In the late 1980s houses were built on Bromsgrove District Council land between Walker's Heath Road and Druid's Lane, which effectively added to the built-up area of the city (Harbinger Road, Chelworth Road). Private ownership of housing has increased dramatically, however, through council tenants exercising their right to buy over the last few decades, so that about a third of the homes on 'The 3 Estates,' for example, are now in private ownership.

New housing made by far the greatest contribution to the development of King's Norton. Industry, mostly confined to the Rea valley owing to the historic location of mills, expanded to the north of Wychall Mill (Eckersall Road) and on the King's Norton Factory Centre between Lifford Lane and Pershore Road South. New factories were built to the north and south-east of the former Lifford Mill, most notably the Sturges chemical works. A large brick works on the south side of Parson's Hill prevented any building over a considerable area. The only other significant consumer of open land in the area was Monyhull Hospital.

TRANSPORT AND COMMUNICATIONS

Suburbanisation depended on both effective public and private transport. From May 1904 a tramway service, operated by a private company, ran from Birmingham City Centre as far as Breedon Cross and by June the line was extended to Cotteridge, where a tram terminus and depot were created.[23] In 1911 Birmingham Corporation took over the operation. The city's radial routes were linked in 1926 by the Outer Circle no. 11 bus route which connected King's Heath with Bournville via Cotteridge, where work was required to straighten Watford and Linden Roads. In the 1930s public transport was further improved by additional routes to the new estates, which followed main roads and almost reached the city's boundaries. When Messrs Bull & Tewkesbury advertised their new development at the Grange Farm Estate in 1939, they could offer potential purchasers ease of access to the city:

> Nos 23 and 23A Corporation 'Buses from Cotteridge Tram Terminus (no. 36 Car) pass Alvesley Road, the estate entrance. Midland 'Red' 'Bus no. 147 from Station Street also pass the Estate. Fare, 5d. single ; 5d. workman's return.[24]

108   *Tram at the Cotteridge terminus, 1904.*

Buses replaced the tramline to Cotteridge in 1952 and the depot was demolished a few years ago to make way for a sheltered housing scheme, Beaumont Park. The West Midlands Passenger Transport Executive, which later took over city transport, has attempted to provide a regular bus service to the outlying estates. While this has helped to lessen the feeling of isolation experienced by some residents, the cost of public transport for low-income families living far from the city centre remains problematic.

Improvements to major highways out of the city were planned in the inter-war years, although the projected dual carriageway between The Green and West Heath was never completed. A gyratory island was constructed at Cotteridge in 1931, at the junction of Pershore Road South and Middleton Hall Road, and another followed in 1934 at King's Norton's 'Five Ways', where Pershore Road meets Wharf Road, Masshouse Lane, Redditch Road and The Green. On Cotteridge hill a dual carriageway was created by the construction of a new south-bound highway, leaving the old road on the western side for traffic heading north.

109 *'Five Ways' junction in 1950 with the roundabout created in 1934. The Methodist Chapel on the corner of Redditch Road and Masshouse Lane had been converted to a newsagent's shop.*

Meanwhile King's Norton railway station continues as a major commuter link and the creation of extended parking, albeit at the expense of the old station buildings, has ensured the station's viability.

THE RURAL ECLIPSE

As housing estates spread into the countryside in the 20th century the problems for the urban farmer, first voiced by J.A. Bridges in the 1880s, increased. Trespass by the children of new residents unfamiliar with the countryside resulted in damage to growing crops and roaming dogs disturbed livestock. Landlords released farmland for building over a protracted period, reducing a tenant farmer's acreage little by little. Dawberry Fields Farm at King's Heath, for instance, lost half its original 52 acres in the 1920s, as land was taken for playing fields, allotments and the Pineapple Road schools. In the face of a lack of security of tenure, and the inevitability of eventual eviction, the ingenuity of the urban farmer was impressive. Redundant farm buildings could provide income from suburban roundsmen needing storage for their vehicles or stock, while the farmer at Wychall had converted his premises to boarding kennels for cats, dogs and birds by the Second World War. He was still able to promote his skill as a horseman when he advertised in the parish magazine his services as a carter.

There were advantages for the urban farmer. Birmingham wholesalers paid a higher price for milk from local farms because their transport costs were lower. Farmers with reduced acreages concentrated on dairy. At Lehing Farm, Headley Heath, a business specialising in nursery milk was established in 1903 by A.H. Johnson which later offered 'healthy milk direct from the farm at 4½ d per quart … delivered in glass' containers. Others, like Jack Bullock of Crabmill Farm, operated their own horse-drawn milk rounds in the new suburbs in the 1930s, serving 'loose' milk from the churns they collected from Primrose Hill and Lilycroft Farms. There was also a ready market for fresh produce, especially eggs and vegetables, sold at the farm gate, together with sundries ranging from manure for gardens to straw bedding for pets.

By the end of the century there were still half a dozen productive farms in the parish between Walker's Heath, Headley Heath and the Maypole. Gay Hill Farm is now the largest working farm and the 600 acre holding stretches into Alvechurch parish. It is a mixed farm with a high reputation for the quality of its beef cattle. Moundsley Farm covers 120 acres with a mix of suckling cows, sheep and horses. Trespass, vandalism and fly tipping continue to blight the lives of King's Norton's remaining farmers, but they somehow manage to hold on, earning a living from agriculture and maintaining the countryside. The majority of the open countryside is pasture, used for keeping horses and ponies owned by suburban dwellers – not unlike those small local farms in the 19th century which supplied the horses needed in the city. In some areas overgrazing has led to 'the creation of unsightly, muddy or dusty wasteland with the characteristic invasion of troublesome weeds such as docks and thistles. Given these conditions horses tend to browse the trees and hedgerows which adds to the general air of neglect. Such damaged pastures are likely to be

110 *Walker's Heath Farm, a 16th-century house on an even older site, with 20th-century tower blocks beyond.*

severely infested with parasites which can affect the animals' health and inevitably threaten any wildlife habitat.'[25] In the last quarter of the 20th century farmland was turned increasingly to other purposes and today there are playing fields, a cemetery, an animal rescue centre and a Business Park in the countryside. Some of the larger country houses, such as the rebuilt Moundsley Hall and Glenfield House at Headley Heath, have found new uses as nursing homes.

THE COUNTRYSIDE AS GREEN BELT

As suburbia spread out towards the boundaries of the city in the 1930s, Cadbury Brothers extended the principles embodied in George Cadbury's model village and acquired agricultural land as part of a 'green lung' around Birmingham's southern edge. The firm bought the Moundsley estate and generously helped the city acquire both Primrose Hill Farm and Hawkesley Hall. These three estates amounted to 691 acres and were transferred to the city on the basis that they should remain in perpetuity as open space.[26] By the late 1950s, however, the city was faced with a housing crisis and attempted to develop the land at Moundsley as part of its bid to

111 *Fourth edition OS 1:2500 map, revised 1935-6, published 1936.*

build on 1,800 acres between Kingswood and Wythall. It tried unsuccessfully on three occasions between 1959 and 1964 to secure permission to build on the Green Belt beyond the city boundary. A fourth attempt in 1969 involved an application to build 11,000 homes at Hawkesley, Frankley and Moundsley together with three balancing lakes at Hollywood. The city gained permission for development at the first two sites, but there was a firm refusal to further encroachment towards Wythall. The covenants on the land given by Cadbury's were eventually lifted after modifications to the scheme increased the amount of open space in the development. Since the 1980s the built-up areas had effectively remained at the boundary of the city and there is no prospect of any significant expansion in the foreseeable future.

Although King's Norton was absorbed into a suburb of Birmingham during the 20th century, it is still only a few minutes drive from the village to open countryside at Redhill Road, Icknield Street, Gayhill Lane and Wythall beyond. Edwardian cyclists and walkers delighted in King's Norton's rural charms and a number of guides set out the best routes to follow and what historical features to observe.[27] Until the late 1920s, when the Lickey Hills became the premier attraction for south Birmingham walkers, King's Norton was a favoured destination. One particularly popular route began at the Alcester Lanes End tram terminus from where excursionists made their way to King's Norton village. After a picnic and wander round the village visitors returned by walking to Cotteridge for the city tram. In the inter-war years poor children from inner city schools were brought to King's Norton in canal boats for their summer outings. On arrival at Wharf Road they would walk up Parson's Hill to Bell's Lane to enjoy a picnic, returning home with bunches of flowers bought from gardeners en route.[28] The tradition of taking exercise and enjoying the countryside around Birmingham was championed in the post-war years by Jack Schatz, who wrote weekly rambles for the *Birmingham Mail* under the initials E.J.S. He lived in Maypole Lane, which explains why several of his walks began on his doorstep at the Maypole or in King's Norton itself.[29]

HOUSES AND HOMES IN THE 1930S

Following the death in 1936 of Charles Pelham Lane, a two-day sale of the contents of Moundsley Hall took place.[30] The auction represents the end of an era, the furniture and furnishings of 29 rooms in the squire's residence being dispersed. The sale particulars list many antiques – furniture, oil paintings, glass and china – as well as an extensive library. Much had clearly been passed down from earlier generations and was old-fashioned, but Pelham Lane's interest in antiquities was reflected in the contents of his library and in the 17th-century panelling he had installed at Moundsley when Masshouse Farm was demolished just a few years earlier. There is hardly a mention of the new labour-saving household devices; Moundsley was still maintained by a small army of servants.

New houses for new residents were creeping closer to the edge of the Lane family's estate. Most were semi-detached or built in short terraces, although in Beaks Hill,

IDEAL HOUSES
in a GARDEN VILLAGE at
Victoria Park Estate,
KING'S NORTON,
BIRMINGHAM.

■

You can have the House you have dreamed
about for less than your present rent —
attractive in style — pleasantly situated —
Built to last — well planned — first-class
building practices followed in every trade.

Price from **£435** Small Deposits

**Tiled Bathroom, French Windows, Large
Bays, Tiled Kitchen, "Savework" Cabinet**

NO { Legal Charges.
Road Charges.
Extras.

Show House open for inspection until
9 o'clock each evening.

■

R. & H. FLETCHER, Ltd.,
VICTORIA PARK ESTATE,
Wharf Road, King's Norton
Telephone No.: King's Norton 1237.

112 *According to this 1933 advertisement for the
Victoria Park Estate in Wharf Road everything the
housewife wanted could apparently be found in these
modestly priced houses at King's Norton.*

Grange Hill and Meadow Hill Roads the detached house predominated and provided opportunities for more individuality. These new houses enjoyed hot running water, tiled kitchens and bathrooms, and French windows to the back garden, and were advertised as affordable 'modern labour-saving dwellings'. They included architectural features such as hipped roofs, curved or canted two-storeyed bay windows surmounted by a gable, mock timber-framing, tile hanging, pebbledash, recessed arched porches and leaded lights, sometimes with coloured glass. Hedged boundary walls and wooden gates added respectability to the perimeter. At the more generous plots there may have been room for a garage to one side of the property.

The new residents preferred these more traditional designs. The only concession to the contemporary Art Deco style is the occasional use of the sunray design on gates and coloured glass, and green pantile roofs. In a sea of traditionalism 53 Beaks Hill Road stands out as a rare exception. It was built in 1935 for Hubert Thornton and was designed by the Smethwick architect T. Dunkley Hogg.[31] It has all the elements of the Modern movement — flat roofs, rendered walls and curved corners with suntrap metal-framed windows.

The compiler of a 1933 guide to the Birmingham suburbs extolled King's Norton's advantages – 'supremely healthy', with well laid out roads, a pure and abundant water supply and a modern and perfected system of main drainage.[32] Yet the same guide applauds these virtues for a number of other outer suburbs. What seems to set King's Norton apart is the following:

> When one considers the nearness of the City centre, it is difficult to imagine that it is also close to delightful country and picturesque scenery, but such is the case; and although the population is ever increasing and many modern well-built houses have been erected and are available, every care has been taken in their planning, so that there is no 'density' or overcrowding, and the whole locality retains a delightful rural aspect.

THE VILLAGE

The Green

In their determination to remove the 'nuisance' of the annual Mop Fair King's Norton & Northfield Urban District Council pushed on with attempts to chain off The Green and prevent wagons and show vehicles encroaching upon it. They had ambitions to transform it into 'a quiet spot where the villagers may resort for rest and meditation'. This involved the creation of a public park with planting and a bandstand. On 19 September 1901 the council's workmen erected fencing posts but that same night, as the public houses round The Green emptied, the villagers removed them all. The following day the process was repeated and a newspaper reporter provided an eye-witness account of the farcical proceedings:

> Barely had the last stroke of ten died away before, in the presence of nigh upon a thousand spectators, violent hands were laid upon the first of the long line of encircling posts. For a few moments it swayed responsively in its half-set concrete foundation, and then a great cheer went up as it was wrenched out and flung down upon the green sward. To the accompaniment of vocal music, of the stirring strains of 'Britons never will be slaves', and a parody on the National Anthem, which ran 'God Save our Lovely Green', the work of demolition went on. The little band of constables, under Sergeant Burford, quietly dotted down names. They saw the humour of the whole business and the crowd treated them most considerately. The work was very expeditiously performed for little more than a quarter of an hour had elapsed before the last of the posts was dragged out of its setting, amid a perfect salvo of cheering. Then there was more singing of national airs, more hearty jest and merriment, as in orthodox fashion, and with a fine sense of humour, the crowd joined in 'God Save the King' and 'Auld Lang Syne'. Soon afterwards the assembled throng began quietly to disperse, and before eleven o'clock tranquillity reigned once more in these rural haunts.[33]

The council had to accept that The Green was not to become a municipal park with bedding and a bandstand. By the time of the celebrations to mark the coronation of Edward VII in August 1902 it had been chained off and a number of trees planted. Two years later the Mop was banished from The Green, first to the Town Field (now Old Town Close) and later to the Lakin, a field behind the *Navigation*. It was not to reappear round The Green until its revival in 1953, during Coronation Year. For a time it was run by the local Round Table, raising funds for local causes, but is now a commercial fun fair. It continues to be held on the first Monday of October and following the tradition of Mop Fairs moves from King's Norton to Alvechurch and other towns before eventually arriving in Stratford-upon-Avon for its fair on 12 October.

113 *The picturesque grouping of 'The Square' on the east side of The Green, demolished* c.1937 *to make way for a cinema.*

Clearance and Conservation

Until the 1930s one of the most picturesque features of King's Norton was the village green and its immediate environs. For builders promoting their developments it was one of the chief attractions of the place. Yet in the 1930s the tide turned in favour of change and many of the buildings which helped to give character to the area were demolished.

The incorporation of King's Norton into Birmingham had a devastating effect on the physical appearance of the village itself. Most people recognise The Green as a historical area, but few historical buildings survive around the distinctively shaped space. One has only to examine photographs of the village in the early part of the 20th century to realise that unnecessary mass demolition has taken place. The blame can be laid at the door of the Housing Act 1936, with which the city council quickly complied. The good intention was to remove houses 'unfit for habitation', but many of these were ancient structures of historical and architectural value. On 8 June 1937 12 'Clearance Areas' were approved, eight on The Green and four on Wharf Road.[34]

With a few applications of a colour wash on the clearance plans, much of the historic village was condemned to demolition. Some took place before the war. Clearance Area No. 5, the site of the attractive grouping of cottages known as the Square, was replaced by a cinema in 1938. The clearance continued after the war so that the historic village suffered a slow decline. This included the cottages demolished about 1960 between the *Bull's Head* and the western end of the *Saracen's Head*. Behind their brick façade was the timber frame of the original late medieval *Saracen's Head* complex. The present pub car park corresponds with Clearance Area No. 7. The eastern side was designated Area No. 8 and functions now more as a back lot to shops facing Pershore Road South. On the south side of The Green only one building of great antiquity survived, nos 10 and 10a, the former Hiron's Bakery. Its timber framing in the left-hand-side gable forms part of a medieval roof. To the west, two pairs of 19th-century cottages (16-19) have managed to survive. Farther along, the King's Norton workhouse complex, later known as West End Cottages, was removed, and there were losses of brick cottages along Masshouse Lane on the corner of Wharf Road, including an important timber-framed farmhouse at 16-14 Wharf Road (Marches Tenement, Holbeche the butchers in the 1930s). For many years after the war the site stood empty, a symbol of needless destruction.

Once the momentum for demolition had gathered pace, other buildings not threatened by the Clearance Orders were demolished. This includes the *Old Bell* in about 1964 and part of the timber-framed building with its profusion of close-

114   *The Green , c.1905. Posts and chains now surround the western Green and street lighting has appeared.*

studding attached to its east side (in 1937 the shop for King's Norton Electrical Co. Ltd). Other villages in Birmingham, such as Yardley and Northfield, and beyond, for example at Alvechurch, did not suffer this degree of destruction. There was resistance to the indiscriminate application of Clearance Orders, as the value of historic buildings was appreciated and defended, and it is not obvious why King's Norton capitulated so abjectly or whether its buildings were really in a worse condition than those of its historic neighbours.

By the time the city council declared King's Norton a Conservation Area on 17 July 1969 the damage had been done.[35] It contained only five statutorily listed buildings, St Nicolas church, the *Saracen's Head*, the Old Grammar School, nos 10 and 10a The Green and nos 16-19 The Green. Without doubt, many of the buildings demolished in the previous four decades would have been listed had they survived. When any of the modern buildings that surround The Green are redeveloped in the future, their size and massing will be controlled so that the domestic scale of the village is retained. But even The Green has changed significantly during the 20th century, and early photographs show no trees and no traffic. In recent times the roads around The Green have become no more than a daytime car park, with vehicles continually circulating, desperate to find a space.

Open space covers a considerable amount of the wider Conservation Area, and traffic is not such a nuisance. St Nicolas church stands within its ancient burial ground with a 20th-century extension to the north. The *Saracen's Head* and the Old Grammar School are considerably enhanced by their location on the edge of the graveyard, which in turn is graced by their presence. The formal part of King's Norton Park is included in the Conservation Area, separated from the rest of the park by an early 19th-century canal feeder from Wychall Reservoir. The open space immediately north of the village provides a green wedge between the old village and Cotteridge across the river Rea to the north east, and is one of the most successful aspects of King's Norton's 20th-century development. Twenty-five acres of land immediately below the churchyard extension were bought by Birmingham Civic Society in 1920 and subsequently presented to the city for use as a park and playing fields. The Society also funded the cost of planning the new park, whose designs included elegant entrance gates, seats and pavilions.[36] In January 1989 the Conservation Area was extended eastwards across Pershore Road South to include King's Norton Primary School (1878/1901-2), King's Norton Library (1905) and the Schoolmaster's House (288 Pershore Road South, 1878/1901), and some property on the corner of The Green and Redditch Road.

Leisure Facilities

King's Norton Library, like many other Edwardian libraries, was built through a partnership between the local authority and the Scottish-born American industrialist and philanthropist Andrew Carnegie. Local subscribers funded the cost of the site, King's Norton & Northfield Urban District Council agreed to meet running costs

115 *The King's Norton cinema opened in 1938 and brought city centre leisure facilities to the suburb.*

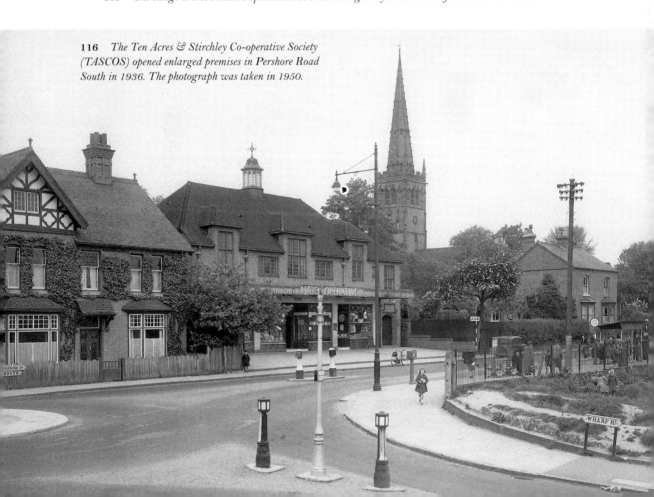

116 *The Ten Acres & Stirchley Co-operative Society (TASCOS) opened enlarged premises in Pershore Road South in 1936. The photograph was taken in 1950.*

once it was built, while Carnegie paid the building costs. Its foundation stone was laid in 1905 by Councillor Edwin Shephard, the head of the local firm of wheelwrights in Wharf Road and it was opened to readers the following year. It is a charming Edwardian building designed by Benjamin Bower and retains much of its original woodwork, plasterwork and other fittings.

When the 'King's Norton' cinema was opened in April 1938 its promoters claimed that 'city centre facilities' had arrived in the old village.[37] Designed by Harold Seymour Scott, who was responsible for over fifty inter-war cinemas, the new building could seat 1,000 people and as such was regarded as a 'supercinema'.[38] It dominated the western end of The Green for the next half century. It closed in 1983[39] and was demolished in 1987 to make way for Grosvenor Court sheltered housing.

Shops and Public Houses

In the Edwardian period Cotteridge developed a wide range of retail outlets, and houses on the north side of Pershore Road South that had only recently been built were converted into shops. A distinctive element was the Ten Acres & Stirchley Co-operative Society (TASCOS).[40] The Society was founded in 1875 'to establish co-operative rather than private trading' and took its name from a field it owned at

117 *The new* Bull's Head *public house under construction in 1901.*

118   *Drinkers at the* Plumbers' Arms *c.1910, when licensee Ann Kimberley kept order.*

Stirchley known as 'The Ten Acres'. Branch No. 2 opened at Cotteridge in 1899 on the corner of Midland Road and the Society's monogram is still to be seen in the step of the present shop. Another branch, designed by architect Francis B. Andrews of the firm Reading & Andrews, was erected near the top of Wharf Road in 1906. By the late 1920s the company had 21 grocery shops, 13 butcher's shops and travelling vans, a Dairy and a Nursery & Gardening Department at Bournville.[41] For a short time during the First World War and up to 1924 the Society experimented with running its own pig farm at Gay Hill, supplying meat and other farm produce directly to its shops. Although the farming initiative failed, TASCOS continued to expand its retail outlets, and elegant additional premises, designed by H.W. Simister of the firm Ball & Simister, were erected on the west side of Pershore Road in 1936. The new premises included departments for grocery, confectionery, butchery, pharmacy and hairdressing, to which a florist's was added in 1960. Upstairs was a meeting hall.[42] The Green retained a number of independent traders through the 20th century which helped to give character to the area.

King's Norton's public houses have fared less well. The *Bull's Head* was rebuilt in 1901 and the *Navigation* in 1906. As part of its rationalisation programme, the brewery giant Mitchells & Butlers closed the *Saracen's Head* in 1930, the *Plumbers' Arms* and the *Bell* in 1931. The only way that breweries could secure licences for the new type of public house – the road house with gardens, where women and families were welcome – was by closing some of their old-fashioned and less profitable houses which had become what one writer has described as bastions of misogyny.[43] The *Grant Arms* at Cotteridge was built in 1929 in a Queen Anne revival style, while the flat-roofed *Cartland Arms* (now a Mcdonald's) was erected in the 1930s on a corner plot at the top of Parson's Hill in Art Deco style with Crittall windows, curved corners and a centrally placed tower. Also from the 1930s, and occupying a prominent corner position, was the now demolished *Maypole* inn. It celebrated traditional English design, with a tall pitched roof pierced by dormer windows, side wings and a central gabled porch with a Tudor-esque stone doorway.

The Saracen's Head

In the early years of the 20th century the *Saracen's Head* saw a rapid succession of licensees before the arrival in 1908 of Frederick George Coombes, who stayed for nearly twenty years. Under Coombes' tenancy the exterior was redecorated and

119   *The* Saracen's Head *photographed in 1910-14. Frederick George Coombes repainted the frontage in 1910. He was keen to promote its beer, as well as his daughter's Tea Rooms in the north range.*

the imitation half-timbering painted over brick at the end of the 19th century was replaced by signs promoting the inn's attractions – 'ales, bottled beers and spirits' and 'good stables'. On the eve of the First World War Coombes' daughter Beatrice took over the grocer's shop which had been run by Charles Cyphus and converted it into 'Ye Olde Village Tea Room'. In 1918 Atkinson's Ltd sold the whole site to Mitchells & Butlers Ltd (M&B), but kept Coombes on as landlord and let the north range and the cottages between the *Saracen's Head* and the *Bull's Head* to a succession of tenants. However, M&B's long-term policy for the site was disposal. They already owned the *Bull's Head* next door and wished to transfer the *Saracen's Head* licence to other premises in Cotteridge, so in 1930 M&B presented the *Saracen's Head* and north range to the Parochial Church Council but retained for their own use the cottages to the south and the bowling green to the rear.[44]

The Parochial Church Council engaged architect Owen Parsons to advise them on the condition of their acquisition and how it might best serve the needs of the parish. His recommendations were to retain the north range, but to cut an entry through the *Saracen's Head* to a new parish hall at the back. This would have meant the loss of an integral part of the 1492 structure, although its architectural importance was not then apparent. Fortunately Parsons' scheme was put aside, and in the 1950s the deteriorating state of the *Saracen's Head*, especially the far end of the north range, became a matter for concern. A number of attempts were made to raise funds for repairs; the Ministry of Works and the Birmingham Civic Society were supportive but Birmingham City Council's Alderman Harold Watton, Chairman of the General Purposes Committee, set back the cause when he ill-advisedly stated that it was 'not as if it were a genuinely ancient building – like Aston Hall'.

In the 1960s the architect F.W.B. Charles, who specialised in the care and repair of timber-framed buildings, showed the PCC the potential of their asset and a long period of restoration was undertaken between 1971 and 1989 under the supervision of architect A.B. Chatwin. It was clear that further work would be needed to the east range fronting The Green, and further deterioration meant that substantial resources would be required if the building was to function in the life of the local community. The opportunity came in 2004 when the *Saracen's Head* (and Old Grammar School) were entered in BBC Two's *Restoration* series 2. Both buildings caught the popular imagination, being presented as 'chocolate box' black and white buildings in a sylvan setting, but in need of rescue. By winning the television series the parish was eligible to make a detailed application to the Heritage Lottery Fund. Through this and via the funds provided by the TV series and the parish's own efforts nearly £4 million was raised, which enabled a major repairs and refurbishment programme to be completed

120 *The completion of the restoration of the* Saracen's Head *and* Old Grammar School, *June 2008. Left to right: Canon Rob Morris, Carole Souter, Chief Executive of the Heritage Lottery Fund, and Mark Thompson, Director General of the BBC, who officially opened the restored buildings.*

121 *The Old Grammar School under repair April 2007 provided the opportunity for close examination of exposed roof structure and a reassessment of the building's development.*

between 2006-8 under the supervision of APEC architects. The work involved the replacement of the late 19th-century south wing with a new block fronting the south and west sides of the courtyard, the overhaul of the timber frame and the provision of modern facilities. As a result the parish has been able to concentrate its activities at the *Saracen's Head* site, which has been renamed St Nicolas Place, and St Nicolas Hall in Westhill Road is to be sold.

The Old Grammar School

The 1891 restoration of the Old Grammar School was followed by more work in 1909-10. A lot of the external frame was replaced – new timbers are identifiable by the Roman numerals MCMX – and the covered stairs, which had been built against the west gable, were replaced by an external stone staircase.

In 1912 the Charity Commissioners authorised the sale of the school. Its purchaser, Theodore Pritchett, immediately presented it to the parish. During the Suffragette campaign it was targeted for destruction by arsonists. In the trial of the movement's leader, Emmeline Pankhurst, at the Old Bailey at the beginning of April 1913 the judge accused her of 'a shameful want of decorum'. Within a matter of days her incensed supporters torched public buildings across the country, including railway stations and sports pavilions, and caused damage to art galleries and museums. The Old Grammar School was broken into by night, and the next day the caretaker found the following inscription written on a blackboard: 'Two Suffragists have entered here, but charmed with this old-world room, have refrained from their design of destruction.'[45]

Further restoration work was undertaken in 1931 (architect Owen Parsons), 1951 and 1988 (architects P.B and A.B. Chatwin respectively). A complete overhaul was undertaken between 2006-7 as part of the implementation of the BBC Two *Restoration* works supported by the Heritage Lottery Fund. Extensive repairs were made to the frame and stonework together with the renewal of services.

CHURCH AND RELIGION

In 1905, when King's Norton was transferred from Worcester to the new diocese of Birmingham, the change anticipated the secular reorganisation of local government six years later. With the population continuing to grow, new churches were established as missions from St Nicolas. Their movement towards independence reflected the spread of the urban area southwards. The Church of the Ascension at Stirchley secured parish status in 1912 and St Agnes, Cotteridge, which had started as a mission in 1898, was rebuilt in 1903 and became a parish in 1916. Under Edward Ashford's ministry from 1949 to 1965 the mission churches at Brandwood (St Bede's) 1963, Longbridge (St John's) 1957 and West Heath (St Anne's) 1966 became separate parishes with new buildings to serve new residential areas.

In the inter-war period successive rectors tried hard to encourage new residents to become regular worshippers. The acquisition of the *Saracen's Head* in 1930 undoubtedly helped by providing much needed space for meetings, and a large number of organisations, from Christian groups, scouts and guides to a Dramatic Society, met there. To relieve the pressure on the building, St Nicolas Hall in Westhill Road was completed in 1960.

However good the facilities near St Nicolas church, the Church was still faced with the challenge of reaching residents on the new estates. In 1976 a new church and Aided Church School at Shannon Road, Hawkesley, was opened in partnership with the King's Norton Methodist Church. Immanuel church in Wychall Lane served people living around the Fairway and Chaddesley estate, the old golf course. At Druid's Heath and on Pool Farm, worship and mission were based at the community centres of Manningford Hall and Greaves Hall.

The clergy strove to serve the spiritual life of the community, but they could not neglect the physical state of the historic buildings in their care. By the late 1940s St Nicolas church was again causing concern and in 1953 a coronation year appeal raised funds to undertake further restoration. A few years earlier some of the Victorian installations, like the heavy reredos and brass communion rails, had been removed and the south aisle chapel was set up as a Lady Chapel for regular worship. The Victorian rectory was demolished in 1970 and a new one built to the east of the old site. Part of the grounds was used for building the St Nicolas Gardens housing development.

THE BATTLE FOR CONSERVATION BEYOND THE GREEN

If the protection provided by designated Conservation Area status arrived too late to preserve the real character of King's Norton's Green, it might be assumed that isolated historic but redundant farmsteads would be even more vulnerable. It is true there were losses in the 20th century of many buildings that today would be regarded as worth saving, such as medieval Wychall Farm, 16th-century Moundsley Hall and 17th-century Masshouse Farm. But two local buildings, both owned by the city, Primrose Hill Farm and Bell's Farm, epitomise the conservation battle fought through the 1970s at a time when public opinion was changing in favour of preservation.

Listed building legislation, which originated under the Town & Country Planning Act of 1947, theoretically gave protection, yet the official lists are not infallible and rely on expert revision or correspondents pointing out errors or omissions. Possibly because of its isolated position, Primrose Hill Farm had escaped listing. It was drawn to the attention of the Department of the Environment in 1972, just when its role as a working farm was coming to an end, but once the Edmonds family vacated the house vandals ransacked it and its future was in doubt. Even after a developer came forward to rescue the building, the site was far from safe. All the traditional farm buildings except the barn, and all within the curtilage, were demolished illegally. The developer disappeared and the site was again exposed to vandals. Fortunately one of the staff in the City Planning Department, Chris Pancheri, made a substantial contribution to saving the building by managing a Manpower Services Scheme which repaired the house. The buildings were subsequently sold to a private owner, who completed their restoration and started a garden centre. Financial difficulties

122   *The restoration of Primrose Hill Farm and Barn in 2008-9 brought to an end a long period of uncertainty about the future of these nationally important listed buildings. They have now found imaginative new use as part of a care village for people with special needs.*

123   *Bell's Farm after its first major fire in 1977. (Restoration followed despite another fire in 1980. For a view of the house after restoration see Fig. 39.)*

led to his disappearance and the house was sold by the mortgagees. It remained unoccupied and, after many years of neglect, was acquired in 2006 by Care through the Millennium (CTTM). The company have spent three years and £5 million restoring the house and barn, and building seven detached dwellings around the edge of the site that can house 39 people with specialised care needs. The farmhouse is used as offices and the barn will be used as a day centre and training facility.

The last tenant of Bell's Farm moved out in 1976 and vandalism and two major arson attacks followed in 1977 and 1980. Birmingham Museums' field officer, Nicholas Molyneux, carefully recorded the building and worked hard to demonstrate its architectural and historic interest to local authority colleagues. By 1978 the Walker's Heath & District Residents Association had begun to take an interest in the fate of the farmhouse and submitted a 1,200-signature petition to the city council. Chris Pancheri of the City Planning Department again became involved with a Manpower Services Scheme. The front part of the house was ultimately restored and a new meetings hall built to one side on the site of the dovecote. The quality of restoration, as well as the achievement of rescuing the house, so impressed the judges of the Jackson-Stops & Staff/*Sunday Times* Country House Award in 1988 that Bell's Farm won the top national award. The Bell's Farm Community Association leases the building from the city and a lively programme of activities and events takes place there. The rear wing is unrestored and in a parlous state, which means the farmhouse remains on English Heritage's Buildings at Risk register.

THE TWO WORLD WARS

The First World War

The youths and men of King's Norton who patriotically joined up shortly after the declaration of war in August 1914 were in the main recruited by the Royal Warwickshire Regiment. A significant number, however, joined the Worcesters, reflecting the area's old ties with that county. Analysis of service records of the people listed on the lych-gate demonstrates that many of them perished in the protracted Battle of the Somme, an Allied offensive on the Western Front in 1916. They are buried in the major cemeteries at Dernancourt, Thiepval and elsewhere in France. The war touched many families. Mr and Mrs J. Farndon of Camp Lane lost their 21-year old son, serving in the 16th Battalion Royal Warwickshire Regiment, on the Somme, while a few doors away Agnes Cogbill was widowed in April 1918 when her husband George, who had joined the 3rd Battalion Worcestershire Regiment, was killed in action in France. The 18-year-old son of the miller Walter Jones and his wife Annie, of Middleton Hall Road, died while serving as a cadet in the Royal Air Force, and at Moundsley Hall, Lieutenant Commander Arthur Lane, a son of the squire, Charles Pelham Lane, died serving on HMS *Assistance*. The following letter, which was found on the body of 20-year-old Corporal Joseph Lowe of the Royal Fusiliers, killed on 25 October 1916 during the Battle of the Somme, embodies the pathos of the First World War and its impact on local families:

In the event of my death, please forward the following to Mrs B. Lowe, 16 Baldwin Road, King's Norton: 'My dearest Ma, Pa, Emily, and Leslie, – again I am called upon as a true soldier of dear England to advance and attack the enemy. I pray that Almighty God may protect me and save me from all harm. Up to the present He has been very kind and He alone knows how little I deserve His protection. Dear folk at home, my heart burns with the pride of a soldier. I am trusting in our Heavenly Father to help me to play the man in this next engagement. I hope that some day we may all meet in Heaven. Best love to all from your loving son, JOE.

Wounded servicemen were treated at Monyhull Colony, where some of the accommodation blocks, which were nearing completion at the start of the war, were converted to a military hospital. Belgian refugees were accommodated at Broad Meadow House and the King's Norton Metal Company turned to munitions production.

The lych-gate to St Nicolas churchyard was erected in 1922 to commemorate the 37 servicemen who gave their lives during the First World War. It was re-dedicated after the Second World War when the names of another 39 men were added.

124 *Lych-gate memorials to local men who gave their lives in the First and Second World Wars.*

The Second World War

For the first years of the war the threat of air attack dominated the life of King's Norton people. Birmingham, as a centre of munitions production, was a key target for German bombers and between August 1940 and April 1942 the city suffered 77 raids by the Luftwaffe. The city centre and armament works in the inner and middle rings took the brunt of the bombings and as an outer suburb King's Norton appeared to contemporaries relatively safe. However, its proximity to the Austin aero factories at Longbridge and Cofton Hackett, the Rea valley factories between Wychall and Lifford, as well as the wartime production at Bournville, made it vulnerable. The official bombing maps record major damage from high explosives and incendiaries in the vicinity of King's Norton village on four occasions. The first, on the night of 28-9 August 1940, destroyed houses in Lindsworth Road, a second, a daytime raid on 4 November the same year, devastated parts of Wychall Lane, while a third, in the early morning of 27 July 1942, caused destruction in Beaks Hill Road, Rednal Road and Grange Hill Road. In another raid on 28 November 1940 three air-raid wardens were killed on duty at the Monyhull Colony and their names are recorded in what is now known as Monyhull church. Personal accounts tell us a lot more about the dangers and difficulties of living through the Blitz. Older residents' stories of

125 *Bomb damage at the corner of Broad Meadow Road and Lindsworth Road following the air raid of 30 August 1940.*

wartime life in the Cotteridge area covered such topics as evacuation, the destruction of Grants' timber yard in Francis Road, and the low-flying German pilot who, in a daytime raid, is said to have shot at workers leaving the GKN factory.

Air-raid wardens patrolled residential neighbourhoods to ensure the effectiveness of the 'black-out', while special arrangements were made to guard premises left empty at night. A fire-watching team at King's Norton Factory Centre[46] was funded by subscriptions from 10 of the firms there, two men and their reliefs being employed to protect the factories. Their equipment – a stirrup pump, shovels, water buckets, ladders, tin hats, boots, overalls and torches – sounds inadequate today, but their presence was effective and ensured that any fires started by incendiaries could be extinguished immediately.

As part of the defence of Birmingham and the Black Country, 100 heavy anti-aircraft (HAA) guns were positioned around the edge of the city. One site was at Kingswood Farm and the bases for the four guns and the radar plinth of the HAA battery are still visible and part of the archaeology of the Second World War.[47]

TRADE AND INDUSTRY

Industry expanded considerably in the 20th century but was largely confined to the valley of the river Rea. Two of the mill sites, Lifford and Wychall, continued to industrialise, but the manorial corn mill site at the corner of Camp Lane and Pershore Road South was eventually abandoned. Large-scale brickmaking was introduced, working a clay pit on the south side of Parson's Hill. Because the development of King's Norton took place mostly during the 20th century, the area did not suffer to any great degree from the inconvenient and unsightly mixture of industry and housing that characterised other parts of the city in earlier periods. In the late 20th century, however, with the national decline of industry and economic recession, several important factories in King's Norton closed.

The Lifford Mill Area
During the first decade of the 20th century Lifford Mill appears to have stood empty. The Orford/Capon connection with Lifford ceased in 1910 when the family sold the estate to George Griffin.[48] He quickly found tenants, for in 1912 a small-time car manufacturer called the Hampton Engineering Company moved into the premises.[49] They made motor cycles, cycle cars and in early 1914 started production of a light car, the Hampton Torpedo, selling at £295. When war was declared in August 1914 production ceased, the workers dismissed on the understanding that hostilities would be temporary. They made perhaps fifty vehicles at Lifford with a workforce of two dozen before shutting permanently; the war did not finish, as hoped, by Christmas 1914. In 1920 the mill was occupied by Fred K. Mountford, a firm of mechanical engineers, and in 1927 by wireless manufacturers and steam insulating engineers.[50] It is not certain when the mill buildings were permanently abandoned but by 1945 they were described as 'old and derelict'.[51] Sturges purchased the site in 1948

126   *Lifford Mill II in the early 1920s with the roof of the original mill building visible at the rear, adjacent to the mill pond; it still contained a redundant water wheel. Lifford reservoir is to the left.*

and in the early '50s demolished that part of the mill that contained the wheel, then still surviving. The buildings on the Tunnel Lane frontage survived a little longer, but by the 1970s only a single wall survived.

The Griffin family of Lifford Hall ran a tea and refreshment rooms on Lifford reservoir and hired out boats to weekend visitors from Birmingham. George Griffin's daughter, Ann, married Samuel Harris, whose son Samuel sold the Lifford estate to Sturges in 1948. The Hall was restored, extended and converted by the chemical company into a workers' canteen and recreation rooms. In 1985 Sturges sold the Hall and immediate grounds and three years later these came into the hands of Pridie Langard, a firm of accountants, who constructed a new block of offices to the east and restored the Hall. Langard are the present owners.

At the time that Lifford Mill was declining as an industrial site, other factories were being constructed in the vicinity. In 1899 the chemical company J. & E. Sturge, established a new factory on Tunnel Lane between Lifford Lane and the canal for the production of precipitated calcium carbonate (PCC). Sturges main works were at Wheeleys Lane, Edgbaston. The site had been a field belonging to Redhouse Farm. The principal products of the firm had been citric acid and Rochelle Salts, but the demand for calcium carbonate had recently risen as an ingredient in compounds for cleaning teeth (dentifrice) as a result of the popularity of tobacco smoking. Production of PCC increased substantially and the works at Lifford expanded accordingly. The buildings gradually spread closer to Lifford Hall on an artificial made-up terrace. Production eventually ceased at the Wheeleys Lane site in the late 1940s and a new plant for making citric acid was established at Selby in Yorkshire. The Lifford site concentrated on PCC, which found a wide variety of uses beyond toothpaste. Sturges was taken over by RTZ Chemicals and in 1990 by Rhone-Poulenc. In 1990-1 a limekiln was constructed in what remained of the mill pool and, as part of the planning permission for the striking tall structure, the site of Lifford Mill II was excavated archaeologically in May 1989 at the expense of the company. In 1998 the chemical division of Rhone-Poulenc was separated to form Rhodia Ltd and immediately the Lifford plant was sold to Mineral Technologies Inc, an American firm which owns the business today. Their products are used in sealants, inks, plastics, foods, pharmaceuticals, rubber and paper. Many of us have brushed our teeth and swallowed pills containing the white powder produced at Lifford.

In the mid-1920s, on the north side of Tunnel Lane and opposite Lifford Hall, a factory producing brass hinges was constructed by a firm called the Worcester Brass Company Ltd. By the early 1990s they were known as Worcester Parsons, still

127 *The Sturges chemical works from the air in the early 1920s – a modestly sized factory compared to today. The present limekiln is situated in the former mill pool visible at the top, beyond which lies Lifford Mill II. Lifford Reservoir is top right.*

producing hinges made from brass, but also using aluminium, mild and stainless steel. In 1998 they were taken over by Basta to form Basta Parsons, but the Lifford factory site was soon closed down, the operations being moved elsewhere. By 2004 part of the site was being used for 'waste transfer' and at the present time skips are delivered to the site and the contents sorted.

Sherborne Paper Mill and Patrick Motors Group

During the First World War J. Baldwin and Sons produced paper and cardboard boxes for ammunition, much of their work in the previous half-century having been government contracts.[52] The number of workers changed very little during the war, although 36 joined the armed forces. In July 1918 there were 114 employees, 96 men and 18 women, the latter figure being lower than in previous years. Women were traditionally employed in picking the raw material and in sorting the finished paper. A government inspector in 1918 noted that there was a reluctance to use women in other duties. The normal working hours were 58 hours per week and 52.5 hours on the night shift, excessive by today's standards and noted at the time as needing reduction. The production per week amounted to 10-15 tons of box board and 60 tons of brown wrapping paper. There were two paper making machines, but one was idle due to lack of raw materials and labour.

The site ceased to be actively used as a paper mill in the mid-1960s and was purchased by Patrick Motors Ltd, primarily to store and prepare new cars for delivery to customers. In the mid-1970s Patrick Motors built new office accommodation and moved their headquarters to the site. In 1982 a purpose-built museum was created which operated until 1994 when the exhibits were gradually sold off. The remainder of the Patrick Collection (as it is now known) can be viewed by appointment. By the late 1990s the Patrick Motors Group had ceased all motor vehicle trading and became PMG Investments Limited, responsible for letting and managing its commercial property, the main holding being the paper mill site. The site is currently occupied by a variety of businesses, including a gymnasium, a nightclub and two blue chip companies, and is known as The Lakeside Centre.[53]

The King's Norton Metal Company and the King's Norton Factory Centre

The factory of the King's Norton Metal Company, which had been established in 1889, was the largest in King's Norton at the time. It also represented the first stage in the development of what was to become the most extensive industrial estate in the area, stretching from Lifford Lane to Pershore Road South. Rolling mills powered by steam engines had been constructed in 1890 and 1900 to produce the copper and brass strip needed for the cartridges manufactured in the plant. A third rolling mill was laid down in 1914 in anticipation of war breaking out. During the First World War about two thousand workers were employed in the King's Norton works.[54]

The ability to make metal strip in copper and bronze and other copper-based alloys led to the establishment of a mint in 1911 and the following year bronze blanks for pennies, halfpennies and farthings were produced. In 1918 and 1919 some five million British pennies were coined for the Royal Mint and these can still be identified by the letters 'KN' next to the date. In 1918 the King's Norton Metal Co. was absorbed into Explosive Trades Ltd, changing its name quickly to Nobel Industries Ltd. At the same time the latter also formed a great new combine with the ammunition makers Kynochs of Witton.[55] In 1926 Nobel Industries in turn became part of Imperial Chemical Industries and in 1930 the minting plant and cartridge making presses were transferred to the Witton works. Part of a poem written in 1928 reflects the devastating effect this had on the local workforce:

> Still full of energy, vigour and tang,
> Ready for anything – tell us before we close
> Who has a job for the King's Norton Gang?

The abandonment of the King's Norton site by ICI led to its sale in 1931 to Slough Estates Ltd. In 1920 the latter had acquired a 600 acre site in Slough and developed it as one of the earliest industrial estates, with light industry renting buildings that could be easily extended and adapted. Slough Estates purchased 55 acres at King's Norton and began to develop the site by adapting the ICI building and constructing new units to the west. By 1938 Melchett Road had been laid out from Pershore Road South, almost opposite King's Norton Mill, and provided the principal access onto the estate. Much of this land had belonged to High House, the medieval Millwards, and the house itself had somehow managed to survive. It disappeared after the war but the avenue of lime trees marks the old entry from the Pershore Road.

The Second World War temporarily revived the King's Norton Metal Company site, supporting ICI's war effort. The 1914 rolling mill was reconditioned to produce aluminium alloy sheet for aircraft and, later, micro-pore filters were designed and manufactured to separate the active isotope 235 from uranium metal. These were used in the first atomic bomb and subsequently in nuclear power stations across the world. In the early 1950s the Birmingham Factory Centre, as it was then called, contained about fifty-five firms employing 3-4,000 workers, and by 1965 these figures had increased to over seventy and 4,500-5,000 respectively.[56] Slough Estates, SEGRO plc from 2007, is one of the largest industrial investment companies in the UK and its local estate, part of a considerably larger property holding, now trades as the King's Norton Business Centre.[57] In 2007 the estate contained about eighty companies in about 180,000 square feet of accommodation, varying between offices, production space and warehousing. Considerable investment has been necessary to update and construct new buildings to meet the exacting demands of commercial operations in the early 21st century.[58]

King's Norton Mill

As the industrial estate on the opposite side of the road grew steadily during the 20th century, King's Norton Mill went into terminal decline from the height of its productive capacity at the beginning of the century. Aaron Jones, who had built himself a house (now a restaurant) below the mill around 1892, died in 1912 and is buried in the cemetery below St Nicolas church.[59] It is not certain how long the machinery that Aaron Jones had installed to grind American wheat lasted. In the late 1890s a 16ft 3in diameter water wheel had been installed, perhaps replacing the turbine.[60] In 1927 Thomas Priest and Son are recorded at the mill for the first time, and William Priest took over in about 1934. The Priests ground only animal feed and it is possible that the wheat rollers had been replaced with more conventional pairs of grinding stones. In 1940 the Public Work Committee agreed to purchase some of the site and, more importantly, his water rights, in order to carry out road and river improvements. This transaction effectively brought milling operations on this site to an end after at least 600 years of more or less continuous use.[61] Photographs taken in about 1940 show William Priest standing by three conventional pairs of stones in timber casing and oiling the gear wheels on the floor below. Under the agreement William Priest was to keep the mill, mill pool and house, but it is not certain when

128 *William Priest, the last miller of King's Norton mill, c.1940, manhandling sacks of flour on the 'stone' floor shortly before the mill's closure. The pairs of grinding stones are enclosed in the barrel-like boxes to the left.*

he sold or left this property. In 1950 seven separate firms occupied the mill, the machinery presumably having been removed.[62] In the 1960s a petrol station was built into part of the mill pool and the rest drained, but the mill was still standing when plans were drawn up in 1972 to demolish it to make way for a 116-bed hotel.[63] The hotel was never built, but the upper part of the mill was dismantled, leaving just the ground floor and an Aaron Jones lean-to still standing. Sometime in the late 1980s the ground floor was removed, the basement filled in and the site incorporated into the garage forecourt. The lean-to has managed to survive and behind it, within the low concrete shed, original mill fabric can still be seen.

Wychall Mill

Although the site of Wychall Mill is now vacant, industry was attracted to a site to the north, which now forms the second largest industrial area in King's Norton. Wychall Mill continued to be used for rolling metal and Charles Ellis and Sons occupied the premises until immediately after the Second World War. In 1920 it was noted that brass, copper and nickel ingots an inch thick were rolled into sheets as thin as paper.[64] The mill was sold in 1946 to Burman and Son, an engineering firm making gearboxes and steering gear. It contained a horizontal steam engine by the Birmingham firm of Mountain, two more ancient beam engines coupled together, now in Millennium Point, two boilers and a water wheel.[65] A photographic survey taken in 1949-50 shows the extent and condition of the buildings, including the position of the water wheel within a timber compartment. Burmans purchased the site in order to demolish the mill and replace it with a new factory, but in the late '40s, at a time of material shortages, this was regarded as low priority and it was not until the autumn of 1947 that work commenced on the new works; they were ready for machinery in the summer of 1950.[66] The mill buildings were not demolished, but were refurbished and used as a store; it was not until the 1970s that they were brought down and the site cleared. Burmans have been closed down in turn and the site cleared (about 1991). In 1998 archaeological evaluation trenches were dug on the site of the mill in anticipation of a planning application to develop the site, but most of the Burmans land still lies vacant.[67] A new industrial road with units has been constructed, which ends near the mill site. Beyond it (west) within the dam of Wychall reservoir can be seen the bricked-up inlet to the mill, the remains of a sluice gate and a now dry spillway. The reservoir, which should not be confused with the significantly smaller mill pool that lay outside its north-eastern corner, has little water in it and forms an important nature reserve.

In 1919 Frank E. Baker, an engine builder from Aston, obtained financial backing from the large Glasgow shipbuilders, William Beardmore, to produce the Beardmore Precision motorcycle.[68] Baker had already set up the Precision Works by 1916 on a green field site between Wychall Rolling Mill and Wychall House and the railway. Road access was from the corner of Camp Lane and Westhill Road. Beardmore shipbuilding ran into serious financial difficulties and the motorcycle works failed by 1924-5. In 1928 Triplex took over the former Precision Works to manufacture safety glass for the Austin Motor Company, which had agreed to standardise its Triplex windscreens. Triplex needed capital for the venture and sought this with Pilkingtons. In 1929 the firms formed a joint company and built a works at Eccleston in St Helens. Safety glass at this time was laminated, and Triplex developed toughened glass as a cheaper substitute. As the car and, to a lesser extent, aircraft industry grew nationally so did the Triplex Glass Works in King's Norton. By 1936 the factory had become the largest in the area. During the war the factory produced laminated glass for military vehicles and aircraft, but the main product was Perspex domes for aircraft. Expansion at King's Norton continued after the war and Eckersall Road was laid out to improve vehicular access. Pilkingtons gradually increased their financial holding in Triplex until it was the major shareholder in 1965. Today the King's Norton site forms part of Pilkingtons Automotive and the factory remains the biggest in the area, the office block competing with the spire of St Nicolas as the tallest building. There has been an independent expansion southwards towards the former Burmans site with new industrial units called Catesby Park.

Guest, Keen and Nettlefolds Ltd (GKN)

In the last decade of the 19th century, before Nettlefolds was absorbed by GKN, considerable expansion had taken place, almost doubling its size. More buildings were added after the First World War on the triangular site constricted by the recreation ground, extending the main factory on the south side and into the north-east corner, including a canteen.[69] The factory, operating roughly within the confines of buildings completed by 1925, finally closed in 1982, when the country was suffering from a deep recession and the GKN workforce was cut drastically. It has been converted into industrial units, using part of the old buildings, Magnet and Do-It-All being erected on the former recreation ground.

Brick Works, Parson's Hill

Around the turn of the 20th century a brick and tile works was established by Hough & Co. on the south side of Ardath Road and beside the Worcester & Birmingham Canal for ease of transport of the finished product.[70] The main building was located at the south end of Cyril Road in a short terrace of houses. A clay pit was opened immediately to the east of the works into part of a field used for allotment gardens; by 1916 the clay pit had expanded to occupy most of this field. The continuing demand for brick and tile between the wars led to the expansion of the buildings and claypits southwards. The two tall chimneys marked the site from afar and were apparently used as navigation aids for Luftwaffe aircraft heading for the Austin Motor Works. After the war the works were owned by the Atkins brothers and a larger clay extraction area was opened to the south and east. The works finally closed in 1958, the clay pits were levelled and industrial units constructed on new roads laid out around the perimeter of the site (Ardath Road and Facet Road). The clay pit area still forms a large open space used as a car park.

129 *Perspective view of King's Norton Brick Company (1916), looking south from Cyril Road with the Worcester & Birmingham Canal to the right and the clay pit to the left. The brick furnace stands closest to the canal, while the clay preparation sheds lie on the other side of the chimney.*

ENVOI

King's Norton in the 21st Century

It is not normal to make predictions in a work of history, as it is hard enough to write an accurate account of the past, without simplification and omission or the unavoidable bias of personal interest and understanding. The documentation on King's Norton that we have consulted over the years is copious and we are acutely aware of how much potential still rests in our research notes and files. Some of this we hope will be published in due course.

It is quite clear that the 20th century witnessed the greatest changes to take place in King's Norton in any single century. An attractive rural landscape has disappeared under houses, factories and roads, but life for the majority of rural King's Nortonians in the preceding centuries had been relentlessly hard and often of short duration, owing to disease and famine and disproportionately frequent acts of violence. The people of King's Norton are undoubtedly wealthier and healthier than they have ever been and enjoy a standard of living that was unimaginable for their rural predecessors. This is not to say that poverty has been eliminated, for, judged by the standards of today, there are stubborn pockets of social and economic deprivation rooted only a short distance from the village Green.

The advance of the city was halted in the 1980s and Green Belt policies have protected the remainder of the ancient parish of King's Norton, though proposals to cover Wythall in bricks and mortar were a relatively recent political ambition. It would be foolish to predict that Wythall will remain rural throughout the 21st century, but we can hope that this landscape survives to remind us of the former appearance of the rest of 'King's Norton under Birmingham'.

This book may serve as a history of the area for a while to come, but it cannot do so indefinitely. At some point we would expect the next generation of historians to take over and develop their insights on this fascinating area. Let us hope they find our history useful.

Abbreviations and Notes

ABG	*Aris's Birmingham Gazette*
BAH	Birmingham Archives and Heritage Service, Birmingham Central Library
BUFAU	Birmingham University Field Archaeology Unit (now Birmingham Archaeology)
BWB	British Waterways Archives, Gloucester
M&B	Mitchells & Butlers Ltd (Brewers/archive)
StratfordRO	Shakespeare Centre and Library, Stratford upon Avon, Warwickshire
TBWAS	*Transactions of the Birmingham and Warwickshire Archaeological Society*
TNA	The National Archives, Kew (formerly the Public Record Office)
TWAS	*Transactions of the Worcestershire Archaeological Society*
VCH Warwicks	*The Victoria History of the Counties of England. A History of the County of Warwick*
VCH Worcs	*The Victoria History of the Counties of England. A History of the County of Worcester*
WarksRo	Warwickshire County Record Office, Warwick
WCL	Worcester Cathedral Library
WHS	*Worcestershire Historical Society*
WRO	Worcestershire Record Office, Worcester

Introduction

1. J. Noake *The Rambler in Worcestershire* (1854) 282-96

2. *ABG* 4 June 1838

3. *The Gentleman's Magazine* vol. LXXVI Part I (1807) 201

4. W.S. Brassington 'Some Account of the Royal Manor of King's Norton, Worcestershire' *Associated Architectural Societies Reports and Papers* 20 part 2 (1890) 332-42; W.S. Brassington 'On the Church of King's Norton' *Associated Architectural Societies Reports and Papers* 21 (1891) 97-118; J.R. Holliday 'The Church and Grammar School of King's Norton' *TBWAS* 3 (1872) 44-62

5. VCH 3 1913, 179-91; H.M. Grant and E.A.B. Barnard 'The Parish and Church of Kingsnorton: being some record of recent documentary researches' *TWAS* New Series 2 (1924–5) 123-45

6. Arthur B. Lock *The History of King's Norton and Northfield Wards* [1925]

7. Charles Parish's series of articles in *The Redditch Indicator* between June–July 1951; J.E.Vaughan 'The Former Grammar School of King's Norton' *TWAS* 37 (1960) 27-36; J. E. Vaughan *Some account of the Parish Church and Ancient Grammar School of King's Norton* (1960 and subsequent editions)

8. A.F.C. Baber (ed.) 'The Court Rolls of the Manor of Bromsgrove and King's Norton' *WHS* (1963)

9. Stephen Price and Richard Langhorne *North Worcestershire Development Hawkesley and Walker's Heath Interim Report on the Archaeological Implications of Development: A field survey undertaken by the Birmingham and Warwickshire Archaeological Society* (1974); [Stephen Price] *King's Norton Trail* (Birmingham City Planning Department and City Museums and Art Gallery, 1983); George Demidowicz 'Rea Valley, Birmingham Archaeological and Landscape survey' *West Midlands Archaeology* 25 (1982)

10. Helen Goodger *King's Norton* (1990)

11. Pauline Caswell *The Archive Photographs Series King's Norton* (1997); Wendy Pearson *King's Norton Past and Present* (2004)

12. Price and Langhorne (1974) *op. cit.* n.9; Demidowicz (1982) *op. cit.* n.9, 85-7; Hugh R. Hannaford *Lifford Mill, King's Norton An Archaeological Evaluation* and *Excavations at Lifford Mill, King's Norton* Birmingham University Field Archaeology Unit (1989); Steve Litherland *An Archaeological Evaluation near Lifford Hall, King's Norton, Birmingham* BUFAU (1990); A.E. Jones *Lifford, Birmingham, An Archaeological Evaluation* BUFAU (1991)

I *Prehistoric, Roman and Anglo Saxon*

1. Some have claimed that Druids Heath takes its name from the Druids and the street names Stonehenge Road and a host of other Wiltshire names have added to the confusion. Druids Heath as a name is a creation of the 1960s, the first part taken from the older Druid's Lane and Farm. But that name derives from a Mr Drew who farmed here in the early 19th century.
2. Sites and Monuments Record, Department of Planning and Regeneration, Birmingham City Council
3. Michael Hodder *Birmingham: The Hidden History* (2004) 28-44
4. Larch S. Goddard 'Berry Mound, Solihull' *TBWAS* 75 (1959) 93-4; David Whitehead 'The Defences of Berry Mound' *TBWAS* 89 (1979-80), 162-3
5. Birmingham Sites and Monuments Record
6. Hodder (2004) *op. cit.* n.3, 64-68
7. Malcolm Hislop, pers. comm.
8. Della Hooke *Worcestershire Anglo-Saxon Charter Bounds* (1990) 59
9. George Demidowicz 'From river Cole to river Rea' *TBWAS* 95 (1987-8), 81-4
10. Margaret Gelling *Signposts to the Past* (1978) 126-8
11. Hooke (1990) *op. cit.* n.8, 58-61
12. G.B. Grundy 'Saxon charters of Worcestershire' *TBWAS* 53 (1928) 164
13. George Demidowicz 'The Lost Lint Brook. A solution to the *Hellerelege* Anglo-Saxon charter and other explorations of King's Norton history' *TBWAS* 107 (2003) 111-29
14. Della Hooke *The Anglo-Saxon landscape: The Kingdom of the Hwicce* (1985) 85-6; Hooke (1990) *op. cit.* n.8, 142

II *Medieval King's Norton*

1. Anne Baker 'A Study of north-eastern King's Norton: ancient settlement in a woodland manor' *TBWAS* 107 (2003) 141, Fig. 8
2. George Demidowicz 'The Lost Lint Brook. A solution to the *Hellerelege* Anglo-Saxon charter and other explorations of King's Norton history' *TBWAS* 107 (2003) 113
3. H.C. Darby *Domesday England* (1986 edition) 205-7; Demidowicz (2003) *op. cit.* n.2, 123-7, Fig. 5
4. Baker (2003) *op. cit.* n.1, 141
5. A. Mawer and F.M. Stenton *The Place-names of Worcestershire* (1927) 350
6. A.F.C. Baber 'The Court Rolls of the Manor of Bromsgrove and King's Norton 1494-1504', *WHS* (1963) 4
7. J.R. Holliday 'The Church and Grammar School of King's Norton' *TBWAS* 4 (1872), 46 and Plate 4
8. VCH Worcs 3, 179
9. VCH Worcs 3, 21-3
10. *Calendar of Patent Rolls, 1258-66*, 167
11. VCH Worcs 3, 23, 182
12. VCH Worcs, 2, 189
13. Stephen Price 'The Early History of Bordesley Abbey' unpublished MA thesis University of Birmingham (1971); Grenville Astill, Sue Hirst and Susan M.Wright 'The Bordesley Abbey Project Reviewed' *The Archaeological Journal*, 161 (2004) 106-58.
14. C.P.S. Platt *The Monastic Grange in Medieval England: A Reassessment* (1969)
15. John Amphlett (ed.) 'A Survey of Worcestershire by Thomas Habington, Vol. 2, pt 2' *WHS* (1897) 219
16. VCH Worcs 3, 31; Holliday (1872) *op. cit.* n.7, 44-5
17. Christopher Dyer 'Bromsgrove: A Small Town in Worcestershire in the Middle Ages', *WHS Occasional Publications* 9 (2000) 13; W. Salt Brassington, 'On the Church of King's Norton, Worcestershire' *Associated Architectural Societies Reports and Papers* 21 (1891), 106-10
18. R.R. Darlington (ed.) 'The Cartulary of Worcester Cathedral Priory (Register 1)' *Pipe Roll Society*, New Series, 38 (1968), 176-8
19. Brassington (1891) *op. cit.* n.17, 107
20. WCL D16
21. VCH Worcs 3, 31
22. Dyer (2000) *op. cit.* n.17, 13
23. WCL C548
24. WCL D324, Vol. A6i
25. WCL B161-162; Toni Demidowicz, 'Monyhull, King's Norton' *Birmingham Historian* 16 (1998) 9-12
26. Gloucester Record Office DR2700 NR 8/1
27. WCL C882
28. VCH Worcs 2, 378
29. W.P.W. Phillimore and W.F. Carter *Some Account of the Family of Middlemore* (1901) 170-1, 261; W.P.W. Phillimore (ed.) 'The Visitation of the County of Worcester 1569' *Harleian Society* 27 (1888) 9
30. *Calendar of Patent Rolls, 1429-36* 167; *1441-6* 384; *1452-61* 384; WRO ref. 009:1 BA2636 176 92493-4 Compotus Roll 1465-6
31. H.J. Jenkins, *Westbury College from 1194 to 1544 A.D.* (1917)
32. WRO ref. 009:1 BA2636 176 92493-4 Compotus Roll 1465-6 176/92493-4
33. *Valor Ecclesiasticus* Vol. II, 434-5
34. Baber (1963) *op. cit.* n.6, 5-6
35. TNA LR2/257
36. H.C. Darby and I.B. Terrett *The Domesday Geography of Midland England* (1954) 240, Fig. 80, 284, Fig. 97 King's Norton statistics under Warwickshire
37. Baker (2003) *op. cit.* n.1, 140
38. Christopher Dyer *Making A Living in the Middle Ages: The People of Britain 850-1520* (2003) 235 Fig. 2
39. J.W. Willis Bund and J. Amphlett (eds) 'Lay Subsidy Roll for the County of Worcester circa 1280' *WHS* (1893) [corrected to 1275]; M. Jurkowski, C.L. Smith and D. Crook *Lay Taxes in England and Wales 1188-1688* (1998) 20-1
40. E.J. Eld (ed.) 'Lay Subsidy for the County of Worcester 1 Edward III [1327]' *WHS* (1895)
41. Michael A. Faraday (ed.) 'Worcestershire Taxes in the 1520s' *WHS* New series 19 (2003) 54-60

42. *Ibid.*, xxxi
43. Dyer (2003) *op. cit.* n.38, 235, Fig. 2
44. George Demidowicz, 'Ridge and Furrow at King's Norton and Northfield, Birmingham' *West Midlands Archaeology* 27 (1984) 117-21
45. WRO ref. 705:7 BA7335/154/1, /155/1A Terrier and Book of Plans of the estates of Bowater Vernon surveyed by John Dougharty Jnr.; Demidowicz (2003) *op. cit.* n.2, Fig. 2
46. BAH CP/KN/12/2/3-4 King's Norton Tithe Map, 1840
47. BAH Lord and Parker 12/2
48. Society of Antiquaries of London, Prattinton Collection, King's Norton, 44-7
49. BAH 292201
50. John Field *English Place Names* (1972); Baker (2003) *op. cit.* n.1, Fig. 9
51. BAH 252473, 206615
52. R.H. Hilton *A Medieval Society: the West Midlands at the end of the Thirteenth Century* (1966) 142 ; Christopher Dyer *An Age of Transition: Economy and Society in England in the Later Middle Ages* (2005) 60-1 and Fig. 2.3
53. TNA SC6/HenVIII/6468; WCL D619
54. TNA SC6/HenVIII/6461; BAH 297359
55. TNA LR2/257
56. BAH CP/KN/12/2/3-4 King's Norton Tithe Map 1840
57. Demidowicz (2003) *op. cit.* n.2, 123-7 and Table 5
58. William Hutton *An History of Birmingham* (1783) 176, 320
59. George Demidowicz and Stephen Price 'Wythall, Blackgrave Moat' *West Midlands Archaeology* 29 (1986) 12-13
60. Adrian Oswald 'Hawkesley Farm, Longbridge' *TBWAS* (1958) 76, 36-50
61. Alison Arnold and Robert Howard 'Primrose Hill House and Barn ... Tree-ring analysis of timbers' *English Heritage Research Department Report Series* 41 (2008)
62. BAH Edwards, Bigwood and Matthews Map 8, 1840
63. WCL 324
64. George Demidowicz 'From river Cole to river Rea, *TBWAS* 95 (1987-8) 81-95
65. WCL E2
66. WCL E30
67. WCL E51
68. WRO ref. b850: Bromsgrove St John the Baptist, BA821/48
69. WCL E92
70. WCL D619
71. Faraday (2003) *op. cit.* n.41, 54
72. Lucy Toulmin Smith *Leland's Itinerary in England and Wales* 2 (1964) 96
73. Christopher Dyer *Lords and Peasants in a Changing Society: The Estates of the Bishopric of Worcester 680-1540* (1980) Appendix 1, 384
74. M. Charles, M. Duncan and M. Hislop *Archaeological Investigations at the Saracen's Head, King's Norton, Birmingham Post Excavation Assessment* Birmingham Archaeology, Project no.

1609.01 (November 2007)
75. Laurence Jones and Stephanie Ratkai 'Excavations at No. 15, The Green, King's Norton, 1992' *TBWAS* 104 (2004), 101-21
76. John Amphlett 'A Midland Architect and his work in the fifteenth century' *TBWAS* 35 1909 (1910) 16-33; John Harvey *English Mediaeval Architects: A Biographical Dictionary down to 1550* (1987) 86
77. *Calendars of Entries in the Papal Registers relating to Great Britain and Ireland. Papal Letters* vol. VI 1404-15, 29
78. TNA C143/273/16, 18 Edw II. no 14 (Inquisition Ad Quod Damnum); Brassington (1891) *op. cit.* n.17, Appendix A
79. TNA E301/60/10
80. TNA E318/28/1607
81. Christopher Dyer 'The Archaeology of Medieval Small Towns' *Medieval Archaeology* 47 (2003) 99 and Fig. 6
82. Jones and Ratkai (2004) *op. cit.* n.75
83. Jean Vanes (ed.) 'The Ledger of John Smythe 1538-1550' *Bristol Record Society* 28 (1975)

III *Tudor and Stuart*

1. John Amphlett (ed.) 'A Survey of Worcestershire by Thomas Habington vol. II' *WHS* (1899), 218
2. Shropshire Archives SA11/851
3. TNA E322/26
4. *Letters and Papers Henry VIII* Vol. XIX (I) 278 (68)
5. Victor Belcher *et al. Sutton House A Tudor Courtier's House in Hackney* (2004)
6. *Calendar of Patent Rolls, 1 Edward VI* 143
7. *Letters and Papers Henry VIII*, Vol. XVII 71 (29)
8. WCL A7 (I), A20
9. TNA SC12/32/1 c1450 Rental; LR2 257 1554-5 Rental, Antony Norton de Bristowe
10. BAH MS 3602/145; 392313
11. TNA SC6/HenryVII/1205
12. TNA SC6/Henry VIII/6473
13. TNA E112/133/260; E134/JasI/Mich41
14. TNA LR2/257
15. TNA E134/22Jas1/Mich41
16. *Calendar of Patent Rolls 1566-1569, Elizabeth I*, 2281; TNA E315/243
17. Michael A. Faraday (ed.) 'Worcestershire Taxes in the 1520s' *WHS* New series 19 (2003) xxxi; TNA E301/20/10
18. TNA E179/260/5
19. Anne Whiteman (ed.) 'The Compton census of 1676: a critical edition' *British Academy: Records of Social and Economic History* New Series 10 (1986) 179
20. BAH EP412/1/1 Parish registers of St Nicolas, King's Norton, 1546-1791
21. Lucy Toulmin Smith (ed.) *The Itinerary of John Leland in or about the years 1535-1543 Parts IV and V 2* (1964) 96
22. BAH 252474
23. VCH Worcs 3 179
24. Thomas Cave and R.A. Wilson, 'The Parliamentary Survey of the Lands and Possessions of the Dean and Chapter of Worcester, made in or about the year 1649 ...'

WHS (1924); 1661 Survey

25. TNA E316/5/342

26. 2,007 acres, 1639 BAH 252474; 3,000 acres 1649 TNA Parliamentary Survey; 3,000 acres, 1650 TNA E320/v18; 1661 1,200 acres, SRO DR37/2/117/8 1661 survey

27. A.F.C. Baber 'The Court Rolls of the Manor of Bromsgrove and King's Norton' 1494-1504, *WHS* (1963); 1661 survey *op. cit.* n.26

28. BAH 206615

29. 1661 survey *op. cit.* n.26

30. BAH, Lord and Parker deeds MS 3882

31. 1661 survey *op. cit.* n.26

32. Henry Robinson *Certain proposals in order to the People's Freedom and Accommodation* (1652), cited by Joan Thirsk *The Rural Economy of England* (1984) 195

33. Alison Arnold and Robert Howard 'Primrose Hill House and Barn ... Tree-ring analysis of timbers' *English Heritage Research Department Report Series* 41 (2008)

34. TNA E179/260/5

35. The principal collections of wills and inventories for King's Norton are in WRO 008.7 BA3585 and in TNA PROB4 and PROB11

36. E.S. Sapcote 'Moundesley [*sic*] Hall, King's Norton' *TBWAS* 64 (1941-2) 118-19

37. Anon 'Transcript of a petition to the Queen of England asking for a licence to sell in the towns of Warwickshire, Worcestershire and Staffordshire' *Transactions of the Midland Record Society* 2 (1897-8) 33

38. TNA C66/2103 14 James I Part 14 No.13

39. TNA LR/76/90 Estreats of Court Rolls for King's Norton (1683 and 1685)

40. *Calendar of Patent Rolls, Phillip and Mary 3 and 4*, Part 1 (no 906)

41. TNA C54/533

42. TNA PROB11/67 Will of Henry Field of Weatheroak Hill, 18 November 1584

43. TNA SC6/HENVII/6460

44. TNA SC6/HenVII/6471; *Calendar of Patent Rolls Edward VI 1550-1553*, 112

45. TNA E117/9/20 Inventory of Church Goods County: Worcester, 1552

46. For the national context see Eamon Duffy *The Stripping of the Altars* (1992)

47. TNA STAC4/4/22

48. Whiteman (1986) *op. cit.* n.19, 179

49. WRO ref. 807 BA 2124 Churchwardens' presentments for King's Norton

50. George Demidowicz 'The Lost Lint Brook A solution to the *Hellerelege* Anglo-Saxon charter and other explorations of King's Norton history' *TBWAS* 107 (2003) 121-3

51. TNA E301/60/10

52. Warks RO CR1291/73

53. TNA E134/3Chas1/Mich24

54. [Thomas Hall] 'A briefe narrative of the life and death of Mr Thomas Hall late Pastor of King's Norton, with a transcript of his will, and a catalogue of books given to the library at Birmingham, and to the parish of King's Norton' [*c*.1662-64] in Dr Williams's Library, London (Baxter Treatises 9.293-9). Photostat in BAH, 467148

55. C.D. Gilbert in *Oxford Dictionary of National Biography*

56. Hall *op. cit.* n.54

57. F.A. Bates *Graves Memoirs of the Civil War compiled from 17th century Records* (1927)

58. TNA E304/7/V18

59. J.W. Willis Bund *The Civil War in Worcestershire 1642-1646 and the Scotch Invasion of 1651* (1905); Malcolm Atkin *The Civil War in Worcestershire* (1995)

60. Hall *op. cit.* n.54

61. William Hamper (ed.) *The Life, Diary, and Correspondence of Sir William Dugdale* (1827) 52

62. *Ibid.* footnote p.52

63. W.S. Brassington *Historic Worcestershire* (1894) 311

64. WRO ref. 008.7 BA3585 1643/94

65. Charles E. Long (ed.) 'Diary of the Marches of the Royal Army during the Great Civil War; kept by Richard Symons' *Camden Society* 74 (1859) 167

66. Demidowicz (2003) *op. cit.* n.50, 123

67. Hall *op. cit.* n.54

68. *Ibid.*

69. TNA E101/141/19

70. WRO ref. 899.77 BA8004/1/vi and BAH Z205

71. Stuart Davies 'A Seventeenth-century Building Dispute' *Worcestershire Archaeology and Local History Newsletter* 24 (1980) 12

72. WRO ref. 705:349 Pakington Collection 12946/478267 and 478256

73. BAH MS206/4

74. BAH 317003 John Cotton's Notes and Queries for Bromsgrove vol. 3, 1912

75. Private collection

76. BAH uncatalogued Taylor Collection, Court Rolls 1721-49

IV *Eighteenth-century King's Norton*

1. Stratford RO DR37/2 Box117/15-16

2. Howard Colvin *A Biographical Dictionary of British Architects 1600-1840* 76-78, 3rd edn (1995)

3. Stratford RO DR37/117/8; DR473/14, 16-17, 22, 23

4. Warks RO L5/182a&b

5. TNA CRES 34/200

6. R.B. Prosser 'King's Norton Church' *Birmingham Weekly Post* 1 August 1891

7. William Hutton, *An History of Birmingham* (1783) 276-7

8. W.S. Brassington, *Historic Worcestershire* (1894) 288-99

9. TNA PROB 31 436/91

10. William Hutton, *The Court of Requests* (1840) 57

11. BAH King's Norton Rural District Building Plan No. 678

12. Stephen Wildman, *The Birmingham School* (1990) 32-3

13. *ABG* 14 February 1757
14. We are indebted to Toni Demidowicz for sharing the results of her extensive research on Monyhull. For a summary see her article 'Monyhull Hall King's Norton' *Birmingham Historian* 16 (1998) 9-12
15. *ABG* January 1770
16. WRO ref: 704:192 BA 5589/95
17. *ABG* 5 March 1764
18. *ABG* 16 May 1768
19. *ABG* 9 October 1775
20. *ABG* 13 June 1774
21. *ABG* 16 February 1792
22. *ABG* 20 May 1794
23. Stephen Price and Richard Langhorne *North Worcestershire Development Hawkesley and Walker's Heath Interim Report on the Archaeological Implications of Development: A field survey undertaken by the Birmingham and Warwickshire Archaeological Society* (1974) 18-19
24. *General Evening Post* 16 April 1771; *ABG* 19 April 1773
25. Stratford RO DR37/117/14,16
26. M&B deeds (private collection)
27. WRO ref.008.7 BA3585 Inventory of Mary Colles, 28 January 1728
28. *ABG* 14 April 1764
29. BAH 297359
30. BAH EP412/1/1 Parish registers of St Nicolas, King's Norton, 18 January 1781
31. George Demidowicz 'The Lost Lint Brook. A solution to the *Hellerelege* Anglo-Saxon charter and other explorations of King's Norton history' *TBWAS* 107 (2003) 121-2
32. Chief Rents *c.*1770-1780, BAH uncatalogued Taylor 61; Rate Book 1782, BAH 378720
33. WRO ref. b705:128, BA1946/9
34. BAH 457114
35. BAH CP/KN/1/1, 1774 Enclosure Award preamble
36. *ABG* 23 March 1752; WRO ref. 008.7 Will of William Shaw of King's Norton, mercer.
37. *ABG* 6 March 1775
38. *ABG* 8 August 1776; 12 August 1777
39. WRO ref. 008.7 BA3585 Will and inventory of John Nickolles the elder of King's Norton, 3 August 1728
40. BAH 617940 A Chronological History of Moseley, Balsall Heath, King's Heath and King's Norton compiled by Henry J. Everson [1920-30] 3, 376
41. *ABG* 1 February 1772
42. *An Act for dividing and inclosing the Commons and Waste Lands within the Manor and Parish of Kingsnorton, in the County of Worcester* (1772) (WRO ref: 705:128 BA1188/8 (i))
43. Only some of the draft maps survive; BAH, Jewel Baillie 35/2, 3
44. *ABG* 17 September 1773
45. *ABG* 1 November 1773; 25 January 1774
46. *ABG* 14 July 1774
47. The enclosure award was transcribed and analysed by Frances Hopkins and girls from King's Norton Grammar School. We are grateful to Miss Hopkins for sharing the results of this work with us.
48. BAH, CP/KN/2/1
49. WRO ref.110 BA1 Quarter Sessions: packet 421/19 Examination of John Woodhouse 26 July 1765
50. BAH 364116 DV358
51. *House of Commons Parliamentary Papers: Abstract of Returns relative to the Expence [sic] and Maintenance of the Poor 1803-04* XIII 576-7
52. Society of Antiquaries: Prattinton Collection
53. Prosser (1891) *op. cit.* n.6
54. WRO BA9135/28 (v) 9 – transcript of Worcester Cathedral Library Muniments D667. Answer to Bishop Hurd's enquiry, 12 April 1782; Mary Ransome *The State of the Bishopric of Worcester 1782-1808* (WHS 1968) 61-2
55. *Ibid.*
56. WRO BA1 Ref: 110 Quarter Sessions 210/75-77
57. *Flying Post or The Post Master* (London) 13 September 1715
58. Everson [1920-30] *op. cit.* n.40, 4, 272
59. William Hutton *A Narrative of the Riots In Birmingham, July 14, 1791, particularly as they affected the author* (1798) incorporated within his autobiography *The Life of William Hutton, Stationer of Birmingham...* (1841 edn) 59
60. *ABG* 13 March 1792
61. *Berrow's Worcester Journal* 22 and 29 December 1796; 22 June 1797
62. *ABG* February 1757
63. BAH Jewel Baillie 83b/4
64. TNA PROB11/558
65. Abstract of Title, private collection
66. Court Roll 1739 BAH, Taylor uncatalogued; Abstract of Title, private collection
67. TNA C38/524
68. *Burke's Peerage* (1826) 349
69. BAH MS3782/12/85/141
70. BAH MS3782/12/85/4
71. BAH j273
72. BAH MS3147/3/888/40
73. BAH MS3147/5/6
74. BAH MS3147/3/888/41-3
75. BAH MS3147/5/107
76. J.R. Harris, *The Copper King* (2003) 165-6
77. 'A Plan of the Worcester and Birmingham Canal through the Parish of Kings Norton ... surveyed in the Year 1799 by Jno Hodgkinson', BWB Archives Gloucester
78. BAH MS3782/12/28/64
79. BAH Lee Crowder 180
80. WRO ref:110 BA1 Quarter Sessions 284/40 and 277/35
81. Alan White *The Worcester and Birmingham Canal: Chronicles of the Cut* (2005)
82. TNA RAIL 886/4
83. White (2005) *op. cit.* n.81, 46
84. *Berrow's Worcester Journal* 6 April 1797
85. Charles Hadfield, *The Canals of the East Midlands* (1966) 163-5

86. TNA RAIL 886/4
87. BAH MS3782/12/44/271

V *Nineteenth-century King's Norton*

1. TNA CRES 34/200
2. VCH Warwicks 7, 95, 109; VCH Worcs 3, 185
3. BAH Lee Crowder 238a-d
4. BAH 428566
5. BAH Uncatalogued Taylor collection – boxes
6. VCH Warwicks 7, 21
7. BAH MS 1452/2/25, E.A. Impey *Ancient and Modern* 10 (Northfield Survey Group n.d.)
8. VCH Warwicks 7, 21
9. By 1881 14 houses had appeared, 26 were built in the next decade and a further 29 by 1901
10. BAH King's Norton Rural Sanitary Authority Building Plans, 945
11. BAH King's Norton Rural Sanitary Authority Building Plans, 11
12. BAH MS 1452/2/24, E.A. Impey *Ancient and Modern* (Northfield Survey Group n.d.)
13. F.E. Hopkins *Cotteridge and its Churches before 1911* 3rd Paper issued by the King's Norton History Society (1986) 5, 9
14. VCH Warwicks 7, 159; BAH MS 1422
15. BAH CP/KN/12/2/1-4 Tithe Map (1840) for the Parish of King's Norton and Apportionment (1838); TNA IR18/11347 Report [by Thomas Hoskins] on the Agreement for the Commutation of the Tithes in the Parish of King's Norton in the County of Worcester, 26 October 1838.
16. Samuel Lewis *A Topographical Dictionary of England* Vol.3 (7th edn, 1849) 444
17. WRO ref. 705:136 BA 4419/1 Diaries of Richard Pountney; Val Lewis *Victorian Village Life as reflected in the diaries of Richard Pountney 1804 to 1891, Farmer, Parish Clerk, Schoolmaster* (2000).
18. John A. Bridges, *Idylls of a Lost Village* (1889); *Reminiscences of a Country Politician* (1906); *A Sportsman of Limited Income* (1910)
19. Bridges *Idylls of a Lost Village* (1889) 4–5
20. Birmingham City Council Deeds: packet 6251
21. BAH MS1446/6,19, 37, 46; VCH Warwicks 7, 390; Arthur B. Lock *The History of King's Norton and Northfield Wards* [1925] 127
22. *Birmingham Daily Gazette* 1 April 1867; BAH King's Norton Rate Books
23. TNA PROB11/1934; M&B deeds for *Saracen's Head*, now lost; 1841 Census; BAH King's Norton Rural Sanitary Authority Building Plan, 1031
24. Birmingham City Council deeds, packet no 21377; 1851 Census; 1838-40 Tithe Survey
25. Bridges *op. cit.* n.19 10-15
26. BAH 387475
27. BAH GP/KN/2/1/1 King's Norton Union Report: Board of Guardians Minutes, 1836-41
28. VCH Warwicks 7, 521
29. John Izon 'King's Norton 'Mop'' *Birmingham Post* 28 September 1956
30. Undated cutting in BAH 1038233 Notes on the History of King's Norton compiled by W. S. Brassington *c.*1880
31. TNA HO 45/9897/B18397
32. *Ibid.*
33. TNA HO129/393 Ecclesiastical Census of 1851, King's Norton Registration District
34. John Aitken (ed.) 'Census of Religious Worship, 1851: The Returns for Worcestershire' *WHS* New series 17 (2000) xvii
35. The remaining denominations in King's Norton were Baptists at Wythall and King's Heath, Methodists at Sparkbrook, Balsall Heath, Stirchley and Rubery, with a Countess of Huntingdon meeting at Rednal.
36. *Birmingham Weekly Post* 12 September 1903
37. BAH EP4/11/8/1
38. J.M.L. Aston *King's Norton in the Olden Time: A Lecture on the Antiquities of King's Norton, with notices of the History of the Parish School, the Royal School, and Old Families connected with the Parish* (1866)
39. J.R. Holliday 'On the Church and Grammar School of King's Norton' *TBWAS* 3 (1872) 52-56
40. Bridges (1889) *op. cit.* n.19 37
41. *The Reports of the Commissioners (commonly known as Lord Brougham's Commission), appointed in pursuance of various Acts of Parliament for enquiring concerning Charities in England and Wales, 1818-1837* (London, P. S. King, 1895) The County of Worcester 598
42. John Noake *The Rambler in Worcestershire* (1854) 293
43. *Schools Inquiry Commission* vol. XV 596
44. W.S. Brassington 'Thomas Hall, and the Old Library founded by him at King's Norton' *Library Chronicle* 5 (1888) 61-71
45. VCH Warwicks 7, 133
46. Stephen Price 'The Nailmakers' Workshops of Birmingham' *The Birmingham Historian* 2 (1988) 5-15.
47. BAH 179416; Birmingham City Council deeds, packet no 9267
48. BAH Jewel Baillie 83b/6, 7a, 8, 9a-b, 10-11; TNA RAIL 886/5
49. BWB, Gloucester 856/81, 81/867
50. BAH.MS275a/161
51. TNA PROB11/1734
52. *ABG*, 24 Dec 1827, 1 March 1828, 11 January 1830, 20 July 1835, 6 March 1843
53. BAH King's Norton Rate Books
54. BWB, Gloucester 168 /90; TNA PROB11/1734
55. WRO ref.b899:31 BA3762/8; BAH Notes and Queries R 144/4060
56. BAH MS275a/226a; *Bentley's Directory of Worcestershire* (n.d.) 53
57. *The Redditch Indicator*, 16 July 1965; there are no paper makers in King's Norton in 1851, but they appear in the 1861 census for the first time
58. VCH Warwicks 7, 133; White's *Directory* (1849); Census 1851
59. W.D. Curzon *The Manufacturing Industries of Worcestershire* (1881) 79-82
60. *ABG* 8 Aug 1808; BAH MS 28/52
61. BWB, Gloucester, 869/81, 870/81, 872/81

62. BWB, Gloucester, 861/81; BAH MS969
63. WRO ref.161/14, 142 BA338
64. BAH 511834
65. Birmingham Museums and Art Gallery Historic Buildings Files – Wychall
66. BAH MS1452 Northfield Survey Group, Vol. 8, letter from S. Shenstone Ellis
67. BAH Jewel Baillie 83b/4; TNA RAIL 886/6
68. BAH uncatalogued Taylor collection, Court Books; *Midland Counties Herald* 16 September 1852
69. BAH King's Norton Rate Books
70. BAH SC/1173; Lee Crowder 238c; uncatalogued Taylor collection, Court Books; VCH Warwicks 7, 108
71. Simmons Collection, Science Museum, London; 1871 Census; *The Miller* 7 July 1902
72. Birmingham Museums and Art Gallery Historic Building Files – King's Norton Mill, Summers correspondence
73. *The Miller* 1 April 1889
74. Bridges (1889) *op. cit.* n.19 89
75. *Dictionary of National Biography* Joseph Henry Nettlefold; Edgar Jones *A History of the GKN Vol. 1 1759-1918* (1987) 146-9
76. VCH Warwicks 7, 133, 155; Walter Showell *Dictionary of Birmingham* (1885, reprinted 1969) 323; BAH MS 298; MS 780
77. BAH MS 1407/2-6
78. 1st and 2nd editions of Ordnance Survey 1:2500 plans, 1884 and 1904
79. Jones (1987) *op. cit.* n.75, Fig. 68
80. VCH Warwicks 7, 159
81. Rex Christiansen *A Regional History of the Railways Vol. 7 The West Midlands* (1991) 57-8.
82. Richard Chadwick *An Historical Note on the King's Norton Metal Company Limited* (12 September 1985) copy in King's Norton Library
83. Iola A. Williams *The Firm of Cadbury* (1931) 68-9
84. BAH 269356, MS1094; MS20/1; WRO ref.161/32-32.1 BA338; Warks ROQS/111/42, 142
85. BAH 269356
86. BAH 383130, 383134
87. VCH Warwicks 7, 28
88. Christansen (1991) *op. cit.* n.81, 55-6; BAH MS 275a – various plans; TNA RAIL 1071/88; WRO ref. f161/62 BA338
89. Mike Hitches *Worcestershire Railways Britain in Old Photographs* (1997) 33
90. TNA RAIL 252/84 (1-2)
91. BAH SC/1365

VI *The Twentieth Century*
1. Census data; www.demographia.com/db-ukcities.htm
2. BAH 238822
3. Asa Briggs *History of Birmingham* vol. 2 (1952) 145-57
4. BAH 256881
5. WRO Worcestershire County Council Minutes 1908-9
6. BAH Jewel Baillie 90/2b
7. *Daily News* 25 October 1909
8. WRO Worcestershire County Council Minutes 12 December 1910
9. WRO ref. 228:1702 BA172/12
10. [Anon] *Bournville Village Trust* [1929] 27 and map
11. 1904 Ordnance Survey 6-inch plan
12. Joseph McKenna *Birmingham: The Building of a City* (2005) 95-105
13. Maureen Messent 'The Mail's six homes in a swift 60 days' *Evening Mail* 25 August 1973
14. Phyllis Nicklin's notes (private collection)
15. Deborah Hutchings *Monyhull 1908-1998: A History of Caring* (1998)
16. McKenna (2005) *op. cit.* n.12, 108-9
17. Birmingham Trade Directories
18. *Expansion of Birmingham into the Green Belt*, reports by the Directors of Cadbury Brothers and Professor M.J. Wise (1968)
19. Hawkesley and Walker's Heath Master Plan, May 1972 plan no. B7805 Birmingham City Planning Department
20. King's Norton 3 Estates Development Study Final Report (2005) Birmingham City Planning Department
21. Wendy Pearson *King's Norton Past and Present* (2004) 66-7
22. McKenna (2005) *op. cit.* n.12, 137-8
23. David Harvey *A nostalgic look at Birmingham Trams 1933-1953 2 The southern routes* (1994) 39; BAH MS1452/2/25 Ethel Impey *Ancient and Modern: King's Norton and Northfield*
24. *The Modern House And Home* (August 1939) 29
25. Hereford and Worcester County Council and Countryside Commission *Draft Management Plan for the Urban Fringe* (1987) 19
26. Cadbury Brothers Ltd *The Expansion of Birmingham into the Green Belt area* (1968)
27. John Hingeley *The Borderland of Birmingham* (1906) 7-9
28. BAH 67653 C.A.P. Rogers 'Some Account of King's Norton in the 20th century, from articles for the parish magazine, 1949-50' (1972)
29. E.J.S. *Weekend Walks* (Birmingham Mail, 1958)
30. BAH SC/735
31. BAH Birmingham Building Plans 63702 (3 August 1935) and 64504 (16 November 1935)
32. Frank Green and Sidney Wolff *Birmingham and District Old And New* (1933)
33. *Birmingham Weekly Post*, 28 September 1901
34. BAH City of Birmingham Minutes of the Estates Committee 20 April 1937; Proceedings of the Council 8 June 1937; Plans to accompany agenda for Estates Committee Meeting held on Tuesday 8 June 1937
35. Planning Committee reports, 17 July 1969, 19 January 1989, Birmingham City Council website
36. William Haywood *The Work of the Birmingham Civic Society* (1946) 17-19
37. *Evening Despatch* 16 April 1938

38. BAH City ofBirmingham Building Plans 66840, 1936

39. Chris and Rosemary Clegg *The Picture Palaces of Birmingham and Solihull* (1984) 40

40. Harry M. Vickrage *The Story of Tascos 1875-1950: Seventy-five Years of Co-operative Endeavour* (1950)

41. *The King's Norton Labour News* February 1928

42. Duncan Chew, Linda Chew and Karen Martin *TASCOS: Ten Acres and Stirchley Co-Operative Society: Past and Present* (1991) 23-5.

43. Geoff Brandwood, Andrew Davison and Michael Slaughter *Licensed to Sell: the History and Heritage of the Public House* (2004) 84

44. BAH EP4/12/1/3

45. *Birmingham Gazette* 9 April 1913; Frederick Lawrence and Emmeline Pethick (eds) *Votes for Women* 6 (October 1912-September 1913) 399

46. BAH MS 1668/1

47. Mick Wilks *The Defence of Worcestershire and the southern approaches to Birmingham in World War II* (2007) 172-4

48. Birmingham City Council, Deed packet 9267

49. Trevor G. Picken, *The Story of Hampton Cars* (1997) 14-19

50. *Kelly's Directory of Birmingham* (1920, 1927)

51. Simmons Collection, Lifford Mill, Science Museum London

52. TNA MUN 3/226

53. Pers. com., Julian A. Pritchard, chairman and CEO PMG Investments Ltd

54. Richard Chadwick *An Historical Note on The King's Norton Metal Company Limited* (1985) available in King's Norton Library

55. Information sheet of IMI Ltd [1950s] IMI- Coin Manufacture; VCH Warwicks 7, 157-9; Ray Shill *Birmingham's Industrial Heritage, 1900-2000* (2006) 12-16, 39

56. The Birmingham Factory Centre, lists of firms and correspondence, 1953, 1964-5 (private collection)

57. SEGRO plc website

58. *King's Norton Business Centre*, brochure [1987]; *Directory of Occupiers 2007, King's Norton Business Centre* [2007]

59. BAH KN Building Plan 1644; *The Miller* 26 February 1912, 4 March 1912

60. Birmingham City Museum, King's Norton file, Summers correspondence

61. *The Birmingham Post* 6 April 1940

62. *Kelly's Directory of Birmingham* (1950)

63. *Redditch Indicator* 4 August 1972

64. *Birmingham Weekly Post* 28 August 1920

65. BAH MS 1452 Northfield Survey Group Vol. 8, Sale Particulars

66. Burmans, Newspaper of Burmans Ltd, July 1988

67. *Wychall Lane/Eckersall Road, King's Norton, Birmingham, Report on Archaeological Evaluation*, Gifford and Partners Report no. B1445A.02R (June 1998)

68. www.madeinbirmingham.org/motorcycle

69. BAH MS1407/1-6, 10, 14, 18, 29

70. Wendy Pearson (2004) *op. cit.* n.21, 108

Appendix

MAPS OF KING'S NORTON 1731-1936

The five maps covering two centuries invite comparison of the detailed changes that have taken place in the village and its immediate environs.

1. John Dougharty drew the first map of the village in 1731-2. The church is shown reasonably accurately with its crocketed spire and weathercock. The Green is depicted as eight grassed rectangles distorting its more triangular shape. The east and west sides of The Green are solidly built up, with the houses shown in elevation, but the south side is more loosely developed. The Green is separated from the churchyard by a fence and a small building is shown which may represent the Old Malthouse, an ancient building known to have stood here until the 1920s. We cannot blame Dougharty for the inaccuracies because his purpose was to map the boundaries of Masshouse Farm and his depiction of the village was a marginal addition.

2. Tithe Map, 1840. Changes in the half century before this survey include the cutting of the Worcester & Birmingham Canal (1794-6), the canal feeder (ref. no. 2478) and the new turnpike road (now Pershore Road South and Redditch Road) to Pershore (1827-34). The workhouse (ref. no. 2335) was built in 1803 at the south-west corner of The Green and extended between 1837-9.

3. The 1st edition of the Ordnance Survey 1:2500 map, published in 1884, shows that little change took place in the next forty years apart from the establishment of the village Board School and Schoolmaster's House (1878) on Pershore Road South and villa residences built along Redditch Road.

4. By 1916, when the 3rd edition Ordnance Survey was published, further school buildings (1901-2) have been erected as well as a public library (1905) and to the north, towards the river Rea, villa residences along the east side of Pershore Road South. Residential development has now spread to Westhill Road and along the recently constructed Beaks Hill Road. Workers' housing has appeared on both sides of Wharf Road and in two side streets (Baldwin Road and Cyril Road) at the foot of Parson's Hill, serving the brickworks established at the turn of the century.

5. The 4th edition Ordnance Survey (revised 1935-6) shows the landscape filling up with detached houses in extensive gardens to the west of the village and higher density semi-detached and terraced housing south of Wharf Road. The outline of a new cul-de-sac, Old Town Close, has appeared at the south-eastern end of Westhill Road. King's Norton Park, the Playing Fields and Recreation Ground form a green wedge between the village and the river Rea. The map shows the layout of the village buildings just prior to extensive demolition in the late 1930s.

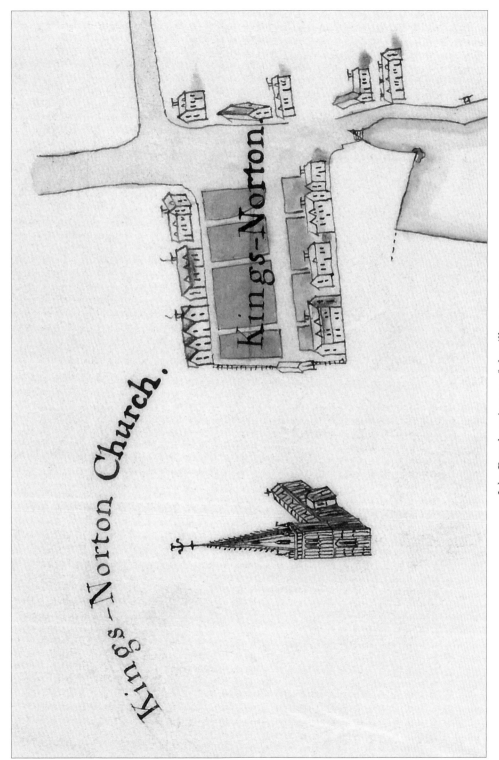

John Dougharty's map of the village, 1731-2.

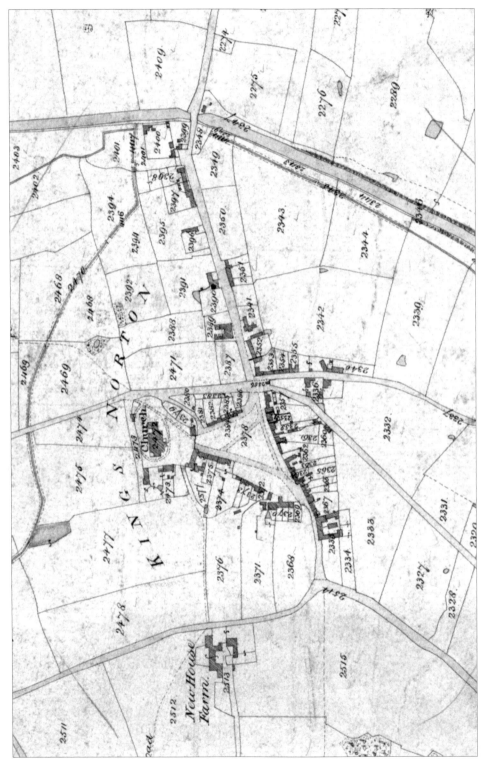

Extract from the King's Norton Tithe Map (1840) showing the village.

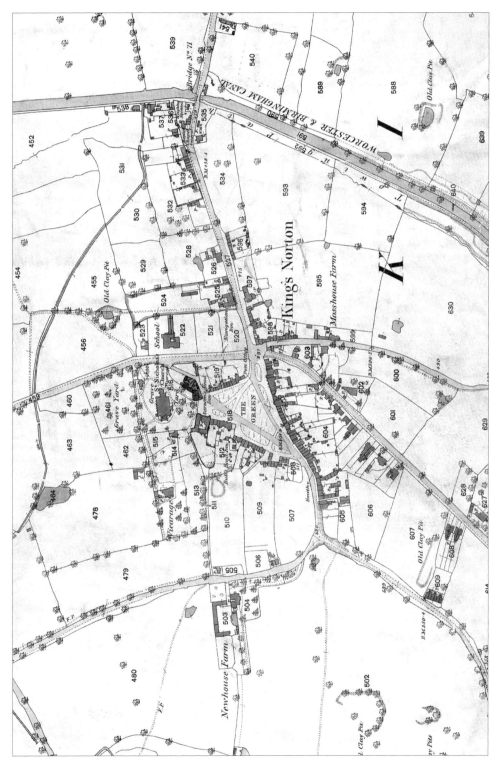

1st edition OS 1:2500 map, surveyed 1882, published 1884.

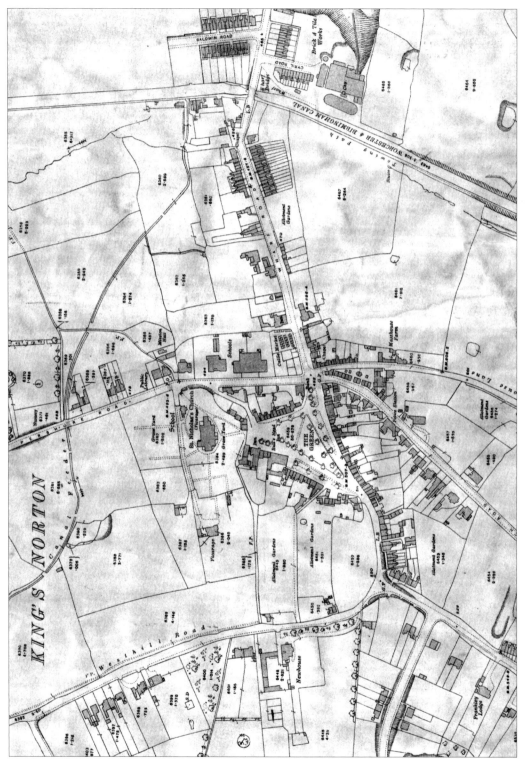

Third edition OS 1:2500 map, revised 1914 and published 1916.

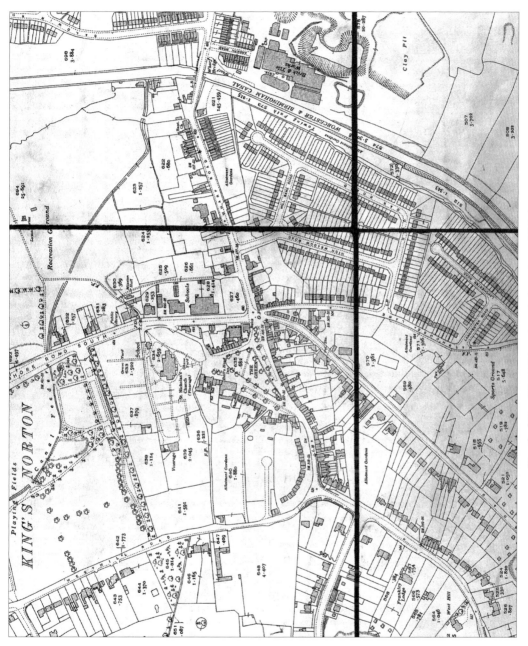

Fourth edition OS 1:2500 map, revised 1935–6, published 1936.

Bibliography

Amphlett, John (ed.), 'A Survey of Worcestershire by Thomas Habington, Vol. 2, pt 2' *WHS* (1897)

Amphlett, John, 'A Midland Architect and his work in the fifteenth century' *TBWAS* 35 1909 (1910)

Anon, 'Transcript of a petition to the Queen of England asking for a licence to sell in the towns of Warwickshire, Worcestershire and Staffordshire' *Transactions of the Midland Record Society* 2 (1897-8) 33

Astill, Grenville, Hirst, Sue and Wright, Susan M., 'The Bordesley Abbey Project Reviewed' *The Archaeological Journal* 161 (2004) 106-58

Aston, J.M.L., *King's Norton in the Olden Time: A Lecture on the Antiquities of King's Norton, with notices of the History of the Parish School, the Royal School, and Old Families connected with the Parish* (1866)

Atkin, Malcolm, *The Civil War in Worcestershire* (Alan Sutton, 1995)

Baber, A.F.C (ed.), 'The Court Rolls of the Manor of Bromsgrove and King's Norton' *WHS* (1963)

Baker, Anne, 'A Study of north-eastern King's Norton: ancient settlement in a woodland manor' *TBWAS* 107 (2003)

Bates, F.A., *Graves Memoirs of the Civil War compiled from 17th century Records* (Blackwood, 1927)

Brassington, W.S., 'Thomas Hall, and the Old Library founded by him at King's Norton' *Library Chronicle* 5 (1888) 61-71

Brassington, W.S., 'Some Account of the Royal Manor of King's Norton, Worcestershire' *Associated Architectural Societies Reports & Papers*, 20 part 2 (1890) 332-42

Brassington, W.S., 'On the Church of King's Norton' *Associated Architectural Societies Reports and Papers* 21 (1891) 97-118

Brassington, W.S., *Historic Worcestershire* (The Midland Educational, 1894)

Bridges, John A., *Idylls of a Lost Village* (Macmillan, 1889)

Bridges, John, *Reminiscences of a Country Politician* (T. Werner Laurie, 1906)

Bridges, John, *A Sportsman of Limited Income* (Andrew Melrose, 1910)

Briggs, Asa, *History of Birmingham* Vol. II, Borough and City 1865-1938 (Oxford University Press, 1952)

Cadbury Brothers Ltd, *Expansion of Birmingham into the Green Belt*, reports by the Directors of Cadbury Brothers and Professor M.J. Wise (1968)

Caswell, Pauline, *The Archive Photographs Series King's Norton* (Chalford, 1997)

Cave, Thomas and Wilson, R.A., 'The Parliamentary Survey of the Lands and Possessions of the Dean and Chapter of Worcester, made in or about the year 1649 ...' *WHS* (1924)

Chew, Duncan, Chew, Linda and Martin, Karen, *TASCOS: Ten Acres and Stirchley Co-Operative Society: Past and Present* (1991)

Christiansen, Rex, *A Regional History of the Railways Vol. 7 The West Midlands* (David St John Thomas, 1991)

Clegg, Chris and Rosemary, *The Picture Palaces of Birmingham and Solihull* (1984)

Colvin, Howard, *A Biographical Dictionary of British Architects 1600-1840* 76-8, 3rd edn (Yale University Press, 1995)

Charles, M., Duncan M. and Hislop, M., *Archaeological Investigations at the Saracen's Head, King's Norton, Birmingham Post Excavation Assessment* Birmingham Archaeology, Project no. 1609.01 (November 2007)

Darby, H.C. and Terrett, I.B., *The Domesday Geography of Midland England* (Cambridge University Press, 1954)

Darlington, R.R. (ed.), 'The Cartulary of Worcester Cathedral Priory (Register 1)' *Pipe Roll Society*, New Series, 38 (1968)

Davies, Stuart, 'A Seventeenth-century Building Dispute', *Worcestershire Archaeology & Local History Newsletter* 24 (1980) 12

Demidowicz, George, 'Rea Valley, Birmingham Archaeological and Landscape survey' *West Midlands Archaeology* 25 (1982)

Demidowicz, George, 'Ridge and Furrow at King's Norton and Northfield, Birmingham,' *West Midlands Archaeology* 27 (1984) 117-21

Demidowicz, George, 'From river Cole to river Rea' *TBWAS* 95 (1987-8)

Demidowicz, George, 'The Lost Lint Brook. A solution to the *Hellerelege* Anglo-Saxon charter and other explorations of King's Norton history' *TBWAS* 107 (2003) 111-29

Demidowicz, George and Price, Stephen, 'Wythall, Blackgrave Moat' *West Midlands Archaeology* 29 (1986)

Demidowicz, Toni, 'Monyhull, King's Norton', *The Birmingham Historian* 16 (1998) 9-12

Duffy, Eamon, *The Stripping of the Altars* (Yale University Press, 1992)

Dyer, Christopher, *Lords and Peasants in a Changing Society: The Estates of the Bishopric of Worcester 680-1540* (Cambridge University Press, 1980)

Dyer, Christopher, 'Bromsgrove: A Small Town in Worcestershire in the Middle Ages', *WHS Occasional Publications* 9 (2000)

Dyer, Christopher, *Making A Living in the Middle Ages: The People of Britain 850-1520* (Yale University Press, 2003)

Dyer, Christopher,'The Archaeology of Medieval Small Towns' *Medieval Archaeology* 47 (2003)

Dyer, Christopher, *An Age of Transition: Economy and Society in England in the Later Middle Ages* (Oxford University Press, 2005)

Eld, E.J. (ed.), 'Lay Subsidy for the County of Worcester 1 Edward III [1327]' *WHS* (1895)

Faraday, Michael A. (ed.), 'Worcestershire Taxes in the 1520s' *WHS* New Series 19 (2003)

Field, John, *English Place Names* (David & Charles, 1972)

Gelling, Margaret, *Signposts to the Past* (Dent, 1978)

Goddard, Larch S., 'Berry Mound, Solihull' *TBWAS* 75 (1959) 93-4

Goodger, Helen, *King's Norton* (Brewin Books, 1990)

Grant, H.M and Barnard, E.A.B., 'The Parish and Church of Kingsnorton: being some record of recent documentary researches' *TWAS* New Series 2 (1924-5) 123-45

Green, Frank and Wolff, Sidney, *Birmingham and District Old And New* (Souvenir Magazines Ltd, 1933)

Grundy, G.B., 'Saxon charters of Worcestershire' *TBWAS* 53 (1928)

Hamper, William, 'The Antiquities of Kingsnorton' *The Gentleman's Magazine* vol. LXXVI Part I (1807) 201

Hamper, William (ed.), *The Life, Diary, and Correspondence of Sir William Dugdale* (1827)

Hannaford, Hugh R., *Lifford Mill, King's Norton: An Archaeological Evaluation and Excavations at Lifford Mill, King's Norton* (Birmingham University Field Archaeology Unit 1989)

Harris, J.R., *The Copper King: a biography of Thomas Williams of Llanidan* (Liverpool University Press, 2003)

Harvey, David, *A nostalgic look at Birmingham Trams 1933-1953 vol. 2 The southern routes* (Silver Link, 1994)

Haywood, William, *The Work of the Birmingham Civic Society* (Birmingham Civic Society, 1946)

Hilton, R.H., *A Medieval Society: the West Midlands at the end of the Thirteenth Century* (Weidenfeld & Nicolson, 1966)

Hitches, Mike, *Worcestershire Railways Britain in Old Photographs* (Alan Sutton, 1997)

Hodder, Michael, *Birmingham: The Hidden History* (Tempus, 2004)

Holliday, J.R., 'The Church and Grammar School of King's Norton' *TBWAS* 3 (1872) 44-62

Hooke, Della, *Worcestershire Anglo-Saxon Charter Bounds* (Boydell, 1990)

Hooke, Della, *The Anglo-Saxon landscape: The Kingdom of the Hwicce* (Manchester University Press, 1985)

Hopkins, F.E., *Cotteridge and its Churches before 1911* 3rd Paper issued by the King's Norton History Society (1986)

Hutchings, Deborah, *Monyhull 1908-1998: A History of Caring* (Brewin Books, 1998)

Hutton, William, *An History of Birmingham* (Pearson & Rollason, 1783)

Hutton, William, *The Court of Requests* (W. & R. Chambers, 1840)

Hutton, William, *A Narrative of the Riots In Birmingham, July 14, 1791, particularly as they affected the author* (1798) incorporated within his autobiography *The Life of William Hutton, Stationer of Birmingham...* (1841 edn)

Jones, A.E., *Lifford, Birmingham, An Archaeological Evaluation* (BUFAU, 1991)

Jones, Edgar, *A History of the GKN Vol. 1: Innovation and Enterprise 1759-1918* (Macmillan, 1987)

Jones, Laurence and Ratkai, Stephanie, 'Excavations at No. 15, The Green, King's Norton, 1992' *TBWAS* 104 (2004), 101-21

Lewis, Samuel, *A Topographical Dictionary of England* Vol. 3 (7th edn, 1849)

Lewis, Val, *Victorian Village Life as reflected in the diaries of Richard Pountney 1804 to 1891, Farmer, Parish Clerk, Schoolmaster* (2000)

Litherland, Steve, *An Archaeological Evaluation near Lifford Hall, King's Norton, Birmingham* (BUFAU, 1990)

Lock, Arthur B., *The History of King's Norton and Northfield Wards* (The Midland Educational [1925])

Long, Charles E. (ed.), 'Diary of the Marches of the Royal Army during the Great Civil War; kept by Richard Symons' *Camden Society* 74 (1859)

Mawer, A. and Stenton, F.M., *The Place-names of Worcestershire* (Cambridge University Press, 1927)

McKenna, Joseph, *Birmingham: The Building of a City* (Tempus, 2005)

Nash, Treadway Russell, *Collections for the history and antiquities of Worcestershire* (T. Payne, 1781)

Noake, John, *The Rambler in Worcestershire* (Longman, 1854)

Oswald, Adrian, 'Hawkesley Farm, Longbridge' *TBWAS* (1958) 76, 36-50

Oxford Dictionary of National Biography (Oxford University Press, 2004)

Pearson, Wendy, *King's Norton Past and Present* (Sutton, 2004)

Phillimore, W.P.W. and Carter, W.F., *Some Account of the Family of Middlemore* (Phillimore, 1901)

Phillimore, W.P.W. (ed.), 'The Visitation of the County of Worcester 1569' *Harleian Society* 27 (1888)

Picken, Trevor G., *The Story of Hampton Cars* (1997)

Platt, C.P.S., *The Monastic Grange in Medieval England: A Reassessment* (Macmillan, 1969)

Price, Stephen, 'The Early History of Bordesley Abbey' (Unpublished MA thesis University of Birmingham) (1971)

Price, Stephen, 'Shephard's Wheelwrighting Business at King's Norton', *The Birmingham Historian* 6 (1990) 5-10

Price, Stephen and Langhorne, Richard, *North Worcestershire Development Hawkesley and Walker's Heath Interim Report on the Archaeological Implications of Development: A field survey undertaken by the Birmingham & Warwickshire Archaeological Society* (1974)

[Price, Stephen], *King's Norton Trail* (Birmingham City Planning Department and City Museums & Art Gallery, 1983)

Price, Stephen, 'The Nailmakers' Workshops of Birmingham' *The Birmingham Historian* 2 (1988) 5-15

Price, Stephen and Demidowicz, George, *The Saracen's Head and Old Grammar School King's Norton, Synthesis of the Historical and Architectural Development and the History of Repairs* (Stephen Price Associates Ltd, 2009); *Historic Images 1731-2008* (Stephen Price Associates Ltd, 2009)

Ransome, Mary, 'The State of the Bishopric of Worcester 1782-1808' *WHS* (1968)

Sapcote, E.S. 'Moundesley [*sic*] Hall, King's Norton' *TBWAS* 64 (1941-2) 118-19

Shill, Ray, *Workshop of the World: Birmingham's Industrial Heritage, 1900-2000* (Sutton, 2006)

Stephens, W.B. (ed.), *A History of the County of Warwick, vol. VII, The City of Birmingham* (Victoria History of the Counties of England, Oxford University Press, 1964)

Thirsk, Joan, *The Rural Economy of England* (Hambledon Press, 1984)

Toulmin Smith, Lucy, *Leland's Itinerary in England and Wales* 2 (Centaur Press, 1964)

Vanes, Jean (ed.), 'The Ledger of John Smythe 1538-1550' *Bristol Record Society* 28 (1975)

Vaughan, J.E., 'The Former Grammar School of King's Norton' *TWAS* 37 (1960) 27-36

Vaughan, J.E., *Some account of the Parish Church and Ancient Grammar School of King's Norton* (1960 and subsequent editions)

Vickrage, Harry, *The Story of Tascos 1875-1950: Seventy-five Years of Co-operative Endeavour* (1950)

White, Alan, *The Worcester and Birmingham Canal: Chronicles of the Cut* (Brewin Books, 2005)

Whitehead, David, 'The Defences of Berry Mound' *TBWAS* 89 (1979-80), 162-3

Whiteman, Anne (ed.), 'The Compton census of 1676: a critical edition' *British Academy: Records of Social and Economic History* New Series 10 (1986)

Wilks, Mick, *The Defence of Worcestershire and the southern approaches to Birmingham in World War II* (Logaston, 2007)

Williams, Iola A., *The Firm of Cadbury 1831-1931* (Constable, 1931)

Willis Bund, J.W. and Amphlett, J. (eds), 'Lay Subsidy Roll for the County of Worcester *circa* 1280' *WHS* (1893) [corrected to 1275]

Willis Bund, J.W. and Doubleday, H.A. (eds), *The Victoria History of the County of Worcester* 5 vols (Victoria History of the Counties of England, Constable, 1901-26)

Willis Bund, J.W., *The Civil War in Worcestershire 1642-1646 and the Scotch Invasion of 1651* (Alan Sutton, 1979 reprint of 1905 edition)

Index

Bold entries indicate that there is a relevant illustration on the page.